CW00497486

C1 984025 60

THE CRIMES OF THE GESTAPO

THE CRIMES OF THE GESTAPO

FROM THE CLOSED FILES OF MI14

ANDREW COOK

AMBERLEY

To Alia

First published 2021

Amberley Publishing
The Hill, Stroud
Gloucestershire, GL5 4EP

www.amberley-books.com

Copyright © Andrew Cook, 2021

The right of Andrew Cook to be identified as the Author of this work has been asserted in accordance with the Copyright, Designs and Patents Act 1988.

ISBN 978 1 4456 9836 6 (hardback)
ISBN 978 1 4456 9837 3 (ebook)

British Library Cataloguing in Publication Data. A catalogue record for this book is available from the British Library.

1 2 3 4 5 6 7 8 9 10

Typesetting by SJmagic DESIGN SERVICES, India.
Printed in the UK.

CONTENTS

ACKNOWLEDGEMENTS

I am greatly indebted to the families of a number of former MI14 officers who have kindly shared material with me and allowed me to use these sources in this book.

My thanks also go to the following individuals who greatly assisted me with various aspects of research, preparation or production of this book: Bill Adams, James Armitage, Alia Cook, Daksha Chauhan, Mary Juraszek, Colin Kendall, Jade Pawaar, Amanda Rossiter, Chris Sillars, Bernard Smith, Phil Tomaselli, George Townsend, Kevin Welch, Oliver White, and Paul Williams

I would also like to thank the staff of the following institutions for their much-appreciated help and assistance: the Bletchley Park Trust, the British Library, the Imperial War Museum, the Ministry of Defence, the National Archives, the United States Holocaust Museum, and the University of London.

Finally, my thanks go to Richard Sutton at Amberley Publishing for his support.

Picture Acknowledgments:
Author's collection: 14, 29, 34, 35
Bundesarchiv, Koblenz: 2, 3, 4, 6, 15, 16, 17
The National Archives, Kew: 1, 4, 5, 7-13, 18-21, 30, 31, 32, 36
US Department of Defense: 22–28

INTRODUCTION

It is probably fair to say that the general public are as unaware of MI14 and the critical intelligence role it played in the Second World War as they are universally aware of the name and sinister reputation of the Nazi state's secret political police, the Gestapo.

To millions, the very word Gestapo conjures up images of repression and torture, and is uniquely associated with dread, fear and foreboding. Nine decades after its creation, the Gestapo still holds a morbid fascination for many. They are part of Second World War folklore, the antithesis of the have-a-go heroes of the prisoner of war camps and those, in Churchill's words, who, despite the odds, 'waged war against a monstrous tyranny, never surpassed in the dark, lamentable catalogue of human crime'.

To write an account of any secret service is a problematic task in more ways than one. Not least of these is the orthodox historian's distrust of the very subject of espionage and counter-espionage in the context of history. Add to this the spectre of Nazi ideology, a world war and the holocaust it triggered, and the task at hand can be seen to be a considerable one.

The men who served the Gestapo are themselves enigmas – contrary to popular belief, only a minority were card-carrying Nazis. Many of them had served in various branches of the police for some considerable time before Hitler even came to power. What drove and motivated such men? What was it that overrode and deadened their consciences in aiding and carrying out some of the most barbaric acts in recorded history?

Over the last nine decades the story of the Gestapo has been blended with a degree of myth, falsehood and sometimes fantasy by an almost unending series of movies and television series which have only muddied the waters still further.

To piece together an accurate picture of the extraordinary story of the Gestapo, it has been necessary to shed all preconceptions and return to square one, starting from scratch in gathering as many primary sources as possible. The ability to draw on a number of classified, restricted and hitherto unpublished sources in Britain and abroad has helped immeasurably. The descendants of a number of those who played such a vital, yet unheralded role in British intelligence during those years have also provided a unique insight into this story, along with the contemporary first-hand testimonies of those who were endeavouring to discover as much as they could about the nature, organisation and modus operandi of the Gestapo.

What better eyes to look through, in telling this story, than those of MI14, the wartime intelligence department created on Churchill's express orders shortly after his appointment as Prime Minister? MI14 were unique in focussing exclusively on Germany. They also effectively acted as a clearing house for intelligence on Germany and worked hand in glove with the likes of MI5, MI6, MI9 and MI19. Materials and reports were circularised within and between these departments, the surviving results of which give us a valuable glimpse of the Gestapo and its development. Each chapter of this book is based upon one or more MI14 files, and/or the papers and retrospective recollections of former MI14 officers. While the book and its chapters run essentially in chronological order, there are a number of overlaps, as inevitably episodes and the individuals involved in them do tend to interrelate as they do in any story.

PREFACE

The index cards cover an entire wall of the 'Topography of Terror' museum on Berlin's Niederkirchnerstrasse. In pink, beige and green, each card is fixed flat to the wall and records the names, dates of birth and biographical details of thousands of individuals. Found by researchers back in 1963, the cards today form one of the main exhibits at Berlin's newest museum, dedicated to one of the most brutal and repressive secret police forces in history – the Gestapo. The cards are not, however, records of the Gestapo's countless victims, but of its employees. From the first day the museum opened in May 2010, one of the most common questions posed by visitors is why, of the thousands of coloured cards on the wall, do sixteen alone stand out at right angles? In fact, on closer inspection, three of the sixteen stand out even further from the wall than the other thirteen. The chilling answer to the conundrum is that only sixteen Gestapo officers out of thousands of cards on the wall were ever charged with war crimes. Even more disturbingly, of the sixteen, only three were eventually convicted.

The Niederkirchnerstrasse, like the 'Topography of Terror' museum itself, is a characterless, concrete and glass creation of the twenty-first century, indistinguishable from all the other concrete and glass buildings in modern Berlin. Originally running from Wilhelmstrasse to Stresemannstrasse near Potsdamer Platz, the street borders the districts of Mitte and Kreuzberg. When it was first built in 1891, it was named after Prince Albrecht of Prussia, who had owned a large house on the site of the new street. In 1905, the Museum of Decorative Art was opened at No. 8 Prinz-Albrechtstrasse. It was this building that was requisitioned by Hermann Göring for the Headquarters of the Gestapo in May 1933.

No. 8 Prinz-Albrechtstrasse, along with the rest of the street, was largely destroyed by heavy Allied bombing in February 1945. After the collapse of Berlin, the boundary between the American and Russian zones of occupation ran directly along the street, resulting in it becoming a fortified 'no man's land'. In 1951 the name of the street was changed to Niederkirchnerstrasse, and the authorities began demolishing the war-damaged buildings. Some West Berlin councillors wanted to reconstruct the unique architecture of Prinz-Albrechtstrasse, but most Berliners preferred to forget this place of horror altogether. The West Berlin authorities later proposed running a freeway through the site, but it never happened. In 1961 the Communist authorities in East Berlin did their part by driving a stake through the area by erecting the Berlin Wall. Finally, in the 1980s, a neighbourhood citizens group campaigned for the site to be excavated and marked as a permanent memorial to the 15,000 individuals who had been arrested by the Gestapo and kept in the underground cells of 8 Prinz-Albrechtstrasse.

Some argued that the project was a pointless one. The architects commissioned to carry out the restoration countered that while the ruins of the buildings above ground level had been demolished, a basement can't be demolished – it's filled in. The project was eventually given the go-ahead and the floors and walls of the basement cells were uncovered. The work took two and a half years, coming in on budget just shy of £20 million, which was met jointly by the Berlin and German federal governments.

Digging up the past, in more ways than one, raises many questions. As Andreas Nachama, the Director of the Topography of Terror pointed out when the museum opened, no exhibition or museum alone can supply comprehensive answers about the past; 'we are', he said, 'pleased if visitors leave us with more questions than they started with'.

How, for example, could the devastation caused by the Nazis have happened in a modern twentieth-century nation? How could the Nazis have taken power through the ballot box in a country that only the previous decade had been seen throughout Europe as an open, tolerant, educated and pluralistic society? And how could the men of the Gestapo who tortured, persecuted and murdered countless thousands simply have slipped away so quietly at the end of the war, to merge back so seamlessly into the new post-war democratic German nation? The answer is not a simple one.

BENEFIT OF HINDSIGHT

For the British public in the 1930s, Nazism meant Adolf Hitler, bullying and screaming, with his Luftwaffe, his army of Stormtroopers, and his grim-faced secret police – the Gestapo. With the benefit of post-war hindsight, people said they'd seen it coming. But perhaps they had not joined up the dots quite soon enough. For years, Nazi rallies had appeared in British cinema newsreels. Everything about these events was alien; it was incomprehensible that such vast numbers of Germans appeared to worship Hitler and admire his boastful parade of warplanes and tanks. So, Hitler, a Jew-hater and a demagogue, became a figure of fun, with his silly moustache and floppy hair. The British press didn't go in for 'scaremongering'. Shocking murders, the abdication of King Edward VIII, football, or whether or not women should wear trousers like Katherine Hepburn – there was so much else to think about.

English people who saw the bigger picture of the 1930s noticed that the conformist, expansionist and ruthless ethos of the Nazis had parallels in Italy's invasion of Ethiopia and Japan's attack on China. Fascists even took over in Spain, with German help. Socialists and Communists were only too aware of these things but they were a minority, barely represented in Parliament.

The passenger on the Clapham omnibus thought about money, family and other things of more immediate importance. Talk of another war was stupid. The newspapers assured them that after the Nazi takeover of Austria and part of Czechoslovakia in 1938, the monster's appetite was satisfied. Prime Minister Neville Chamberlain himself had said that there would be 'peace in our time' since Germany and Italy had promised France and Great Britain that there'd be no more marching, uninvited, into foreign countries.

The following year, on 23 August 1939, Hitler's Germany and Stalin's USSR signed the Molotov-Ribbentrop Pact of mutual non-aggression. On 1 September Germany and Russia jointly invaded Poland.

So, Britain and Germany went to war. It would clearly become another world war, yet when it began, even the best-informed British intelligence services had failed in every attempt to make Neville Chamberlain, Lord Halifax and their colleagues move to action. These ruling politicians continued to dither, to discuss some kind of peace settlement, and left others to confront the horrifying situation.

There were, however, very fewer 'others' who were either sufficiently senior or determined enough to be able to influence events. The state of inertia in the form of appeasement had pretty much washed over the entirety of Whitehall. While a relatively small number of career diplomats and military officers saw the roots of a potential Second World War in the aftermath of what was, prior to 1939, still known as the Great War, others buried their heads in the sand.

One man whose head was firmly above ground, and knew Germany and the Germans probably better than almost anyone else in military intelligence circles, was Major Kenneth Strong. Commissioned into the 1st Battalion Royal Scots Fusiliers in 1920, Strong became an Intelligence Officer in Ireland before being posted to the British Army of the Rhine as an interpreter at a critical time in Germany's post-war history – 1922. As an interpreter, he gained a unique picture of literally every aspect of the country and its people. He saw at first hand the destitute state of Germany following the economic collapse and hyperinflation brought about by the victorious Allies' demand for reparations, and was one of the first to see this as sowing the seeds of a second, future conflict with Germany.

Reparations were essentially a claim for damages against Germany, resulting from the destruction and devastating human losses suffered on the western front and elsewhere and codified by the Treaty of Versailles of 1919. None of the Allies felt that the war had been justified; it had, in their view, been caused by German aggression and the Germans were going to pay – never mind that according to other conditions of the peace treaty, Germany was about to lose major sources of income and employment, including, among others, the coalfields of Silesia and Alsace.

Almost immediately on taking up his new post in Germany, Strong began committing to writing his personal impressions of everyday life in Germany, economic and political developments as well as his observations about the German army, 4,500,000 strong at the end of the war, but now radically shorn back to a maximum of 100,000 by the Treaty of Versailles. Strong continued this chronicle for the best part of two decades, by which time he'd reached the rank of Major-General and intelligence advisor to Allied Supreme Commander General Dwight D. Eisenhower. It was in this capacity that he would eventually take part in the negotiations which led to Germany's unconditional surrender in May 1945. That, though, was all very much in the future. In the here and now of 1923, Strong couldn't help but feel a degree of sympathy towards the German people. Those he met from all walks of life complained bitterly that the country had simultaneously been crushed by debt and required to shell out huge sums for decades to come. Germany had also been humiliated, as well as impoverished, by the loss of territory.

For Adolf Hitler, the Austrian who had fought for Germany in the war, everything he had identified with seemed to be blown apart by Germany's defeat. The old problem of how to make a living, conveniently put to one side for the four years of the war, now once again confronted him. In December 1918, he volunteered for guard duty in a prisoner of war camp in Traunstein on the German/Austrian border. Six weeks later, however, the camp was closed and Hitler returned to Munich, where shortly afterwards he got a job in VII Army District's Press and News Bureau as an Instruction Officer. One of his first assignments was to investigate a small, newly formed political grouping called the German Workers Party. It had no more than forty members and held its meetings in an obscure beer-house, the Alter Rosenbad, on Munich's Herrnstrasse. Here Hitler encountered a small circle of angry men whose opinions – anti-capitalist, anti-Freemason, anti-communist, anti-Semitic and fervently German nationalist – happened to mirror his own. It wasn't long before he'd resolved to leave his Press and News Bureau job and throw in his lot with the fledgling party. Thanks to his electrifying oratory, the small circle soon grew to a couple of thousand and in 1921 renamed themselves the National Socialist German Workers Party, or Nazis, with Hitler as their leader.

Naturally, there was in-fighting. Hitler's instinct was to eject or otherwise destroy those who disagreed with him. Capitalists and communists must be expelled from Germany, and since both capitalism and Marxism were the result of a Jewish conspiracy to disrupt the inevitable destiny of the Fatherland, Jews must be expelled first of all.

Jews had emigrated west into Germany for centuries and were fully assimilated, yet Hitler's message reached an increasingly susceptible audience, especially in the countryside where although there were Jewish families, they were fewer, and people were more ready to isolate whoever was conspicuous. Hitler constantly told them that while they, good Germans, had been getting poorer in Germany's crippled post-war economy, the Jews had been getting richer.

This was untrue for many reasons, starting with the economy itself. The question of how to pay 'reparations' due in foreign currency, when Germany was too disadvantaged to earn any foreign currency, was temporarily solved by printing more paper Marks and buying currency. But that could only be done once. When the second instalment of the reparations didn't arrive, French troops marched into the Ruhr Valley, where much of Germany's income stream came from. The government advised the Ruhr's coal miners to strike, and so that they wouldn't starve without work, the government printed more money to pay their wages. Inflation became hyperinflation. In 1921 – and again, even more seriously, in 1923 – hyperinflation made the currency worthless. The only people who benefited were the heavily indebted, because if the money had been borrowed against something tangible it could be paid off with a stack of worthless Marks. In that case, the creditor lost.

So, there were aggrieved people. And frightened people, frightened mostly of Communists, and more particularly of the threat of the type of violent revolution that was currently sweeping Russia. There were people who didn't know why life had got so darned difficult but it must be somebody's fault. Hitler, the demagogue, told them how to get revenge and 'reparations' of their own. He was still under thirty, and had no intellectual credibility, but few dared to question him. His henchmen were with him always, and nobody who contradicted their leader was safe from violence.

Most of all, he attracted unemployed people. Men who had been in the services and believed that Germany only lost the war because of a Jewish communist conspiracy. Men who were disappointed and angry and argued with their fists.

Quite early on, in 1923, 600 of those men had become Hitler's personal band of street bullies, and took orders from a short, scar-faced ex-army captain called Röhm. They wore brown shirts and were known as the Stürmtruppe. Should Hitler be heckled, or even mildly challenged, they would identify the offenders and beat them up.

At this early date the Nazis were prominent only in Munich, Bavaria. On 8 November 1923 a State of Emergency had been declared by an interim Bavarian government and its new leader, Gustav Kahr, was to make a speech in the Bürgerbräukeller, a huge Munich beer hall. Kahr duly arrived and was in mid-oration when – defended by Stormtroopers with a machine gun, and surrounded by a posse that included hatchet-faced Rudolf Hess, wartime air ace Hermann Göring, and for still greater credibility, old General Ludendorff – Hitler leapt unannounced onto the stage, smashed a stein of beer, fired a pistol into the ceiling and declared a march on Berlin to oust 'the Berlin Jew government'.

The crowd howled their enthusiasm and Nazis all over town simultaneously attempted to take over major buildings, but they were outnumbered by armed police. Hitler was hustled away to safety. The following day, he and his troops met 3,000 Bavarian state police in a shoot-out in the city centre; three policemen and sixteen Nazis were killed. Hermann Göring, the former hero of the German air force, was injured and bundled away. He fled abroad and returned two years later a fat, ill-tempered morphine addict.

Hitler also ran for his life, but he was caught, arrested and brought to trial. He made an opportunity of it. He was notorious now: the press was interested. He used his twenty-four days in court to expound his views at length, so that the whole nation knew what he stood for: national pride and expulsion of the Jews.

He was sentenced to five years' imprisonment and on 9 November 1923 the Nazi Party was banned. However, he eventually served only one year and nine days at Bavaria's Landsberg prison and emerged from obscurity, a martyr to the cause, with his plan in book form: *Mein Kampf*.

The Beer Hall Putsch had been chaotic but it had raised his profile and enlarged his supporter base. He managed to have the ban on the party lifted on a promise of good behaviour. *Mein Kampf*, along with the continuing menace of Röhm's Stormtroopers and Göring, when he returned from hiding abroad in 1927, did the rest. Hitler's movement was growing and brooked no opposition.

Hitler took half-baked ideas from all over the place and bashed them into his warped master plan. *Mein Kampf* promoted Germany as a 'pure Aryan' civilisation which would dominate humanity for a thousand years. The creation of a master race meant ethnic cleansing of non-Aryans. Hitler found it all too easy to convince ordinary people that by ridding Germany of people who did not conform to his imagined ideal genetic type, the nation would be immeasurably stronger. All this went down very well in those parts of Germany where Hitler's followers were numerous.

During his time in Germany, Kenneth Strong observed the steady growth of support for the Nazis, a growth that was considerably accelerated by the Wall Street stock market crash of October 1929 and the international economic depression that followed hot on its heels. As Strong observed in his journals, German banks had been large investors in US companies and suffered huge losses as the share prices of these companies fell. This in turn created a banking crisis in Germany as savers began to fear for their money. Several big German banks went bust as customers attempted, en masse, to withdraw their money. Those banks that survived did so by recalling business loans, which in turn led to a significant number of companies failing, triggering a sharp rise in unemployment. Rising unemployment led to falling demand for goods and services, reinforcing the downward spiral. Between September 1929 and January 1933, unemployment in Germany rose from 1.3 million to 6.1 million.

Despite the growing dole queues and the darkening Nazi thundercloud beneath which they lived, millions of Germans did not hate Jews and thought Hitler was poisonous. Although some spoke out, most remained unprepared for what happened at the elections in 1930. Hitler had been well supplied with funds even in 1925 when he emerged from prison to ride around in his own Mercedes, but at the end of the decade the party was suddenly powerful indeed. The federal elections held on 14 September 1930 catapulted the Nazi Party from minor party status to second largest party. Although losing ten seats, the Social Democratic Party remained the largest party in the Reichstag, taking 143 of the 577 seats, while the Nazi Party dramatically increased its seats from 12 to 107.

Three years later, in 1933, Hitler had a war chest, a strategy and a highly effective propaganda machine run by Joseph Goebbels. In the federal elections on 31 July 1932, Hitler's party finally became Germany's largest in terms of seats, leapfrogging the SDP into first place. Although the Nazis now had 230 seats to the SDP's 130, they lacked an overall majority in the Reichstag. There then followed another election less than four months later on 6 November 1932, which would, although nobody knew it at the time, be the last free and fair election before the Nazis came to power. The results were a great disappointment to the Nazis, for although they clung onto first place, their vote fell by 4 per cent and their tally of Reichstag seats fell from 230 to 196.

However, Hitler duly persuaded a few smaller nationalist parties to support the Nazis. By the end of January 1933, after much horse-trading, Hitler became Chancellor. Four weeks later at the end of February, the Reichstag burned down. Göring, Minister of the Interior at the time, immediately blamed Moscow. The whole party claimed that this was a Communist plot, and when a young Dutch communist was accused, they seemed to be vindicated.

Again, Hitler seized the moment. Rising on the tide of popularity for its anti-communist stance, the party was able to pass the Enabling Act in May. Thereafter, the Nazis could legislate as they wished, approve whatever treaties with whatever foreign states they chose, and amend the Constitution at will. They were no longer required to consult Parliament; the Reich's Cabinet would dictate what Germany did. Nazi-appointed state governors would have extensive local powers but would always have to 'carry out the general policy laid down by the Reich Chancellor'.

In the three years between Hitler coming to power and his first escapade in the quest to row-back on the Treaty of Versailles, Kenneth Strong looked on with concern as Hitler and his Nazi followers marched towards the promised land.

2

HEADS IN THE SAND

The population of the Saarland, on Germany's western border, could have been forgiven for believing they lived in a parallel universe following the end of the war in 1918, for under the Treaty of Versailles, the Saar region of Germany was separated from the rest of the country and administered directly by the League of Nations. On top of this, the French were given control of the Saar's coal mines as part of the clauses of the Treaty.

After fifteen years of League of Nations administration, a referendum was scheduled under the treaty to decide the long-term future of the region. In November 1934, the League of Nations Council met and determined the arrangements for the vote and more importantly, its supervision. Fearful of Nazi intimidation and possible voting fraud, the League decided that a peacekeeping force would be necessary during the plebiscite period. On 8 December 1934 the Council unanimously passed a resolution creating a 3,300-strong international force, that would be under the command of General John Brind and comprised of 1,500 British, 1,300 Italian, 260 Swedish and 250 Dutch troops.

Brind was keen to have British officers on his staff who knew Germany and the Germans, and Kenneth Strong was an obvious choice. Not only had he been highly recommended by the War Office, he was someone already known to Brind by reputation. Strong had no hesitation in taking up the post and spent the weekend before leaving London immersing himself in all that he could read about the Saar.

The plebiscite, while being a comparatively short episode in the events leading up to the Second World War, was, without doubt, a major watershed moment, not only for the future peace of Europe and the world, but for Kenneth Strong and those of his colleagues who witnessed the plebiscite campaign and the forces it unleashed.

Once the preparations began, the population of the Saar would then be asked to decide whether they wished to return to being a sovereign part of Germany, retain their separate identity or became part of France. The outcome of the vote was by no means a certainty. Since the Nazis had come to power two years before, many anti-Nazis, Jews and dissidents had fled to the Saar. Seeing what Hitler was doing in Germany, communists and social democrats formed a 'united front' for the purposes of the Saar plebiscite campaign with the objective of campaigning to retain League of Nations status. The Nazis, for their part, formed the 'German Front' and with the covert assistance of the Saar police, the Gestapo began a campaign aimed at boycotting, beating and generally intimidating their opponents.

The Gestapo began work in earnest on 1 March. It was through the Saar that, during the fourteen months which had elapsed since the Nazis had come to power, the refugees living abroad had smuggled their clandestine anti-Nazi literature into Germany. From there, it was circulated undercover, preserving hope among the opponents of the regime. The Gestapo had already spent some months reconnoitring those they regarded as opponents, assembling as much data as they could on them. They then began inciting the population to lynch 'separatists' and 'French spies'.

Non-Nazi Saarlanders and members of the foreign press complained to the Plebiscite Commission about interception of telegrams and letters, listened into telephone calls and kidnappings. The Commission were only too well aware of the reality of what was going on, but were afraid to intervene, let alone stop, the plebiscite for fear of Nazi riots.

Strong saw examples of intimidation while walking the streets in civilian clothes and drew these to the attention of Plebiscite

Commission member Sarah Wambaugh, an American college professor. She dismissed Strong's complaints out of hand, as in her words, 'they were made by non-Nazi Saarlanders and the foreign press'. An incredulous Strong dryly retorted that they would hardly have been be made by pro-Nazis! While he had heard of the Gestapo before returning to Germany, this was the first time he had come face to face with their activities. He was, from this moment on, only too painfully aware of the threat posed by a secret police force with the powers and tools deployed by the Gestapo and equally determined to learn more about this secretive and deadly foe.

When the vote finally took place on 13 January 1935, to the surprise of neutral observers, over 90 per cent voted in favour of reuniting with Germany.

Unification with Germany:	477,089	90.7%
Remain a League of Nations Mandate:	46,613	8.8%
Unification with France:	2,124	0.4%
Invalid/blank votes:	2,161	0.4%
Total voting:	527,987	100%
Registered voters:	539,542	97.9%

Strong noted in his report to the War Office that every voting district in the Saar saw at least an 83 per cent turnout of voters supporting a return to German rule. He also noted with a mixture of concern and irony that despite there being 150,000 French citizens living in the Saar, only 2,124 of them had apparently voted for annexation of the Saar by France, which was less than 1 per cent of registered French voters.

Some five years later, with the benefit of hindsight, Strong astutely observed that it was in many ways 'the first step to war'. It had validated Hitler and the Nazi regime by seemingly demonstrating that the German people were not being browbeaten into supporting the Nazis and that Germans living outside Germany, in the Saar, had shown the world that they were more opposed to the Treaty of Versailles than they were to Hitler. The vote also gave Hitler a considerable boost of prestige and provided him with no little measure of moral authority to advance his demands for unity on others such as Austria, and the Sudeten Germans in Czechoslovakia. Finally, and most importantly for Strong, the episode showed him that the League of Nations and the western powers were unwilling and unable to confront the violence and intimidation deployed by the Nazis. This would inevitably embolden Hitler and lead him to conclude that Britain, France and the League were in no mood to block or oppose his dreams of further territorial expansion.

With the plebiscite over and resolved, Strong returned to London where he pondered on his future in the British Army and how best he could convince his superiors of the danger posed by Hitler. In little over a year, the chain of events that would lead to a new crisis began on 7 March 1936, when German military forces marched into the Rhineland. This was a significant move for two reasons. Firstly, it was a blatant violation of the Treaty of Versailles. Under articles 42, 43 and 44, Germany was 'forbidden to maintain or construct any fortification either on the Left bank of the Rhine or on the Right bank to the west of the line drawn fifty kilometers to the East of the Rhine'. Secondly, any violation of this clause, 'in any manner whatsoever, shall be regarded as committing a hostile act'.

When Hitler called the collective bluff of the western powers, British Prime Minister Stanley Baldwin told a Cabinet meeting on 11 March 1936 that Britain lacked 'the resources to enforce the treaty guarantees and that public opinion would not stand for military action anyway'.

The Chiefs of Staff, relying on War Office intelligence reports, expressed the view that war with Germany was inadvisable on the grounds that the deep cuts imposed by the Ten-Year Rule, together with the fact that rearmament had only begun in 1934, meant that the most Britain could do in the event of war would be to send two divisions with backward equipment to France after three weeks of preparation. If ever this position were to improve, intelligence would be the key.

Intelligence gathering is as old as human history. Twentieth-century British Military Intelligence, whose officers would try to develop an informed understanding of the motives and capabilities of foreign powers, had been set in train by the Committee for Imperial Defence in 1903. All intelligence organisations collated information at a central point while deploying, and often paying, a network of independent agents. Only the Gestapo, originally a policing rather than military organization, had exploited this system to subdue an entire populace. The British MI system, originally divided into departments and subsections, identified by numbers and letters, tended to expand in times of war and contract in times of peace and appeasement. At the time of the Rhineland crisis in March 1936, the MI structure, like the armed forces themselves, was in poor shape and was comprised of five departments:

MI-1 (five subsections) The organization and coordination of Military Intelligence.

MI-1(a) co-ordination of questions affecting personnel employed by the War Office; training in intelligence duties; security; administration questions affecting British Military Attaches; policy affecting the completion and issue of intelligence publications.

MI-1(b) censorship policy; co-ordination of Engineer intelligence; questions relating to publicity and propaganda; trade questions in time of war; policy regarding ciphers and liaison with the Government Code and Cipher School; wireless intelligence; questions connected with the security of ciphers; training of cipher officers.

MI-1(c) 'special duties' or Secret Intelligence Service. This section would, in 1939, be renamed MI6.

MI-1(d) interior economy of Military Intelligence.

MI-1(e) coordination of artillery, small arms, explosives and mechanized intelligence; scientific research connected to ammunition manufactured in foreign countries.

MI-1(f) military translations.

MI-2 (three subsections) The collection, collation and dissemination of information regarding the organization, equipment, training and education of the undermentioned countries.

MI-2(a) Egypt, Sudan, Abyssinia, Cyprus, Palestine, Trans-Jordan, Saudi Arabia, Yemen, Trucial Coast, Aden, Iraq, Persia, Afghanistan, India, Burma, Sinkiang and Tibet.

MI-2(b) USSR, Poland, Finland, Estonia, Latvia, Lithuania.

MI-2(c) Japan, China, Siam, Dutch East Indies, Indo-China and Philippines.

MI-3 (four subsections) The Collection, collation and dissemination of information regarding the organization, equipment, training and education of the undermentioned countries.

MI-3(a) France, Belgium, Luxembourg, Spain, Tangier and Portugal.

MI-3(b) Germany, Holland, Austria, Switzerland, Norway, Sweden and Denmark.

MI-3(c) Italy, Albania, Hungary, Yugoslavia, Romania, Czechoslovakia, Bulgaria, Greece and Turkey.

MI-3(d) USA, Mexico, Guatemala, Salvador, Honduras, Nicaragua, Costa Rica, Panama, Cuba, Haiti, San Domingo, Porto Rico, Columbia, Venezuela, Ecuador, Peru, Brazil, Bolivia, Chile, Argentina, Paraguay and Uruguay.

MI-4 (seven subsections) Geographical duties for the War Office and Air Ministry; Collection of maps and survey data; making of maps for military and air purposes; Liaison with the Colonial and Dominions Survey Departments and the Hydrographic Department of the Admiralty.

MI-4(a) Geographical work for the Army.

MI-4(b) Geographical work for the Royal Air Force.

MI-4(c) Geographical work and maps of Asia, Australasia and Oceania.

MI-4(d) Research work in connection with Air Surveys.

MI-4(e) Geographical work and maps of Africa, North and South America, and West Indies.

MI-4(f) Geodesy of the world. Liaison with the Air Survey Committee.

MI-4(g) Indexing and storing all published topographical maps of the world.

MI-5 (three sections) Inter-departmental Security Service. Defence Security Intelligence. Military policy in relation to civil authorities, civil police, aliens, and War Department Constabulary.

MI-5(a) security intelligence services home and overseas.

MI-5(b) visits by foreigners and civilians to military establishments; credentials for military services and purposes; military permits and passes.

MI-5(c) executive duties; War Department Constabulary.

With his foreign languages, and his knowledge and experience of Germany, it was perhaps not unsurprising that Kenneth Strong saw his future in intelligence work and in MI-3(b) in particular. Not long after joining the German Section, it was decided that Strong should go to Berlin as an Assistant Military Attaché.

Berlin at this time was not only the centre of Britain's intelligence interest but was also a growing worry in terms of security leaks. There was a growing concern and suspicion in British intelligence circles that Britain's embassies in Rome and Berlin had been penetrated by the Gestapo and their Italian counterparts. Until January 1937, Sir Eric Drummond, Britain's Ambassador in Rome, resentfully rejected any suggestions that moles were at work in his embassy, despite the fact that several Italian newspapers had actually quoted directly from a number of secret British documents on their front pages.

He was forced to think again when his wife's diamond necklace was stolen from their bedroom at the embassy. The theft was the perfect opportunity for Major Valentine Vivian, head of counter-espionage at SIS, to be sent in to the embassy to review security. Vivian arrived incognito on 8 February and made a tour of the building during the lunch hour and siesta period. What he saw confirmed his worst fears. In his report he highlighted unlocked office doors, open windows and lax security at every level. He entered the chancery offices where he remained undisturbed and unchallenged for half an hour. A piece of paper was also found on which was written the combination number of the chancery safe. The same key was found to fit all the embassy red dispatch boxes, and key copies were in wide circulation among employees. There was in addition, no awareness that telephones might be bugged and significantly a new telephone had recently been installed in the cipher room. The overall conclusion was that 'security was virtually non-existent' at the embassy. Vivian also voiced concern that key chancery servants were Italian nationals and had ample opportunity to remove embassy documents and take wax impressions of keys. One in particular, Secondo Constantini, was named in Vivian's report as the prime suspect for the 'loss of two copies of the "R" code' along with his brother.

Vivian was later sent to the Berlin embassy to size up security there, and found that the ambassador Sir Neville Henderson had no better appreciation of security than Sir Eric Drummond in Rome. Henderson's notorious indiscretion during telephone conversations was also found to be of great concern. The Gestapo, it was unkindly suggested, did not need a key to British ciphers at the embassy, they had only to lure Sir Neville to the telephone. The British embassy porter was a German, and the Ambassador's residence had no proper guard on it during Henderson's annual two-month leave; and the embassy as a whole, outside of working hours, was at the mercy of the German porter. Vivian's report concluded the following:

> This means, in fact, that the Gestapo could, if they were so minded, introduce nightly and for a practically unlimited period each night any number of lock-smiths and experts in safe-breaking, thereby having continuous access to current papers, telegrams and prints without leaving any trace. There is, of course, no evidence that the porter has admitted Gestapo agents, but, having in view the situation in Berlin and the German mentality, it would be sheer lunacy not to act on the assumption that, a) the porter is in the pay of the Gestapo, and b) that the latter have at their disposal as expert lock pickers as the criminal or professional world can produce.

Vivian's report impressed on British diplomats that Germany, Italy, Japan and Russia should be treated as 'enemy countries' for intelligence purposes and urged 'the replacement of certain native or domiciled members of staff by 100% British subjects recruited from the United Kingdom'. While the Foreign Secretary, Sir Anthony Eden, appears to have adopted Vivian's report in principle, the recommendations were far from completely implemented by the time Eden resigned the following year, to be replaced as Foreign Secretary by the appeaser Lord Halifax. In particular very few foreign employees were dismissed; in fact, Constantini, Vivian's prime suspect in Rome, continued to work at the embassy until 1940 when Italy declared war on Britain. He then worked at the Vatican embassy until June 1944 when he was finally exposed as an Italian intelligence agent.

This then was the Berlin embassy to which Kenneth Strong was assigned. It would seem that he was already aware, from a briefing he had received before setting off for Germany, that circumstances at the embassy were far from satisfactory. He had also been fully drilled on matters of security that would be so vital to the assignment he was now embarking upon. He would arrive in Berlin on the very day that a sleepy Spanish market town would become an everlasting symbol of the atrocity of war.

3

SLEEPWALKING TO WAR

German bombers first appeared in the skies over Guernica around 4.30 p.m. on the afternoon of 26 April 1937. What followed was witnessed by Noel Monks, a correspondent covering the Spanish Civil War for the *Daily Express*:

> Over the top of some small hills appeared a flock of planes, but down much lower, seeming just to skim the treetops were six Heinkel 52 fighters. The bombers flew on towards Guernica but the Heinkels, out for random plunder, spotted our car, and wheeling like a flock of homing pigeons, they lined up the road.

The Heinkels made several runs along the road, machine-gun bullets strafing the car, and as Monks recalled, 'plopping into the mud ahead, behind, and all around us'. Monks and his driver had the luckiest of escapes, leaping from the car into a muddy bomb crater by the side of the road.

Guernica would not be so fortunate. Monday was market day and there were more than 10,000 people in the former Basque capital. They had no idea of what was about to befall them. Over a period of three hours, Dornier DO17 bombers, escorted by Messerschmitt BF 109s, dropped 100,000 pounds of high-explosive and incendiary bombs, reducing the town to a smouldering ruin.

For the Luftwaffe, it was the ideal opportunity to test for the first time its blitzkrieg doctrine of terror bombing, a tactic to deliberately target civilians in order to break their will and resistance. The atrocity is today considered to be the first deliberate air attack on a civilian target.

Noel Monks records:

> I was the first correspondent to reach Guernica, and was immediately pressed into service by some Basque soldiers collecting charred bodies that the flames had passed over. Some of the soldiers were sobbing like children. There were flames and smoke and grit, and the smell of burning human flesh was nauseating. Houses were collapsing into the inferno.

The *Manchester Guardian's* correspondent Frank Jellinek was not too far behind Monks, arriving in Guernica less than an hour later, and lodged a report to London in which he observed, 'Even flocks of sheep were machine-gunned. The fires were so extensive that many bodies will never be recovered.'

Two days after the attack, George Steer of The Times asserted that:

> The raid on Guernica is unparalleled in military history. Guernica was not a military objective. A factory producing war material lay outside the town and was untouched. The objective of the bombardment was seemingly the demoralization of the civil population and the destruction of the cradle of the Basque race.

Within hours of arriving in Berlin, Kenneth Strong, accompanied by his travelling trunk and two suitcases, was taken by an Embassy official, to what would be, for the next two years, his home from home.

The small unfurnished flat on the western edge of Konigsplatz Square, near to the Kroll Opera House, was the height of luxury compared with billet in the UK. The Opera House was originally built in 1844 as an entertainment venue, but following the Reichstag fire in February 1933, which provided a pretext for Hitler to seize dictatorial power, it became the new home of the German Parliament. Overlooking the Victory Column, the flat had the most efficient of central heating, constant hot water, double-glazed windows and insulation, all of which, he recalled, were unheard of in Britain in 1937.

Within a few days of his arrival, Strong was to meet the man who more than anyone else would kindle his fascination and foreboding for the Gestapo and give him the foundations of the knowledge about the organization that would prove an invaluable asset to him in the not-too-distant future. Their paths crossed for the first time at an Embassy reception hosted by the British Ambassador, Sir Nevile Henderson. During the course of the perfunctory round of hellos and handshakes, Strong was introduced to the British Passport Control Officer, Captain Frank Foley.

At this time few, if any, fellow guests knew or even suspected that the post of Passport Control Officer was effectively a cover for the Head of the Berlin SIS Station, as indeed was the Passport Control Office for the SIS station itself. Life in this guise was often precarious, Foley would later tell Strong, due to the fact that although attached to the British Embassy, Passport Control staff did not have diplomatic status, and therefore had no diplomatic immunity.

The fifty-two-year-old Foley, a genial ex-army officer wounded on the Western Front, was a seasoned SIS veteran who had been Station Head in Berlin since 1923, four years after the outpost was established in late 1919. He and Strong soon became firm friends, but took care never to meet on their own in public, only at functions and other official gatherings, for as Foley warned him, the Gestapo were only too well aware of the intelligence function of the Passport Control Office.

Foley had worked closely with the German police from the time he arrived at the height of the 'red scare', pooling intelligence on the activities of the Russians and home-grown German communists operating in Berlin and north-east Germany. These early police intelligence contacts had provided a smooth seam by which Foley had managed to maintain his covert contacts even after the new Nazi regime had taken over the Prussian police. Indeed, in 1933 Foley had early awareness from his police contacts that Hermann Göring, the Interior Minister with responsibility for Prussia, was about to create a new 'mailed fist' to take the battle to Hitler's opponents. On 26 April that year, Göring detached the political and intelligence sections from the Prussian police and merged them to create a new, autonomous Secret State Police (the Geheime Staatspolizei), which became better known in its abbreviated form, the Gestapo. According to Foley's police connections, Göring had originally wanted to call it the Secret Police Office (Geheimes Polizeiamt). However, its initials, GPA, were considered too similar to the those of the Russian Secret Police, the GPU, so Gestapo it was.

While the Gestapo and their Prussian police predecessors knew precious little, if anything, about the SIS as an organization, they did know that Foley was a British intelligence officer and someone with a shared interest in the GPU (known from 1934 onwards as the NKVD). At this early point of the Nazi regime, this common interest in Soviet activities provided the glue that, at least for the time being, gave the relationship with Foley traction. However, by the time of Strong's arrival in Berlin, Foley's relations with the Gestapo were becoming somewhat strained due to his refusal to 'satisfy the Gestapo lust for information on the subject of anti-Nazi Germans in England on the false grounds that they were communists'.

The Gestapo were, at the same time as pushing Foley harder for intelligence, beginning to take a much more proactive line against British intelligence and anyone they thought was involved or associated with it. This became evident on 17 August 1938 when the Gestapo arrested Tommy Kendrick, the SIS Head of Station in Vienna (now, since the Anschluss, part of Germany). SIS personnel in Vienna immediately burnt everything secret and headed for London.

Unlike Foley, Strong, as an Assistant Military Attaché, had diplomatic immunity, but this was not something anyone wanted to put to the test, least of all Strong. He kept his every movement circumspect and was forever alert to the possible attentions of the men from No 8 Prinz-Albrechtstrasse.

Despite the shadow of the Gestapo, Strong deliberately pursued an active social life in order to maximize the contacts that he made:

> The Opera and the theatres in Berlin were packed every night. Occasionally, while we awaited the rise of the curtain at the Winter Garden or some other place of entertainment, there would be a sudden hush and the audience would quietly rise to its feet. Hitler and his entourage would enter and take their places in one of the boxes in the auditorium. In those days it was still possible to meet prominent Nazis socially at receptions and dinners. Göring came frequently to our embassy parties and was always friendly.

In this way Strong met an array of Nazis such as Dr Robert Ley, whom he described as:

> ... an uncompromising agitator. We had many beers together after hot, stuffy meetings, when he would valiantly try to explain to me the tenets of Nazism. I also met Goebbels. A small man with an enormous head, large ears and paralyzed in one leg. But he was highly intelligent and, after Hitler, the best orator in the party. His speeches, shorn of propaganda, were always worthy of the closest attention.

Strong's duties as an Assistant Attaché were to maintain contact with the German armed forces and to obtain all possible information about them. The attack on Guernica by Germany's Condor Legion and the Legion's wider role in the Spanish Civil War was of critical importance to MI3, who saw Germany's involvement in Spain as little more than a dress rehearsal for a wider European conflict. The war between Franco and the left-leaning Republican government was the perfect opportunity for the German armed forces to trial ideas and tactics that, to date, had been confined to training and policy lectures.

MI3(a) and MI3(b), who were responsible, respectively, for Spanish and German intelligence, were keen to learn more about the Condor Legion, and in particular its strength, tactics and methods. Strong had also picked up from Captain Frank Foley that the Germans were also using their Spanish expedition as a proving ground for more covert methods of controlling and administering subjugated territory.

The Gestapo had been in on the Spanish venture from day one and saw it as an ideal opportunity to road test ideas for the weeding out and eliminating of anti-Nazi elements. Paul Winzer was appointed head of the Gestapo's Spanish operation in 1936 and immediately set about the setting up of a network of Francoist concentration camps in areas of territory controlled by nationalist forces. By 1938, the camps held more than 170,000 prisoners. Camp inmates were in the main republican ex-combatants, as well as socialists, communists and homosexuals. While many were executed, the majority were used as forced labour. While no reliable figures can be established regarding the number of inmates who survived the civil war, it is known that many were later 'subcontracted' to private companies and landowners who effectively used them as slave labour.

Strong, at the behest of MI3, wrote at some length about German support and aid to Franco in Spain. An early note on the Condor Legion outlines a host of details concerning its foundation. Recruited mainly from the Luftwaffe, it also included tank and supply units. Initially under the command of General Warlimont, Strong noted that its personnel were rotated frequently so that maximum use could be made of the Spanish Civil War for training the German armed forces. As Strong concluded:

> The operations of the Legion in Spain were also said to have been a considerable drain on German financial resources, but undoubtedly the armed forces gained a great deal of experience from them in bombing effects, air support for ground forces, tank deployment, and the transport of large parties of troops by air.

Not long after committing these notes to paper, Strong related 'a great stroke of luck' that came about as the result of the Legion's frequent rotation. A contingent of tank units from the Condor Legion were returning to Berlin and would be taking part in a military parade through the city centre:

> I was in my flat in the Tiergarten just after lunch on the day before the parade. The telephone rang and I recognized the voice of one of my friends in the German High Command. He enquired politely after my health, hoped he would see me next day at the parade and then suggested that, as the day was fine and sunny, I should take an evening stroll through Berlin to observe for myself how enthusiastic people were at the prospect of tomorrow's events. He even suggested the names of the streets where I should find the greatest and most loyal enthusiasm.

This seemed a rather curious message, and so Strong decided to take a walk and see for himself what was happening. To his astonishment, he found that the Germans had marked on the pavements the names of the units which were to assemble that evening before the next day's parade. This was a real bonanza, but the difficulty was to remember all he had seen written down in chalk. As he could not afford to attract attention to himself by openly taking notes, he had to try and commit as much as possible to memory, and quickly returned to his flat and wrote it down. As things turned out, he'd acted just in the nick of time: an army of charwomen with buckets and mops suddenly appeared in the streets. Someone in authority had belatedly discovered the German blunder and was now trying to redress it.

When Hitler moved, in 1938, to argue that the Sudetenland in Czechoslovakia, where large numbers of German speakers resided, should be ceded to Germany, a new international crisis was triggered. Fearing that if the Czech government was unwilling to acquiesce, which clearly, they were not, Hitler could be tempted to invade, thus triggering a European conflict involving France and Britain.

The War Office were keen to monitor the build-up and movements of German troops potentially heading to the border with Czechoslovakia. Strong was therefore deputed to carry out a reconnaissance in the Dresden area, which he undertook with some care, knowing that the Gestapo would be watching British Embassy personnel with an ever-watchful eye:

> We had heard that troops were being moved southwards ready for action against the Sudentenland, and I set off in my car (which had a German number plate) to see what I could discover. I parked it at the side of a road near Koenigsbrück, a vast military camp about twenty miles north of Dresden, where I felt sure that newly arrived German divisions were being assembled. I had guessed correctly. Every few minutes trains were steaming into the nearby military sidings packed with soldiers, tanks and a variety of military equipment.

When Strong returned to his car, he was concerned to find a German soldier standing by it. Fearing the worst, that he was about to be arrested for spying, he was mightily relieved when the soldier instead asked him for a lift to Dresden. Apparently, the young man wanted to say a final goodbye to his fiancée who lived in Dresden, and spent the first part of their journey unburdening himself of his personal worries. Strong unhesitatingly played the role of a sympathetic and understanding listener and their conversation soon moved on to talk of his unit, their movements, and the instructions they had been given about the future. The soldier belonged to a tank battalion which was stationed in Berlin but had just moved south towards Czechoslovakia. When they reached Dresden, and the soldier was dropped off, Strong immediately went at once to the British consulate, where he encoded a message to the War Office in London forwarding the information he gathered.

While Strong remained resolute in his view that the outbreak of a new European war was only a matter of time, and saw the Munich Agreement, concluded on 30 September, as a naive and unapologetic act of appeasement, he found that it had unexpected advantages so far as his intelligence-gathering mission was concerned. Chamberlain's concordat had:

> ... unexpectedly given us an unparalleled opportunity to get a close view of the German array. The Agreement had been preceded by preliminary discussions between Chamberlain and Hitler, and the

task of conveying the results of this conference to our Embassy in Prague was entrusted to myself and Mason-MacFarlane. To get to Prague we had to pass through the Czech frontier fortifications and defences.

On returning to Berlin, Mason-MacFarlane and Strong reported to the British Embassy and gave a pessimistic account of what they had seen. The report could only be superficial because of the speed with which the task had been undertaken, but nevertheless, they saw enough to become convinced that the Czechs would be incapable of any prolonged military resistance to a German incursion.

Strong also noted the high morale and confidence in the future among the officers and men of von Reichenau's Army Group. When reporting back to Sir Nevile Henderson at the British Embassy after his return from Hof, Strong described

> ... all I had seen and heard, and said that the morale and efficiency of the German Army now seemed to be at its highest point; I could not see how this could be maintained indefinitely without further military adventures. I was given to understand that Henderson did not agree with this view. It was not thought to be of sufficient importance to report to London.

The intelligence-gathering operation undertaken by Strong and Mason-MacFarlane was, however, seen as a valuable exercise by Ambassador Henderson, although the War Office continued to draw the wrong conclusions from what Strong saw as growing evidence of further German aggression. Among Strong's Wehrmacht informants were Ulrich Liss and Karl Schuchardt. Five years later, both men would be among those involved in the July 1944 plot against Hitler. According to Strong's notes:

> One of them confided in me that another war would mean disaster for Germany. If war came, Germany would be beaten and he would once again be back to being a salesman. Such officers believed it was essential to ensure that the British were in possession of the fullest possible information about German military capabilities

in the hope that the British Government would realise the real importance of what was happening in Germany and would curb German ambitions.

Such was the fear among a number of Wehrmacht officers, that when war did eventually break out in September 1939, removing Hitler became their only logical move. The plot, and how the Gestapo exploited it to draw first blood from the SIS in the opening months of the 'phoney war', was to prove a farce in multiple acts, as we shall see in chapter 5.

Strong's arrival back in Berlin coincided with what he described as 'one of the saddest and most disturbing experiences I had in Berlin and one which brought me close to the essential character of the Nazi movement'. On the night of 8/9 November a pogrom against the Jews was carried out by the SA paramilitary forces across the country. The rioters ransacked Jewish homes, synagogues, schools and businesses in what came to be known as Kristallnacht ('Crystal Night'), named after the shards of broken glass from the smashed windows of Jewish properties.

It is estimated that by morning, over 7,000 Jewish businesses had been smashed, burnt and looted, 30,000 Jewish men arrested, and hundreds reported dead. On his way to work at the British Embassy on the morning of 9 November, Strong personally witnessed the aftermath of the night before:

> Our Passport Office was in the same building and I remember, on my way to work, having to pass a long line of distressed Jews, weeping, waiting, hoping and begging to be given passports to leave Germany. They grabbed at me as I passed, old men and women, young children, all desperate to get out of Germany; but there was nothing I could do to help them.

Strong related what he had seen to Frank Foley, who was already well versed in the modus operandi of the SD and the Gestapo. The two men spoke at some length about what Foley referred to as 'bestial depravity'.

Most people in SIS knew exactly what cruelty the Gestapo were capable of. There were British Consuls and Vice-Consuls in cities such as Frankfurt and Hamburg, and they sent memos to the Foreign Office. One of these memos, unsigned but still in the records, mentions a Jew 'who was in the trenches during the [First World] war, who had a good business here and is a well-educated man. I knew him as a member of the golf club and he is on friendly terms with Vice-Consul Dowden'.

The memo goes on to recount the man's experience of being telephoned by the Gestapo and told to stay at home. They came to collect him. He asked to take a change of clothes. He was told 'no; bring some money'. He was taken to a police station and then by lorry with scores of others to the large Exhibition Hall. Crowds outside hurled abuse at each lorryload of Jews as they arrived (the place would hold well over 20,000 people). They lined up. His money and handkerchief were taken 'for return later'. Many of those who had been there since the previous night had had no food or water. Everybody was made to kneel, forehead to floor and hands behind backs. Those who could not do this were kicked in the back of the neck. Some were made to run around the building. Some who vomited had their faces and hair rubbed in it.

The SS arrived and drove them with sticks into lorries bound for a railway station. Driven by blows, they were herded through a tunnel towards a platform and stopped. They were told to face the tunnel walls. 'The guards passed up and down behind them kicking and beating them.' They were entrained for Buchenwald. In the train, the guards knocked out teeth, bashed heads, and blacked eyes. Then, again beaten, they were forced into a lorry from Weimar to nearby Buchenwald. Once there they were driven into enclosures; the wire fencing carried a dangerously high current which inflicted burns. The camp Kommandant harangued them about the sin of being Jewish. SS men approached them with scissors and hacked off their hair and their beards, attacking the rabbis (for whom facial hair was sacrosanct) with particular glee.

In the camp the men were accommodated in sheds. These were around 20 feet by 80 feet, with bunks to the ceiling. With each bed in a bunk having to hold three men, this meant 2,500 individuals. The camp at Buchenwald wasn't quite ready yet, so there was no water to drink the first day, and no latrines, and no water for washing.

On the first night, men were picked at random to be taken outside and flogged, feet strapped onto footplates, body bent over a pole, head held rigid between two horizontal bars. Strokes were limited to fifty as punishment, but there was no limit as this was 'sport'. Some died. If they survived, they were kicked back to the shed. Some lost control, and were chained up with sacks round their heads to muffle their screams.

> During the first night men were not allowed to leave the shed to relieve nature. They used their hats. I cannot enlarge on these filthy details. ... I cannot spare you one other horror which shows the sadistic nature of some of the SS men, who are supposed to be the flower of the party manhood: they forced men to urinate into each other's mouths to give them sport.

Arthur Dowden, who is mentioned above, together with his Consul Robert Smallbones, are today commemorated as Holocaust heroes by the British government. At Kristallnacht, with her husband in London, Mrs Inge Smallbones hid scores of Jews in their house. Their teenage daughter had been traumatised by the sight of a line of Jews hanging at a remote spot when she was out riding. The consular staff also hid Jews, in the Consulate. They told nobody, especially not Consul Smallbones, for his own safety. In London, he and Vice-Consul Dowden nagged a reluctant Home Office until a visa scheme was devised and quietly passed into law. It allowed Jews to enter Britain for up to two years pending their emigration to the United States. This stamp on a passport saved the lives of many thousands.

Frank Foley, more than anyone else, knew a considerable amount about the ever-growing tentacles of the Gestapo. Having been in close cahoots with the Prussian State Police from the time of his arrival in the early 1920s, he had seen the organisation's birth and growth at first hand. He had catalogued its development in detail, a task in which he had been greatly assisted by a British businessman, John MacLaren-Clarke, who had business interests in several European countries including Germany and France. 'M.C' had sought to cultivate a number of German officials over the years, purely in the interest of smoothing the way for his numerous business deals. This, more often than not, extended to showing his gratitude to officialdom 'in the usual way', or to coin his own phrase, 'baksheesh'. Foley had become acquainted with MacLaren-Clarke through the Embassy's social circles and had, after satisfying himself of MacLaren-Clarke's bona-fides, enlisted him as a source and eventually as a confederate. Strong was eventually introduced to 'M.C' by Foley, and it was principally through these two key sources that Strong built up a detailed pen-picture of the Gestapo, recognising the importance not only of this new and disturbing phenomenon in the world of espionage, but equally for the oldest of adages: 'know thine enemy'.

4

THE WATCHERS

On a hot summer's day in early August 1938, two men in a Citroen 7 sedan cruised slowly through the streets of the exclusive Alto de Santo Amaro district of the Portuguese capital. Lisbon in the late 1930s was a twilight zone awash with a heady mixture of glamour and menace, succinctly described by John Masterman, in his classic post-war novel *The Case of the Four Friends*, as a busy ant heap of spies, hustlers, wheeler-dealers and profiteers.

While officially non-aligned, the government of dictator Antonio de Oliveira Salazar was, in the view of many, hand in glove with Franco's Spain and more in sympathy with the fascist cause than that of France or Britain. The power of his 'Estado Novo' National Union movement was underpinned by the Portuguese Secret Police, the PVDE (Policia de Vigilancia de Defesa do Estado). They had been well trained and organised by the Gestapo, and were well known for keeping an eagle eye on foreign nationals, particularly those from France and Britain.

The two PVDE agents in the Citroen 7 had picked up a subject for surveillance they had code-named Antonio. The man was approximately thirty-eight–forty years old and around 6 feet tall. He had dark hair, a moustache, glasses, and had a camera around his neck. On this particular day he was wearing a white shirt and dark trousers. They began following 'Antonio' from his hotel. He was driving a black Fiat 1500. Once in the Alto de Santo Amaro district, 'Antonio' parked his car and continued his journey on foot. His route took him along several streets that had magnificent views over the River Tagus and past some of the most important monuments in the city. As one might expect of any tourist, he stopped and took photographs of the river and several other buildings along the way. However, it was his interest in one of the nondescript ordinary-looking houses a short distance from the Valle Flor Palace that aroused suspicion. 'Antonio' stopped at house No. 37 and knocked on the door. There was no answer. He then spoke to a woman from the neighbouring house. He asked her something. The surveillance team were not close enough to overhear the exchange but noted in their report that the woman pointed to one of the doors on the opposite side of the street. 'Antonio' knocked on that door too; again, there was no answer. He then turned back in the opposite direction, retracing the route back to his car.

The entire duration of the surveillance was less than four hours. The two PVDE agents filed their report later that same day. At that point, they had no idea who he was, or what he had been doing in the Alto de Santo Amaro district. All they knew for sure was that Antonio had not found who or what he was looking for.

When, several days later, Antonio's hotel registration records were checked, he was identified as a British national by the name of John MacLaren-Clarke. A copy of the surveillance report was sent to the Lisbon office of the Gestapo, who responded to the PVDE to the effect that MacLaren-Clarke was known to the Gestapo and that they could vouch for him. This was somewhat of an understatement, for MacLaren-Clarke had for some years cultivated senior officials in Göring's circle in order to oil the wheels of commerce. He had also apparently had dealings with von Ribbentrop in London when the Nazi was Germany's Ambassador to Great Britain. MacLaren-Clarke is referred to in the exchange as having chemical, mining and mineral interests in several European countries and addresses in London, Paris and Berlin. While his motives for joining forces with Foley are unclear, it seems apparent that MacLaren-Clarke used his German contacts, official and social, to assist Frank Foley in his quest to compile a detailed dossier on the Gestapo.

Much of the early and rudimentary awareness SIS and MI3 had of the German secret police centres around the personality and activities of Hermann Göring. Almost from the moment that Hitler had succeeded in gaining the office of Chancellor, Göring had been given control of the Office of the Prussian Ministry of the Interior in Berlin. This office stored useful personal and political information about Berlin's Communists, Socialists, and others likely to undermine the regime. He immediately decided that this system must now be extended, first throughout Prussia – by far the largest state – and as soon as possible throughout the whole country. As Minister of the Interior, Göring decreed that his new State Secret Police, the Geheime Staatspolizei, shortened to Gestapo – would take over all such pre-existing records nationwide and – most importantly – add to them. Hitler also began, in due course, implementing his covert plans to rearm Germany by stealth, and recreate a German Airforce. To this end he renamed the Air Supply Corps the Reich Ministry of Aviation. While the Ministry was responsible purely for civil aviation it was clearly a stalking horse for the next step in the plan – the Luftwaffe. This was forbidden by the Treaty of Versailles, hence the need to tread carefully. Göring was now appointed Minister for Air on the inception of the new ministry and to add to his already growing collection of uniforms was also appointed General of the Reichswehr (the German Army). Despite the elderly President Hindenburg's misgivings, he had been persuaded that the man who would eventually command the new Luftwaffe could not possibly do so from the rank of captain. With his new self-designed general's uniform, Göring began to take a less active interest in the affairs of the Gestapo. Having spent some time polishing Göring's ego and presenting him with a new toy in the shape of the soon-to-be Luftwaffe, Hitler now began to move forward with a plan for a Germany-wide secret police apparatus. It was suggested that this was the result of gradual lobbying by Heinrich Himmler, whom Hitler had already appointed President of the Munich Police Department in April 1933. While seen by many in the party as a backwater post, it nevertheless provided an effective bridgehead from which Himmler plotted a gradual takeover of all German police departments and organisations.

Himmler wasted no time in creating the Bavarian Political Police (the Bayerische Politische Polizei or BPP). Like Göring in Prussia, Himmler gave the new department independence from the jurisdiction of the criminal police headquarters in Munich. He began by recruiting 152 additional officers that had also been recruited by the Munich Police Department. Some were already Nazi Party members, although the majority were not. Himmler soon dismissed Julius Koch, the President of the Munich Police, but kept the vast majority of rank and file officers. He also acted to promote Heinrich Müeller, who had a growing reputation for his expertise in matters of Marxist and socialist parties operating in Bavaria. Another Munich police officer Himmler decided to befriend was Franz Josef Huber. Two years older than Müeller, he was also a man with considerable political experience in the police force. Surprisingly, he had been responsible for monitoring the Nazi Party during the Weimar period and had reputedly been anti-Nazi prior to his recruitment in 1933. Himmler no doubt saw him as an asset and he very quickly won him over as a sympathiser and follower.

Müeller and Huber were effectively redeployed and promoted due to the influence of Reinhard Heydrich, Himmler's chief confidant. Heydrich had been fast-tracked by Himmler from the moment he had recruited him in 1931, after being introduced through an acquaintance of his wife, not long after Heydrich had been discharged from the navy. Himmler was thinking seriously at the time about developing a counter-intelligence division of the SS, and asked Heydrich at their first meeting to present him with ideas and proposals.

Within days, Heydrich had come back to him with page after page of ideas which Himmler was apparently most impressed with. The young Heydrich's early ambition was to be a chemist. As well as excelling at sports, he also had a fascination with detective and spy novels and had apparently cribbed many of the ideas he presented to Himmler from a number of his boyhood spy books. Ironically, another unacknowledged key source was the 1929 book *The Secrets of Espionage – Tales of the Secret Service* by the German-Jewish writer Winfried Ludecke. One of the most fascinating sections of the book was about the British secret service and the Russian adventures of Captain Sidney Reilly. It is unlikely that Heydrich knew Reilly was, in fact, a Ukrainian Jew by the name of Rosenblum, who had fled to London in the 1890s and adopted a new Irish name and identity.

Ludecke himself quickly left Germany not long after the rise of the Nazis, and was later to find himself on Hitler's 'Black Book' list (along with Sidney Reilly) as an enemy of the Reich who faced arrest and death at the hands of the Gestapo in the event of being tracked down.

Apart from an irrational belief in the racial superiority of his nation, Heydrich played the violin to near professional standard, spoke several languages and had distinguished himself as a naval officer.

Heydrich was at first tasked with spying on the Nazis' political enemies in Bavaria. He and his wife (also a Nazi) flung themselves into the work, following leads they found in pre-existing files in Munich. So successful was he that by 1932 he was head of the SD, the SS intelligence service. So, when in 1933 the call came – essentially, ordering that all political opponents in Bavaria should be rounded up and arrested, with the possibility of transfer to a concentration camp – the SS and SD knew exactly whom to pursue. The SD's initial brief was to spy on political opponents, collecting useful information on parties opposing the Nazis and identifying dissent within the party. Heydrich was soon collecting information on party members and allies. He began by filing such information by hand on index cards. At first, he did almost all the work himself on a borrowed typewriter having few staff in his employ. Unlike the Gestapo, whose employees were on the state payroll, SD members were employed by the Nazi Party.

Heydrich was firmly of the view that in terms of recruitment, not always having Nazi connections or sympathies was a distinct advantage. From day one Himmler's police terrorised one group of Nazi opponents after another. Within two weeks of taking over as President of Police some 3,000 KPD members and supporters had been arrested and put into the 'protective custody' offered by the SS and SA concentration camps that had recently been set up in Bavaria. In a BPP report dated 25 May it was claimed that the KPD had been effectively eradicated. This may have been a little optimistic as other BPP files indicate that a further wave of KPD arrests took place shortly afterwards based on intelligence provided by BPP agents planted in the KPD. There followed arrests of SPD members and members of their paramilitary wing the Reichsbanner. Members of the Bavarian Peoples' Party too were arrested and placed in protective custody. The Jews were unsurprisingly an early target and the BPP responded with enthusiasm to the national edict of 12 May 1933 instructing all police forces to search the offices of all Jewish organisations for subversive and treasonable materials. Over 200 arrests took place although no subversive materials were found. By August 1933, 4,152 individuals were in Himmler's protective custody in Bavaria, which compared to a nationwide total of over 100,000.

Two months later in October, Himmler took over the Hamburg Police Department; during the following two months he added Mecklenburg, Lübeck, Württemberg-Baden, Hesse, Thüringen, and Anhalt to his tally. In January 1934 he mopped up Oldenburg, Bremen, and Saxony. By April 1934 it would seem that Göring was finally persuaded to hand responsibility for the Prussian Gestapo to Himmler. While this was no doubt the result of Hitler's influence, it is also highly likely that others too had encouraged Göring in the conclusion that heading the secret police would only hinder his efforts to cultivate the popularity he craved. With the Gestapo under Himmler's belt, he now held all the aces and was in de facto control of all police forces in Germany.

Heydrich moved to Berlin and was immediately appointed de facto director of the Gestapo, while remaining head of the SD. A system of card indexes and files had already been developed by the Gestapo. It was expanded by Heydrich and improved upon. In both the Berlin headquarters and the local departmental offices, all known enemies of the state were recorded in what the organisation referred to as the A index. This card index consisted of three groups of cards. Group A1, denoted by a red mark on the left side of each card, was for enemies of the state who were to be apprehended. Group A2, denoted by a blue mark, consisted of those who were to be arrested upon the proclamation of a mobilization. Group A3, however, were citizens who were not classed as enemies of the state but were, in Heydrich's words, 'in times of hard tests [to] be regarded as politically so dangerous that their apprehension and special surveillance must be considered'.

On the right-hand side of the cards was another mark. A dark red mark, for example, signified a Communist, a light red mark a Marxist, a brown mark a terrorist, and a violet mark a 'troublemaker'. The card index system was thoroughly reviewed twice a year, on 1 April and 1 October, to ensure that information remained valid. The filing system was highly modern and the most advanced in Europe if not the world. It was estimated that the system comprised of some half a million cards. There was apparently an 'inner system' which was comprised of those individuals who were considered to be the most significant individuals from the point of view of the Gestapo. This 'inner system' was stored in a large horizontal circular card index machine, described by Kenneth Strong as 'a forerunner of the punched-card reader'. The machine was operated by an electric motor which could apparently find any card within two to three minutes.

The card index system, however, would have counted for very little had it not been for a highly complex grass roots system of informers. Germany had thirty-two administrate districts or *Gaue*. Each district was in turn divided into circles or *Kreis* and subdivided into groups of municipalities or *Ortsgruppen*. Every municipality had cells or *Zellen*, similar to wards in the UK. Finally, these were broken down into groups of approximately sixty homes known as blocks or *Zelle*. Each of these administrative areas was headed by a Leader. The Block Leader (*Blockleiter*) was the key player so far as the Gestapo system of informers was concerned. While Himmler and Heydrich perfected the system of informers, it was an earlier order issued by Göring on 22 June 1933 that required every official to report any anti-German behaviour. By implication this made it a crime not to inform on neighbours, acquaintances and work colleagues.

The Nazis were most meticulous in ensuring that there was a Party organisation in every factory and company throughout the Reich and although the Trades Unions had been banned and dissolved, a new German Labour Front (the DAF) had been created to take their place. The DAF was ultimately to emerge as the largest mass organisation in the Reich, eventually having a membership of some 25 million. DAF officials too were covered by Göring's June 1933 order.

Other organisations were to follow, such as the Reich Farmers Organisation, youth groups such as the Hitler Youth, and vocational and cultural groups like the Chamber of Writers. Officials of these organisations in turn also became subject to Göring's order. In addition to voluntary information supplied by informants, Göring was also credited with enabling the means to obtain involuntary information. In 1933 he had founded the Research Institute Hermann Göring, which due to its non-governmental status was not officially part of either the police or the judiciary. The Institute taped telephone switchboards, the telegraphy system and radio traffic, and also took an interest in international telephone calls made by foreign citizens.

The Gestapo also had its own section of specialists who worked under the guise of the telephone service, installing telephone taps on the pretext of carrying out repairs and checking telephone lines and electrical equipment. The Gestapo could therefore call on either of these services to record conversations in the homes and offices of suspects. Telephone conversation transcripts were then typed up at Gestapo offices and transferred to a complex system of individual files.

Göring had created his own enormous secret telephone tapping unit based in Berlin and Heydrich now had access to that too, with predictable consequences for the regime's enemies. For example, when the former Chancellor, Franz von Papen, delivered an incendiary speech at Marburg University on 17 June 1934, the speech writer, Edgar Jong, was identified, abducted and murdered. His dismembered body was brought all the way from Munich to the outskirts of Berlin, where it was found in a ditch.

Göring and Himmler disliked one another but for a long time had been united in opposition to Ernest Röhm. Röhm's Störmtruppe, who were now called the SA (Stürmabteilung), presented a challenge. Röhm seemed to take his own superiority for granted and the force was too unpredictably aggressive. Himmler's SS had shown themselves to be a better trained, better controlled and more vicious bodyguard for the Führer than the SA (to whom they were officially subordinate). The Wehrmacht generals had never had any time for Röhm. Göring and Himmler now formed an alliance of convenience to unite in the liquidation of Röhm and his SA followers in a massacre that was soon to be known as 'the Night of the Long Knives'.

Heydrich also moved to create a Gestapo counter-intelligence unit that would specialise in recruiting V-persons. V-persons were German employees of foreign consulates, recruited as 'agents' tasked with informing their Gestapo handler what was going on inside, for instance, the American, British or French Consulate in Frankfurt, Berlin or Hamburg. They could be offered exemption from military service. In return, they would smuggle documents out of the Consulate, or open incoming letters, photostat them and seal them again. This was not a quick process. Photostat machines took two minutes to produce a single page, white on black. To reverse the copy to black type on white paper meant another two-minute pass on the machine.

Many policemen and justice officials had the power to hold individuals without trial 'to protect society'. They could have letters and telegrams opened and read, phone calls listened to, and houses raided. There was no need for any judicial imprimatur such as a warrant. The Gestapo could effectively do as they pleased. The lives of all citizens were open to investigation, and curiosity was encouraged. There was constant talk of enemies, of people who posed a huge threat to the Reich and the Führer himself. Anyone who let slip a leftist opinion could be reported, rounded up and taken for interrogation followed by dispatch to a concentration camp. Communists would be sent to camps from which they were unlikely to return. It was so important to root out the enemy within. If one's neighbour drank too much and insulted the regime or – worse still – the Führer, one must of course report that immediately to the local Gestapo unit or become an accessory to the crime. Good record-keeping was vital. Party members were told to set up a card index: who did they know, and what did they know about their political affiliation?

Journalists or anyone else known to have been dismissive of the regime were fair game.

Arrests were arbitrary. Communists and socialists were taken away. Next came those other categories who were surplus to requirements in the Reich. Hitler's list of human misfits was lengthening all the time. Allowing for subtle variations in time and judgement, it consisted of the following.

Non-Aryans of all types and Jews. Jews were defined as people who had Jewish grandparents (even if they or those grandparents had converted to some other religion; even if they had become nuns or priests). Whole families must go and most alluringly, Jewish businesses and Jewish homes and possessions could be removed from their owners – who would be paid, of course, at a set price chosen by the authorities. Such people would be sent to 'correction camps'. Their businesses, homes and possessions would be repurposed by worthy Aryans.

Also to be removed were Mischlinge (people of mixed race, including the children and grandchildren of Jews who had married out, or Gentiles who had married in). Mischlinge must also go to the camps, as must disabled people, the mentally ill and the chronically sick, homosexuals, Communists and Socialists.

The Nuremberg Laws of 1935 locked down all these strictures and exclusions as the will of the Führer, although the Gestapo had already been enforcing them for some time. Marriage with a Jew, a Roma, or any other 'subhuman' was not permitted. Association with Jews was forbidden. If an 'Aryan' person had a friend who looked Jewish, and a self-righteous neighbour noticed this, the neighbour was duty-bound to report both of them. The Gestapo raided synagogues and removed precious records, the better to find families. Jews could not work in the civil service, only a few could go to university, and they were prohibited from owning certain property or practising law – or, if they were doctors, from treating a non-Jew. Economic and social survival were made almost impossible.

Detention was 'for the protection of society'. There was no *habeas corpus*, no right to escape unmerited imprisonment according to the judgement of a court. After some time in a cell, under interrogation if necessary, the detainee would be moved to a concentration camp. Some of these were set up in the first months of Hitler's rule as Chancellor, others later. They were largely the Gestapo's concern. At first people were put anywhere – empty warehouses, dirty old cellars, for instance. Dachau, a disused power station near Munich, was the first to be redesigned for this purpose. Himmler was keen on the idea of 'correction' camps, and at the coalface was Heydrich. At the correction camps, guards ill-treated the inmates, and the Gestapo interrogated them and (at first) released them when they were broken and cowed. Black people were sterilised. Everyone had reason to be afraid.

Later, concentration camps proved useful as providers of forced labour and live or dead bodies for medical experiment. But in the early years they were more of a deterrent, because on release Jews and sub-humans would be likely to leave the country – to conveniently deport themselves, leaving their property to be 'confiscated'.

Heydrich instructed Heinrich Müeller to root out all Communists in Munich. Müeller had long been obsessed by the Red Menace. When he found a civilian couple who had made a list of known correction camps and 'reception centres' he was infuriated, and minded to charge them with treason. He could not; their list alone was insufficient proof. But he made sure that the law was tweaked so that any interest in, or description of, such places became treasonous. His SS file in the early 1930s pointed out that he 'tolerates none who might stand in his way. He knows how to display his efficiency.' Every Socialist and Communist he could lay his hands on went to jail.

In 1936 Heydrich decided to put Müeller in operational charge of the Gestapo. Under his authority Gestapo officers did their job with such exemplary enthusiasm that the number of camps multiplied to accommodate all the 'communists' and rather fewer 'sub-humans'. This had an unexpected result. Local leaders in Munich were exasperated by high-handed orders to seize land and facilities for camps. Such orders expressed the will of Berlin, which they resented. Dachau, 10 miles from Munich, had been built in 1933, and quite soon spawned the first sub-camp in the area. Then another, and another. But complainers could expect a brisk reprisal, so pretty soon any resentment was silenced.

The Kripo, the German criminal police, did nothing to intervene. Even if the law had permitted them to do so, Heydrich's Gestapo under Müeller admitted no boundaries. In the search for genuine informers, it had turned on a tap of spite and was flooded with streams of information from the public, much of it completely redundant. An early head of the organisation had complained of an 'army of snoopers and tittle-tattlers'. There seemed no limit to the number of disappointed lovers, angry neighbours and aggrieved purchasers who sent petty accusations to local offices. But in an atmosphere of fear, where people could only suspect what powers the Gestapo might deploy, conformity – even a willingness to stand out as being a good citizen of the Fatherland – was the safest option.

In true Teutonic fashion, the emphasis in the Gestapo, from its very inception, was the mantra of efficiency, bureaucracy and effective systems. While Göring, Himmler, Heidrich and Müeller were, in many ways, very different personalities, they all shared the belief that senior and even middle-ranking Gestapo personnel should be drawn from those with good educational qualifications, with a preference for graduates. Pay, pension and employment packages for new Gestapo recruits were also highly attractive, in order, in Heydrich's own words, 'to draw the best brains into the service'.

In February 1936, Göring, as Premier of Prussia, and Frick, as Interior Minister, signed the decree, subsequently known as the 'fundamental law' of the Gestapo. This law stipulated that the duty of the Gestapo was to investigate throughout the entire State all forces hostile to the State. It further declared that the orders and the affairs of the Gestapo could not be subject to revision before administrative tribunals. It meant too that the Gestapo had authority to order measures valid throughout the whole state. One paragraph in particular alluded to the Gestapo 'administering' the concentration camps. Himmler subsequently arranged that the application of this clause should not be implemented, and instead, a specialised section of the SS was entrusted with the administration of the camps.

A further decree of 17 June 1936 consolidated Himmler's powers by naming him Supreme Commander of All German Police Forces. This ensured the entire services of uniformed and civil police came under his authority. In practice this centralisation existed de facto since Himmler had ensured control of all the political police forces in the spring of 1934, but it had only been vested in him without any formal legal instrument to confirm it. The decree of 17 June finally gave a legal status to the Gestapo. It withdrew the police forces from the jurisdiction of the Länder and transferred it to that of the Reich. Although police officials continued to be paid from the budget of the Länder, from 19 March 1937 their salaries and expenses came under the Reich's budget. The 17 June 1936 decree also placed the Gestapo under the Ministry of the Interior; however, the same day Himmler became the Minister of Police, a post directly responsible to Hitler, which gave him access to cabinet meetings of the Reich whenever police matters were discussed. This was the first step in him achieving another ambition of his, to become Minister of the Interior, a post which he finally obtained in 1943.

During this same period of time, it has to be said that the state of Britain's espionage and counter-espionage services were in a particularly poor state of repair. Ironically, the reputation and prestige of the British Secret Services stood higher in the imagination of adversaries than it did in government circles in London. The popular press of the 1920s and '30s was full of serials such as the *Evening Standard*'s 'Master Spy', which featured the adventures of the legendary 'Ace of Spies' Sidney Reilly. This archetypal agent of infallible ability, who by cunning and derring-do manages to photograph secret naval plans in the dead of night, under the very noses of the opposition, existed only in the imagination of thriller writers and Fleet Street hacks. Foreigners, however, took at face value the yarns of John Buchan and Cecil Mercer (Dornford Yates) in which athletic British officers, often sporting false moustaches, outwit the enemy in what many writers came to refer to as the 'Great Game' (originally the 19th-century confrontation between Russia and the British Empire over Afghanistan).

This perception was of such magnitude that any chance event that thwarted the plans of a potential adversary was often attributed to the work of the British Secret Service. The reality was sadly somewhat different. Admiral Hugh Sinclair, the Chief of the Secret Intelligence Service (SIS) and successor of the legendary Mansfield Smith-Cumming, who headed the service in the previous war, was a man under considerable pressure. Due to the progressive tightening of government purse strings in the interwar years, particularly in the later days of appeasement, Sinclair was running the service on a shoe string. He was not alone among the heads of the other intelligence departments in his ongoing and often frosty dialogue with mandarins at the Treasury. In 1938 he pointed out in one contemptuous memo to the Chief Secretary of the Treasury that the amount of money allocated to SIS was less in one year than the cost of maintaining a single destroyer operating in home waters. As a consequence, secret service salaries were poor, even by 1930s standards; there was no pension and pay increases were exceptionally rare. To counter this, SIS relied to a great extent on personnel of independent means, in other words private incomes or inherited wealth. Penny-pinching by the treasury also had further unwholesome repercussions. The temptations were great, particularly in the Passport Control Offices that were used as official cover for many SIS stations abroad. The Foreign Office, to whom SIS was politically accountable, had introduced a system of charging for visas, which was originally seen as a covert way of boosting SIS income. In the Hague, for example, SIS Head of Station, Major Hugh Dalton, and a colleague, Jack Hooper, pocketed bribes and PCO funds. When their private enterprise came to light in an audit in 1936, Dalton shot himself and Hooper was dismissed and arrested. The government's hair-shirt mentality to the intelligence services also meant that Sinclair himself was forced to work into the early hours of the morning for lack of administrative support and forego his annual leave for several years.

On top of this, relations between the counter-espionage service (MI5) and SIS were at a very low ebb. The tales of economic woe and shoe-string existence were also a fact of life at MI5. Few of the senior staff in either service were university graduates. Between the wars SIS and MI5's tiny establishment of staff were mainly engaged in identifying Russian attempts to cause mutinies in the British and Empire armed forces and in infiltrating and influencing the leaderships of Britain's trade unions. Both Hugh Sinclair at SIS and his MI5 counterpart Sir Vernon Kell were tired men by the close of the 1930s. Sinclair's health deteriorated rapidly and broke down completely in 1939 when he died in a London clinic at the age of sixty-six.

It would be one of the last operations authorised by Sinclair that would, more than anything else, demonstrate the contrast between the reality and myth of the British Secret Service. It would ultimately prove to be a reputational disaster of epic proportions – in reality an impeccably organised Gestapo entrapment operation. History would record it as 'the Venlo incident'.

5

PLOT AND COUNTER-PLOT

The Venlo incident, as it would be known, was linked to an attempt on Hitler's life. Every year on 8 November, he commemorated the failed Beer Hall Putsch of 1923, which had brought him national notoriety, by returning to the Bürgerbräukeller in Munich to deliver a rousing speech.

In 1939 he arrived to make his speech as usual. As everyone knew, the Führer was never succinct. His speeches went on, and on, and on. Surprisingly, this one took less than an hour. At 9.07 p.m. he excused himself to the 3,000-strong audience of party faithful, and he and his entourage, which included Joseph Goebbels, Reinhard Heydrich, Rudolph Hess, Robert Ley, Alfred Rosenburg, Julius Streicher, August Frank, Heinrich Himmler and Hermann Göring, swept away in a motorcade to Berlin. Just thirteen minutes later, a tremendous explosion destroyed the podium, brought down the ceiling, the gallery, and an external wall. Eight people died and sixty-two were injured, sixteen of them to devastating effect. Horror, panic, screaming, blood: a ghastly scene.

Hitler heard the news of his narrow escape while on the way back to Berlin. He immediately instructed Himmler to place Arthur Nebe, the Head of the Kripo (Criminal Police), in charge of the investigation. This Himmler did, but also placed Gestapo Chief Heinrich Müeller in overall charge of the case. Nebe's first step was to order a fingertip search of the auditorium, sifting through the debris, which went on throughout the night. Shortly before dawn, Nebe was able to cable Himmler the news that the remains of the brass plates, bearing patent numbers of a clockmaker in Schwenningen, had been found. Despite this proof that the clock was made in Germany, Himmler released a press statement asserting that 'the metal parts are of foreign origin'.

Hitler blamed the British government for the attempt on his life, declaring that he had been the intended victim of foreign aggression. The British, who had nothing to do with it, were suspicious of Hitler's unexpected exit from the stage; they figured it was a set-up. After all, by blaming them, the Nazis had been able to position the Führer as the victim of a malevolent foreign power: a perfect vindication of the narrative he was spinning.

Three days later, a carpenter, Georg Elser, was arrested trying to cross the German border into Switzerland. A search of his pockets produced strong circumstantial evidence linking him with the explosion. In addition to round-the-clock beatings that resulted in his relatives being unable to recognise him, he was worked on for three days by Gestapo doctors, who injected him with sizeable doses of Pervitin. While eventually making a full confession, Elser firmly asserted that he, not the British, had hidden the fatal bomb at the Burgerbraukeller. No amount of beatings at 8 Prinz Albrechtstrasse would make Elser change his mind. He persisted in simply describing how and why he made the attempt to kill Hitler and despite being cruelly tortured never deviated from it.

Himmler, on releasing the news of Elser's confession to the press, offered a 500,000 marks reward for information leading to the arrest of Elser's co-conspirators. This inevitably led to the Gestapo being inundated with information from the public on literally hundreds of suspects. Otto Rappold of the Gestapo's counter-espionage arm preferred the tried-and-tested method of rounding up every family member and possible acquaintance of Elser and taking them all in for interrogation.

Rappold also decided to go one step further, by sending Gestapo detachments to Elser's home village of Konigsbronn, where countless residents were also taken in for questioning. According to a Gestapo enquiry report, the local quarry owner, George Vollmer, and his employees were severely beaten during interrogations about the origin of the explosives Elser used. Vollmer was later sentenced to a term of twenty years in the Welzheim concentration camp for negligence. Max Niederholer, the Munich locksmith who unknowingly supplied Elser with parts for the detonator, was bound and beaten over a period of two weeks. The fact that Niederholer had been born in London was an added bonus so far as the story of foreign involvement was concerned.

Elser himself was never to stand trial. After a year of hell at the Gestapo's Berlin headquarters he was sent to the Sachsenhausen concentration camp. In early 1945 he was transferred to Dachau, where he was shot on Hitler's orders on 5 April 1945. The Gestapo interrogation report on Elser concluded that he, and he alone, was responsible for the bombing. However, not wanting the truth to get in the way of an irresistible propaganda opportunity, Goebbels recommended to Hitler that the story of British involvement in the assassination attempt be milked for all it was worth. On 22 November German newspapers began reporting Elser had been funded by British intelligence and that two British agents had been arrested and were in custody. Their names, Sigismund Payne-Best and Richard Stevens, were very soon released along with photographs.

Best had not long been attached to the MI6 station at The Hague in neutral Holland, working under Stevens, the Head of Station. He and his Dutch wife belonged to the Dutch royal family's inner circle. He was an accomplished musician and linguist, and had been decorated for work in intelligence in the First World War. A cultured but reckless man, working for SIS in the First World War he had been caught in an affair with the wife of one of the Belgian resistance leaders he was supposed to be helping. SIS Chief Mansfield Cumming had been furious.

Twenty years later, in the autumn of 1939, he was about to embark on the tragi-comedy at Venlo which is still associated with his name. He was pushed: senior figures in Chamberlain's government knew there was resistance to Hitler at high levels in the German military and wanted to 'negotiate'. And he was pulled: a trusted source had introduced Best to a German refugee called Dr Franz.

The following is based largely on his account of what happened, an account in which he plays centre stage, along with

SIS reports copied to MI3b (who would soon evolve into MI14). But for SIS in London, it was Major Richard Stevens who was the main protagonist and the person with whom they communicated, and the tone of their responses was far tougher than their tone as reported in Best's account (in which all the names, except those of Stevens and Seidlitz, are fake).

Dr Franz had already received useful information from a Major Solms, serving in the Luftwaffe. Solms was now insisting that he had vital news to impart but it must be given only to a British officer, face to face. Had the tidbits of valid intelligence been bait? Best, in his own later version of what happened, doesn't even raise that possibility. There was so much at stake. If this 'vital news' related to peacemaking moves, untold lives could be saved. It might come to nothing, but he must take a risk. Major Solms suggested a meeting at Venlo, a little Dutch town only a few kilometres from the German border. Serving German officers were allowed to go there.

Solms turned out to be, in Best's own words, a 'big, bluff, self-confident fellow' from Bavaria who talked a lot without saying very much. He said he had to get permission from a more senior figure before he revealed anything. They would meet again in a week.

On this second occasion Solms 'seemed to be acting under definite instructions' and when asked technical questions about the Luftwaffe, answered them correctly. Yes, there was a high-level conspiracy to remove Hitler, but he could say no more. His General wanted direct contact with a British officer.

Solms and Best devised a coded message to take back to Germany, for confirmation of his credentials. Dr Franz received that coded message in a phone call from an officer he claimed to know in Berlin. A letter then arrived. Yes, an important general wanted a meeting, but for reassurance a certain news item must be broadcast on the German News from the BBC. The precise words of the item were in the letter.

It was duly transmitted, twice, on 11 October. At the same time a message arrived from Solms, who thought the Gestapo were watching him; he'd lie low for a while. Best did not feel at all unnerved, but he needed support.

These latest developments seemed to indicate that I might be on to quite a big thing and, as I feared that the job might prove to be more than I could manage alone, I asked Major R. H. Stevens, a British official at The Hague, whether he would be willing to lend me a hand. He agreed to this without demur and from that time on we worked together as partners.

Major Stevens worked in Passport Control at the Embassy, but certainly the Dutch, and almost certainly the enemy, knew that was a blind: he was an MI6 officer. Already at least four people knew everything, and two of them were Germans. To make matters worse, a meeting would be devilishly hard to organise. The Netherlands now expected an invasion at any time and the border was bristling with roadblocks and soldiers checking papers. The chance of a German general getting into Holland was not optimal.

Stevens and Best came up with a plan. Maybe the Chief of Dutch Military Intelligence would help? He certainly would – Major van Oorschot knew that mere Dutch neutrality would not stop the Wehrmacht from sweeping straight into the Netherlands, and if there was even a chance of bringing Hitler down, it had to be encouraged. So, when the two British officers approached him, he agreed at once. They could meet the General on Dutch soil. He would provide an escort, Lieutenant Klop, to take them through the cordon before the frontier and to pass the General safely into the Netherlands.

> The only stipulations which he made were that this officer should be present at our interviews with the Germans, and that we would ourselves refrain from putting forward any proposals which might endanger Dutch neutrality.

They agreed. At least seven people now knew of the meeting: two British, two Dutch, and three German (or four, if the General arrived with an aide-de-camp.)

On 19 October their German contact communicated again. The meeting would have to be at Dinxperlo, 120 miles from The Hague, tomorrow morning at 10 a.m.

Dinxperlo was slightly closer than Venlo, but at least a three-hour drive in the late 1930s. Best was a fluent German speaker and had a good description of the General. There would be four people in the Buick: Best driving, Stevens, Lieutenant Klop, and Dr Franz. Best's account does not explain why Franz was there. Already a dangerous enterprise begins to seem like a wizard adventure.

Lieutenant Klop spoke perfect English, so they decided that he would pass himself off as an English 'Captain Coppens'. Twenty kilometres from the border they stopped at Zutphen. Klop and Franz went on ahead by taxi to collect the General and bring him back to the café where Best and Stevens would be waiting. They waited in Zutphen until after midday. Klop then called them (presumably at the café's number) and said no General had turned up, but two other men were coming back with him and Franz in the taxi.

Here was another chance to say 'forget it'. But Best had begun digging this hole – and if the Germans were genuine, there was so much to gain.

When the taxi arrived, Dr Franz introduced a Colonel von Seidlitz and a Lieutenant Grosch and said he knew them both well. They were nervous and reluctant to talk. The Englishmen, having hung around for four hours in the café, speaking English, were now speaking German – the party were getting suspicious looks from the waiters. So, all six men climbed into Best's Buick, which he drove out to the countryside and parked at a roadside café where they could eat lunch as they talked. Franz fussed around them, interrupting Best's questions to the Germans; he was a nuisance.

A couple of Dutch soldiers came in, noticed them and stared. This was uncomfortable, so Best used the café's phone to ring a friend in Arnhem, around 14 kilometres away, and ask if he could borrow his dining room for a private discussion. They could. They sat around the table in Arnhem. The Germans explained that they knew nothing and were only following orders – they had been sent simply to ensure that the meeting would be safe for the General, who was very nervous. They would of course report back that it was perfectly safe, and he'd be sure to come next time.

They heard a tap at the door and their host entered, agitated. His house was surrounded, he said. The gendarmes had accused him of harbouring Germans here.

Klop and I went out and sure enough the street seemed full of side-car combinations and men of the Dutch gendarmerie. ... Klop had some difficulty in preventing the police from bursting into the house and arresting the lot of us, but after some argument they agreed to take him to their barracks where he quickly allayed the suspicions of the officer in command.

This was turning into a copper-bottomed nightmare for everybody. The Germans tried to escape out of a window. Stevens sprang up to manhandle them back. Dr Franz seemed about to faint.

At last Klop returned, and they all sat around the table. The Germans said 'We want to go home' and nothing else, so Best asked Klop to escort them to the frontier – which in the circumstances, was asking a lot. Dr Franz was now having trouble with his gallstones, so Payne-Best and Stevens put him on a train and drove back to The Hague without him.

Having survived what was by any measure a bungled operation, Best agreed to another meeting at Dinxperlo on 25 October. This was then postponed to 30 October. The long-suffering Klop was sent to collect whoever turned up and bring them all the way to The Hague. He got there in plenty of time but the Germans, instead of waiting as instructed, tried to come into Holland through a wood, and were promptly arrested. Klop, pulling rank (Dutch gendarmes were part of the army), took the opportunity to scrutinise their papers, which were perfectly in order. He brought the Germans back to The Hague.

Now there were three: Grosch, as before; a Colonel Martini; and – the most articulate and friendly – Major Schaemmel, his face disfigured by duelling scars. He brought them back to The Hague. Where, exactly, Best is in his account he does not say.

Schaemmel was a man Best could do business with. Not only did he confirm that the Wehrmacht had suffered severely in the Polish campaign, but also that Hitler must go. The Führer must not be martyred. He would remain as a figurehead but would be forced to relinquish power to a competent junta. A negotiated, honourable peace with Britain and France was what Germany needed.

Between them they worked out the terms of a possible protocol. The Generals would accept Hitler only as a figurehead in their military government; there would be no other Nazis. How to negotiate this? Maybe a royal? All parties conceded that they had no authority to finalise anything and the ideas must be passed up the chain of command for consideration. Before the Germans left, they were given a wireless set through which they could transmit and receive messages.

Best then wrote a 'full report' to London. He received 'a carefully worded and rather non-committal reply' to be relayed to Schaemmel. He and Best were to 'follow it up with energy' but to 'be cautious and avoid risk'.

The SIS' reply isn't non-committal at all and it is addressed by C, the Head of MI6, to Stevens:

A. Immediate considered reply impossible, but general impression given is that proposals make little advance whilst retention of Hitler might prove insuperable obstacle to any progress in negotiations.
B. Does Wehrmacht plan envisage complete elimination of Party control with disappearance of leading figures?
C. Proposed Royal contact hardly likely to appeal but with W/T [wireless telegraph] facilities more considered reply will be sent.

Messages were exchanged and another meeting arranged for 7 November. Stevens had by then received a telegram from C, to be relayed to the Germans:

It is only fair to say that it would be extremely difficult, if not impossible, to convince people in this country that a change of regime in Germany, which left Hitler in office, was a genuine change.

In any case, not only would Germany have to right the wrongs done in Poland and Czechoslovakia, but she would also have to give pledges that there would be no repetition of acts of aggression.

It is difficult to see what pledge would be convincing short of a renunciation by Germany of her <u>power</u> to pursue the policy she has followed in recent years. There would have to be practical proposals for cooperation with other countries in the peaceful rebuilding and development of Europe and a reversal of the policy whereby German effort is devoted primarily to the maintenance of overwhelming military strength.

Further than that - it is difficult to see how there could be mutual confidence and cooperation between England and Germany unless the latter abandoned her methods of religious and political persecution.

It is not for H.M.G. to say how these conditions could be met, but they are bound to say that, in their view, they are essential to the establishment of confidence on which alone peace could be solidly and durably based.

These questions have been put to us, and we can only answer them on our own behalf, but we have every reason to believe that the French Government would give a similar answer.

Neither France nor Great Britain, as the Prime Minister said, have any desire to carry on a vindictive war, but they are determined to prevent Germany continuing to make life in Europe unbearable.

This would indeed be a big ask and almost impossible in practice. Hitler and the Nazis would somehow have to fade into oblivion – fine. But that could hardly happen unless Germany's entire economy, which since 1933 had, in contravention of the terms of the Armistice, depended heavily on arms manufacture, aeronautics and warship building, was broken down and repurposed. And unless the entire population was psychologically and socially re-educated after more than a decade's repression. And unless enormous amounts of money and stolen property were returned to compensate millions of private families and businesses in half a dozen countries.

Best agreed with Klop's suggestion that the 7 November meeting would take place in Venlo. It was safer (for the Germans, presumably, in Best's over-empathetic mind). On the day, the two Englishmen booked into a hotel in Venlo while Klop went to the frontier to collect the German party. He rang Best at the hotel. The Germans were scared; they wouldn't come back with him. But there was a café here, near the frontier, which was perfect for a meeting – better than the hotel.

Another chance to pull the whole thing. But Best, still convinced that he was dealing with honourable people, didn't want to put the Germans in a difficult position, and Klop knew the terrain, so...

They set off – 'a pretty drive through pine woods' – to the café, a big family-friendly sort of place within sight of the frontier. They were given a side room in which to talk. Schaemmel and Grosch said the General would like to meet them and entrust to them some secret papers about the projected coup. So, could they come again tomorrow?

At last, Best's internal warning bells began to sound. Too late. The next day, Wednesday, they drove to the café... There was no General. Just Schaemmel. The General had been detained by an urgent meeting to discuss today's appeal to peace from Queen Wilhelmina and the King of the Belgians. How about tomorrow in the afternoon?

That would be Thursday 8 November. These people had told Best that the coup was planned for Saturday 10 October.

> Neither Stevens nor I liked the idea of coming here again. The weather had turned dull and in the waning evening light we seemed a long way from home and far, far too close to Germany.

They consciously subdued their instinctive fear. On Thursday morning Best kissed his wife goodbye and set off once again to collect Stevens and Klop and get on the road. He had brought his driver, Jan, with him this time in case he needed him after what would surely be a long, tiring day. They stopped for lunch and then set off for the café at the frontier. This time the two SIS officers carried Browning pistols, loaded.

Otherwise nothing had changed, except the weather; this was a much colder, greyer day. They approached the café and Best had just parked the Buick and was getting out when

> ...there was a sudden noise of shouting and shooting. I looked up, and through the windscreen saw a large open car drive up around the corner till our bumpers were touching. It seemed to be packed to overflowing with rough-looking men. Two were perched on top of the hood and were firing over our heads from sub-machine guns, others were standing up in the car and on the running boards; all shouting and waving pistols. Four men jumped off almost before their car had stopped and rushed towards us shouting: 'Hands up!'

Young Lieutenant Klop made a run for it.

> He was running diagonally away from us towards the road;
> running sideways in big bounds, firing at our captors as he ran. He
> looked graceful, with both arms outstretched - almost like a ballet
> dancer. I saw the windscreen of the German car splinter into a star,
> and then the four men standing in front of us started shooting and
> after a few more steps Klop just seemed to crumple and collapse
> into a dark heap of clothes on the grass.

The English officers and Jan the Dutch driver were
frogmarched by the Gestapo men across the border into
Germany. It would not be out of character for Best, at least, to
hope to talk his way out of this – saying perhaps that he had
hoped for nothing more than an attempt to make peace – and
receive lenient treatment. What he didn't know about was a
coincidence of timing. That night the bomb would go off in
Munich, and the Gestapo would need to blame a foreign enemy
for it. They might conveniently use two British intelligence
officers as scapegoats.

In London it was clear that nobody knew how to respond. As
for Venlo, they were not sure whether the elusive General and
coup plot had been genuine, or if German counter-intelligence
had been behind the whole thing. SIS trusted Best and Stevens
completely. In their view, a few weeks after his capture:

> The balance of evidence shows that the 'feelers' we received
> were not, originally at any rate, part of a plot organised by Herr
> Himmler. On the other hand, if we assume that it was – and
> perhaps still is – still genuine, then it is clear that the Gestapo
> must have had wind of it before they framed the incident of
> 9 November; and it is also clear that they must by this time have
> been able to extract by torture everything that one or both of our
> representatives knew.

It was a ghastly mess. In response to the German accusation, SIS
had to decide whether to deny any involvement, or what to say to
whom – including their French allies. Apart from anything else:

Owing to the glaring indiscretions of Mrs Stevens and Mrs Best large numbers of private persons know all about the 'negotiations' and the wireless.

It was all leakier than a colander. In Britain, Venlo was kept secret; journalists were not allowed to write about it. The French Ambassador reassured the Foreign Office that 'nobody believed what the Germans said anyway'.

At the café in Venlo that afternoon in November, the first anniversary of Kristallnacht, Nazis achieved two objectives. They seized two important British sources of information, and since a Dutch intelligence operative had been complicit, the Venlo incident could be used as an excuse to invade Holland the following year.

Elser, Best and Stevens, although separately interned, would spend most of the war in concentration camps awaiting trial for conspiracy to murder Hitler. They may have revealed, under torture, much of what the Germans wanted to know about British intelligence, including names. Unlike Elser, the Englishmen survived the war.

6

DOWN IN THE BASEMENT

Almost all British households had received instructions about what to do in case of war: 'warning' and 'all clear' sirens were tested, anti-blast sandbags were stacked outside public buildings and nearly everyone had been issued with a gas mask and knew how to use it. Anderson shelters were soon to be a common sight in back gardens, air-raid shelters were signposted and pillboxes disguised. It seemed unreal, but the fact was inescapable. No attack had yet occurred, but it would.

On 3 September, when Prime Minister Neville Chamberlain announced to the nation that war had been declared, rigid covered-trench shelters had been dug in the parks. From then until Christmas, thousands of heartbroken people had pets put down, knowing that dogs and cats would be driven crazy with fear when bombs fell. The National Evacuation Scheme transported 1,300,000 children from London in 4,000 special trains in the first three days. Everyone tried to wear a brave face as little girls and boys, with and without their mothers or older siblings, but often with their school and teachers, piled onto trains in their thousands from cities, to lodge with strangers in the country. 'Have you Forgotten your Gas Mask?' asked the posters. London schoolteachers moved hundreds of miles with their pupils, and set up classes in the outbuildings of provincial schools. Men who were not in 'reserved occupations', but who were fit enough, were conscripted into the army, navy and air force. Every building was to be blacked out at night. Cars were to be fitted with blackout headlights.

There were no air raids in London in the winter of 1939–40, but from November 1939 onwards, German ships were blatantly laying mines across the estuary near Southend. An incoming convoy was mined in December and there were raids throughout 1940 on Southend's pier, yacht club, RAF station, airfield, shipping in the estuary and of course, the town.

The BBC reported these raids, but were vague about the location. Radio and newspapers would mention 'a town in the south of England' for instance. The first of thousands of barrage balloons around every port and city went up across the Thames Estuary and around South London: balloon curtains of huge tethered blimps, 1,500 metres above ground, intended to deter or entangle low-flying bombers and mine-laying planes.

The police ordered revolvers and half a million rounds of ammunition from the US. Christmas in a stranger's house made people homesick. At the start of 1940 evacuees started returning home. Spring came, beautiful as ever. Days lengthened and the hours of blackout were shorter. A third of the population now thought either that Hitler would not invade and all this was a waste of time, or that if he did, Britain couldn't expect to win.

However, there were more jobs to be had in the armament's factories. Millions also volunteered for services such as the ATS, the WRVS, the Land Army, the Ambulance Service and to do their duty as ARP (Air Raid Precaution) wardens. The Ministry of Information was certainly doing its bit. 'HELP THE RAF – JOIN THE WAAF' pleaded a poster. Procedures and protocols seemed to rain from the skies. Everyone was encouraged to 'Dig for Victory' and 'Waste Not Want Not'. There were ration books (food coupons, clothing coupons, petrol coupons). 'Join the Royal Armoured Corps!' Up and down the country, men who were too old or young to join up, or in a reserved occupation, joined the men-only Home Guard – a network of uniformed local militias who, in the first year of the war, were desperately undersupplied with weaponry and transport.

This 'quiet before the storm' has since been dubbed the 'phoney war' by historians. The phoney war, however, soon came to a thundering end, when on the night of 8/9 April 1940, Hitler unleashed his blitzkrieg warfare on neutral Norway and the Low Countries. Britain and France went at once to the aid of the Norwegians, but had been forced into an embarrassing and humiliating retreat by a much stronger German enemy. On 26 April, Britain decided to evacuate from Norway.

Ten days later, a shell-shocked and angry House of Commons dramatically seized the initiative from the government in a debate that Sir Stafford Cripps famously described as 'the most momentous that has ever taken place in the history of parliament'. In the six minutes that it took MPs to vote on what was, on paper, an Adjournment debate, the government would be brought to its knees, sparking a chain reaction that would ultimately change the destiny of the country irrevocably.

Of all the Members who spoke in this memorable and historic debate, none made such a deep or indeed dramatic impression on the House as a man of sixty-seven, who only seldom rose to speak. Today, however, was to be different. In full-dress uniform, complete with six rows of medal ribbons, Admiral of the Fleet Sir Roger Keyes, Conservative MP for Portsmouth North, slowly rose to his feet, having finally caught the eye of the Speaker. Although the official motion for debate that day, Tuesday 7 May 1940, was 'that this House do now adjourn', it was clear to all in the chamber that to all intents and purposes this was in reality a confidence motion in the Prime Minister Neville Chamberlain. His government's shambolic handling of the defeat and retreat from Norway in the face of Germany's invasion was the only subject now engaging the minds of members.

In a rare moment of hush, in what had so far been a bad-tempered debate, the House listened intently to the Admiral's cutting account of the Norway campaign:

> I came to the House today in uniform for the first time because I wish to speak for some officers and men of the fighting, sea-going Navy who are very unhappy. I want to make it perfectly clear that it is not their fault that that the German warships and transports which forced their way into Norwegian ports by treachery were not followed in and destroyed as they were at Narvik. It is not the fault of those of whom I speak that the enemy have been left in

undisputable possession of vulnerable ports and aerodromes for nearly a month, have been given time to pour in reinforcements by sea and air, to land tanks, heavy artillery and mechanized transport, and have and have been given time to develop the air offensive which has had such a devastating effect on the morale of Whitehall. If they had been more courageously and offensively employed, they might have done much to prevent these unhappy happenings and much to influence unfriendly neutrals.

As the House listened in silence, Keyes delivered his coup de grace, asserting that the campaign had been

> ... a shocking story of ineptitude, which I can assure the House should never have been allowed to happen ... one hundred and forty years ago, Nelson said, 'I am of the opinion that the boldest measures are the safest,' and that still holds good today.

He sat down to thunderous applause. The debate continued into the following day, when former Prime Minister David Lloyd George joined the fray, by rebutting Chamberlain's appeal, in opening the debate, for the nation to make sacrifices for victory:

> There is nothing which can contribute more to victory than that he should sacrifice the seals of office.

It was, however, left to Chamberlain's constituency neighbour, Leo Amery, the MP for the Birmingham Sparkbrook, to deliver the knock-out blow. Winding up his speech with the same words Oliver Cromwell had contemptuously hurled at the 'Long Parliament' in 1651, Amery told Chamberlain:

> You have sat too long here for any good you have been doing. Depart I say, and let us have done with you. In the name of God, go!

When MPs finally walked through the voting lobbies at the end of the debate, the government's usual majority of over 200 had been drastically whittled down to eighty-one. Forty-one of his own MPs had voted with the opposition and fifty others had abstained. Within forty-eight hours, Chamberlain was forced to resign and Winston Churchill was summoned to Buckingham Palace on 10 May to kiss the hand of the King as the Prime Minister of a new coalition government. At sixty-six years of age, he was an inspirational orator, former war correspondent, and Boer War hero who had successfully escaped a prison camp and had been defiantly anti-Nazi for a long time. Churchill proved himself capable of changing the public mood. His fierce opposition to Nazism inspired a defiant unity: the British were going to fight on and win. The 'we might as well give up' brigade melted away.

On 13 May Churchill made his first speech to the House of Commons as Prime Minister, telling the assemblage:

> I have nothing to offer but blood, toil, tears and sweat ... you ask, what is our policy? I can say: It is to wage war, by sea, land and air, with all our might and with all the strength that God can give us; to wage war against a monstrous tyranny, never surpassed in the dark, lamentable catalogue of human crime. That is our policy. You ask, what is our aim? I can answer in one word: It is victory, victory at all costs, victory in spite of all terror, victory, however long and hard the road may be; for without victory, there is no survival.

Two days after the famous speech Churchill moved with speed to galvanise the intelligence services, who he saw as a vital tool in Britain's fight for survival. Having appointed himself Minister of Defence, he set about transforming the standing of intelligence in Whitehall. Churchill recognized that the problem was not so much the collection of information, but in how it was utilized.

On 15 May, Churchill ordered the creation of a new intelligence agency to focus entirely on Germany. MI3's Lieutenant-Colonel Kenneth Strong, and the small staff of three regular officers that had comprised MI3's 'German section', immediately had conferred on them the status of a full-blown intelligence department that would henceforth be known as MI14. The man who had been a lone voice in intelligence circles for the best part of five years, warning his superiors of German intentions and the inevitability of another war, was the obvious choice to head the new department. He was now tasked by Churchill with the immediate recruitment of specialist staff with expert knowledge of Germany and the methods by which to assess the new intelligence.

It is likely that Strong and Churchill had been loose, low-key acquaintances for at least two years. Strong was among several anti-appeasement civil servants and service personnel who unofficially provided Churchill with statistics and data that enabled him to counter the government's pro-appeasement policy in the House of Commons, one of the most notable occasions being Churchill's forty-five-minute intervention in the government-sponsored debate on the Munich Agreement on 5 October 1938. Although the government won the vote 366-144, Churchill scored a moral victory in using the occasion to expose the folly of appeasement and the reality of German expansion.

So far as Strong was concerned, statistics and intelligence were now no longer the fodder of parliamentary debates, but matters of life and death. As Churchill wrote, four weeks after the creation of MI14:

> What General Weygand called the Battle of France is over. I expect that the Battle of Britain is about to begin ... upon this battle depends our British way of life, and the long continuity of our institutions. The whole fury and might of the enemy must very soon be turned on us. Hitler knows that he will have to break us in this island or lose the war. If we can stand up to him, all Europe may be free and the life of the world may move forward into broad, sunlit uplands. But if we fail, then the whole world, including the United States, including all that we have known and cared for, will sink into the abyss of a new dark Age made more sinister, and perhaps more protracted, by lights of perverted science. Let us therefore brace ourselves to our duties, and so bear ourselves that if the British Empire and its Commonwealth last for a thousand years, men will say, this was their finest hour.

So much for the rhetoric. Strong needed manpower and that was very much in short supply. Almost the only factual evidence about German army intentions at this time came from the reports provided by Captain Peter Earle, who was one of only three officers in the British army at the time who knew how to interpret aerial photographs. Noted for his gold-spectacle frames, slow-moving eyes and almost permanent glazed expression, Earle was far from indolent. Once his interest was engaged, he underwent a spectacular personality transformation. A man of many interests, particularly fast cars, his corner of the beehive-like War Office basement conveyed all the calm and order of a country house. Strong needed more people like Earle: men with specialist skills, men who were who permanently focused on the job in hand. In particular, he needed someone who could assist Earle in interpreting aerial photography, but such men were gold dust.

Most intelligence recruits were found via the 'old boy network', and this was Strong's first port of call. Typical recruits came from families who had served the nation for generations as soldiers, politicians, or civil servants. They tended, if they did not know one another already, to have mutual friends. Or they might belong to the same London club. When an extremely delicate, confidential job had to be done, Military Intelligence officers would pick from a pool of people they knew, or who knew people they knew. Secret service work was no ordinary job. Lives depended on it – sometimes one's own. There was nothing reprehensible in an 'old boy network' for such purposes, any more than there would be if a ship's captain chose a crew he had worked with before. In some circumstances it paid to be on the safe side.

Strong eventually found his aerial photography man by pure chance. Dining one day at his London club, he was introduced to Osbert Crawford, the noted archaeologist. Having no particular interest or enthusiasm for archaeology, Strong was only half listening to Crawford's dining table banter until he chanced to mention that ordnance survey maps were much dependent on good aerial photography. While he had been aware for some time that Crawford was an archaeologist, he was not aware that for the past twenty years his dinner table guest had acted as Archaeology Officer for Ordnance Survey. While Crawford confessed that he had pioneered the use of aerial photography to identify archaeological sites in the Middle East, he had no specialist ability of his own in the field. However, after some gentle probing, Crawford did volunteer that a younger colleague of his, one Harry Pickering, had been fully involved, not only in the actual photography, but in the processing and detailed analysis of the developed films.

As a result of this conversation, Pickering received, in double-quick time, a letter from the War Office, with a railway warrant from Southampton to Waterloo enclosed, instructing him to report to the War Office in Whitehall in two days' time. The War Office was, he later remarked, a strange trapezium-shaped building, built in Renaissance style (now called 'Edwardian Baroque'), its design dictated by the need to use all available space on a site already surrounded by other buildings. MI14 had been given subterranean basement space below the War Office and adjoining accommodation in Whitehall Court immediately behind it; a tunnel ran under the street between the two buildings. When Pickering arrived at the Horse Guards Avenue entrance, he was met by the tall, frock-coated head porter in his gold-braided top hat, who made several telephone calls before summoning a messenger to escort him. He was eventually taken on a route march down a steep, narrow flight of stairs, and along a maze of subterranean, rabbit warren-like passages. As the descent continued, the décor of light green and cream paint was enlivened by a large, square-sectioned air-conditioning plant painted bright red. When work began on the new War Office building in 1899, it had to be constructed on an enormous 'tank' with 6-foot-thick concrete walls and base 30 feet below street level in order to support the huge weight of the new building. This subterranean world below the War Office was to prove a godsend during the Blitz.

At the end of one of these subterranean passages was a room no bigger than a broom cupboard in which was to be found a striking moustachioed figure wearing the epaulettes of a captain and medal ribbons from the First World War. The room was so small there didn't seem enough room for both the captain and his desk. After squeezing awkwardly from behind the desk, Captain 'Sandy' Sanderson introduced himself. A former business executive and territorial army officer, Sanderson had joined MI3 at the start of the war, before being seconded to MI14, from where he now coordinated invasion intelligence. With no other formalities or small talk, Sanderson asked Pickering what he knew about aerial photography. Pickering told him that, in fact, he knew quite a lot about it since his first Ordnance Survey assignment in Samaria, Iraq, some five years before. Since then he had worked on a series of projects on areas of archaeological significance.

'Splendid, splendid,' retorted Sanderson, gesturing for Pickering to follow him out of the windowless 'broom cupboard' and down more narrow corridors which eventually led them to a marble staircase that took them back up into the daylight. The elegant surroundings at the top of the staircase suggested that this was a totally different building from the one he had entered earlier on in Horse Guards Avenue. A lift then took them slowly upwards to what seemed like the top of the building. Sanderson knocked lightly on the door immediately opposite the lift cage. As they entered from the threshold of the doorway, the sitting room was bathed in bright sunlight and everything momentarily appeared in silhouette against the bay window overlooking the Thames. Sitting behind a paper-covered desk at the far end of the room was the man who Sanderson introduced simply as 'the Chief'. Pickering immediately noticed that under the desk he was sporting a particularly loud and colourful pair of tartan trousers.

Sanderson and Pickering sat in silence for what seemed like several minutes, while the man in the tartan trousers drew what looked like a series of wavy lines and circles on a large buff pad of paper. Eventually he introduced himself as Lieutenant-Colonel Strong and continued with his sketching. Strong could never tell you anything without drawing a diagram, Pickering later recalled. In this case the wavy lines and circles were an introduction to Strong's short and succinct explanation as to why Pickering had received the call to arms. He had been recruited to MI14's Section G, and would be assisting Captain Peter Earle in H Section with aerial photography. Section G was but one spoke in a hub Strong was putting together in order to carry out what Churchill had decreed was to be their first and most pressing task – to find out as much as was humanly possible about German plans for invading Britain.

All information concerning German preparations was reported in detail to the Cabinet by a special 'Invasion Warning

Committee'. Captain Sanderson, responsible for invasion intelligence, reported via Strong to Lieutenant-Commander Denning at the Admiralty, who would be coordinating the work of the committee. Norman Denning had joined the navy as an officer cadet in 1922 and had served as a Lieutenant on the aircraft carrier HMS *Courageous* and the cruiser HMS *Effingham*, before being promoted to the rank of Lieutenant-Commander and seconded to the Naval Intelligence Division in 1936. By the outbreak of war he was working for the Naval Intelligence Department's Operational Intelligence Centre at the Admiralty in Whitehall. It was Denning's job not only to service the committee but to report directly to Churchill, at any time, day or night, should there be any intelligence updates about the threat of invasion.

Most mornings Pickering had a rough file of material deposited on his desk from a variety of other MI departments, naval intelligence (NID), the Air Ministry, and the newly created Ministry of Economic Warfare and Weapons Production. These included production statistics, estimates of how many divisions, air squadrons, bombers, U-boats and capital ships were in place and operational at any one time, their locations and potential future movements. Frustratingly, some sources often conflicted or contradicted others, and judgement and experience were therefore called upon in such questions of reliability.

Once a week there was what was called 'the intelligence digest' which included copies of air photographs, prisoner of war interrogations, captured documents, reports from other MI14 sections, information from diplomatic sources, reports from businessmen abroad, stories filed by foreign newspaper correspondents – whose sources of information could often be more reliable than diplomatic sources – summaries of radio broadcasts from across the globe, and articles from specialist periodicals.

The invention of the modern photocopier was still some time away, and the foolscap sheets of paper in Pickering's digest were either carbon copies of typed letters and reports or, for items circulated in greater quantity, the faintly sweet aroma of pages fresh off the spirit duplicator. These hand-cranked duplicators were, eighty years ago, at the cutting edge of document technology. Using two-ply 'spirit masters' the top sheet was typed, written or drawn. The second sheet was coated with a layer of coloured wax. The pressure of the pen or typewriter on the top sheet transferred coloured wax to its reverse side, producing a mirror image. The wax colour was aniline purple, a cheap, moderately durable pigment that provided good contrast. The machines used by the War Office were purchased directly from the manufacturers, Associated Automation Ltd of Willesden, London NW10. These machines, a little more sophisticated than the standard model, had the ability to print multiple colours in a single print run, making them ideal for intelligence reports and maps. However, the Achilles heel of the spirit duplicator was that, notoriously images would gradually fade with exposure to light, limiting their usability for permanent archiving.

Pickering soon learnt off by heart the various other sections within MI14:

MI14(a) German Strategy
German Intentions
MI14 (b) German Order of Battle & Locations
German Army Personalities
MI14(c) German Operations in Western Mediterranean
German Troop Movements in All Occupied Countries
MI14(d) Nazi Party
Nazi Party Personalities
SS & Gestapo Police
Information from Special Sources
MI14(e) Pigeon Intelligence
Study of Special Intelligence
MI14(f) German Tactics, Morale & Manpower
German Publications
MI14(g) Invasion Intelligence
Defences & Installations
MI14(h) Air Photographs
MIRS Captured Documents

After the formality of working at Ordnance Survey's head office in Southampton, he found life at MI14 more like a university common room, which perhaps wasn't too surprising, bearing in mind the number of academics that had been recruited. Eric Birley, a professor of classical studies, was an archaeologist and an authority on the Roman army. Ably assisted by Lloyds underwriter Colin Tangye, he employed, in Sections (a) and (b), the same methods of card-indexing that he had applied to Roman legions, in order to build up the German order of battle and predict, as best he could, its next move. MI14's only senior female officer, at that point, Captain Winnie 'Pooh' Malcom, quickly became an expert on the German battle order and henceforth had responsibility for liaising with the Americans on battle order matters. Before too long, there were two MI14 officers in the section by the name of Tangye, when Colin and Winnie married.

Alyn Price-Jones, a well-known author and literary critic who had lived in Austria before the war, worked in Section (c). Section (d) was headed by Brian Melland, a theatrical character whose job it was to assemble information and intelligence on the German secret services and their activities, in particular the Abwehr, Gestapo and Sicherheitsdienst (SD). His deputy was Leo Long, a seemingly able officer, who two decades later would be exposed as a Russian agent and a confederate of the Cambridge spies Burgess, Maclean, Philby and Blunt. Also working in Section (d) was a civilian Kenneth Strong had first encountered three years previously in Berlin – John MacLaren-Clarke, who was working on a resumé of Gestapo and Nazi Party personalities.

The former England and Middlesex cricket captain George 'Gubby' Allen headed Section (e), which sought to establish the whereabouts and strengths of German anti-aircraft regiments. Working in close harmony with the code-breakers and RAF Bomber Command, he was responsible for seeing that British pilots flying over enemy territory were thoroughly briefed on the conditions they were likely to encounter.

One matter that Churchill raised several times with the Invasion Committee was not to discount the possibility that the Germans might direct their immense resources to the task of building a Channel Tunnel, using the exploratory workings begun by the French in the 1870s. A Channel Tunnel had long been a fixation of Churchill's ever since he had seen the 1907 film *Tunnelling the English Channel* by pioneer filmmaker Georges Melies. At the 1919 Paris Peace Conference, Churchill's ally, Prime Minister David

Lloyd George, repeatedly raised the issue of building a Channel Tunnel as a way of reassuring France of Britain's willingness to defend them against another German attack. The French, however, showed no enthusiasm for the idea and it was dropped. Churchill, though, continued to advocate such a tunnel throughout the 1920s and wrote an article in the *Weekly Despatch* newspaper, 'Should Strategists Veto a Tunnel'. In it he vehemently dismissed suggestions from opponents that the tunnel could be used by an invading continental army in an invasion of Britain. As late as 1936 he had written another article, 'Why not a Channel Tunnel', this time in the *Daily Mail*, following interest created by the recent release by Gaumont studios of the science fiction film *Tunnel*. Clearly, the shock and surprise of the rapid German victory over France had caused him to rethink.

Not long after the French surrender, Pickering, Earle and Sanderson were called in to see Lieutenant-Colonel Strong. 'Sorry to drag you into this fracas, but we've been called into an Invasion Warning Committee meeting,' explained Strong. He was clearly agitated as he'd seen the agenda and had learnt that a Royal Navy officer by the name of Lieutenant Goodfellow, from the Directorate of Miscellaneous Weapons Development at the Admiralty, had tabled a report in which he had calculated that the Germans could dig two Channel Tunnels in a matter of eighteen months if they used slave labour.

MI14 had barely been able to take the proposition of a German tunnel seriously when it had first been mentioned some months earlier. However, Earle had kept a wary eye on aerial photographs of the Calais area for signs of digging, of which there were absolutely none. Now they feared that Goodfellow's report would needlessly reignite discussion and indeed workload at their end. With an air of resignation, Strong, Sanderson, Earle and Pickering walked the short distance from the War Office to the Admiralty, on the opposite side of the road, next door to the Whitehall Theatre. Entering through the courtyard gate, they headed for the porch under which hung an immaculately polished brass lantern – inside, a doorman in a frock coat directed them past a life-sized statue of Lord Nelson to one of the committee rooms. By the time Goodfellow's report came up on the agenda, Sanderson had seemingly plucked from nowhere a strategy to defer consideration of the report. Lavishing praise on Goodfellow's endeavours, he proposed that Goodfellow be asked to take the report back, pending further research on the amount of soil that might reasonably need to be dug out from under the Channel, and the various means the Germans might deploy for the disposing of the soil. There appears to be no record of Goodfellow's report ever again seeing the light of day so far as the committee's agenda was concerned. While MI14 had no desire to spend any further precious time on the subject of tunnels under the sea, Sanderson's estimate was that ten years was much more likely than Goodfellow's eighteen months. Despite such scepticism in this instance, MI14 was often pressed to take seriously every rumour and every theory concerning possible German plans and intentions. Kenneth Strong was even asked on one occasion to evaluate the prognostications of an astrologer and a water diviner whom he nicknamed 'Smokey Joe'.

MI14's view about the likelihood of invasion was based on its knowledge of the Germans. In their view, neither Hitler nor Ribbentrop had really thought that they might have to fight Britain. They thought or hoped that Britain would throw in the towel if sufficiently threatened or cajoled. Strong was fairly certain that an invasion of Britain had never really entered into German pre-war military planning. There was no German air force organized for the specific purpose of conducting a strategic air offensive against British cities and industries; all talk of its existence before the war had been bluff. The Germans were, as a nation, accustomed to large armies and land-based warfare.

While a German invasion of Britain never came to pass, it remained one of MI14's tasks to try and anticipate what Germany's plans might be for administering an occupied Britain or indeed a large part of it. Would the Germans have sought to cut Britain into two parts as they had with France, or would they have sought direct control over the entire country? Who were the puppets that the Nazis had lined up to rule Britain and how did the Gestapo plan to spread its tentacles across every facet of British life?

7

GESTAPO GB

When the French surrendered on 22 June, the Nazis divided France into an Occupied Zone (the north and Channel/Atlantic coast as far as the Spanish border) and what the Allies knew as Vichy France: the south and east, administered at Vichy by the puppet leader Marshal Philippe Pétain.

The Wehrmacht, Hitler's army, appeared to be preparing to invade Britain. Ships were massing along the Channel coast. Dunkirk had marked the start of the war's most terrifying year; but from June onwards, the British would fight back whatever the cost.

On 18 July Hitler stood up to say his piece to the Reichstag. He moderated his tone. He spent a long time on the inevitability of German triumph and its successes so far, but he presented himself as a peacemaker. He suggested that Churchill, the strident aggressor, would bow to the inevitable, and that he must surely wish to prevent further loss of life. He talked for over two hours.

His interpreter, primed with a copy of the text, read out the English version and it reached London via the Berlin Broadcasting station.

Less than an hour later a response was broadcast on the German Service of the BBC. Hitler knew the speaker personally.

He wasn't Churchill, or a translator. He was Sefton Delmer, a regular broadcaster on the German Service. As a British subject born to Austrian parents he had been born and brought up in Berlin and educated there until his teens. As a journalist, he had been embedded with the Nazi leaders from around 1930 until after they came to power. Speaking perfect, demotic German he now said: 'Let me tell you what we here in Britain think of this appeal of yours to what you call our reason and common sense. Herr Führer and Reichskanzler, we hurl it right back at you, right in your stinking teeth.'

This apparently left the Führer and his band dumbfounded. It was *rude*. They assumed that it was officially sanctioned; of course, it was – that was the way things *worked*. Actually, it wasn't the way it worked in Britain, but it did very nicely. Churchill had nothing further to say. The Wehrmacht had not yet fully established their force in France, so Hitler decided to postpone the invasion until mid-September. Göring's Luftwaffe would have two months in which to destroy British industries, airfields and the RAF's capacity to return fire. That would surely force Churchill to sue for peace.

If the Luftwaffe had decimated the RAF, and the Germans crossed the Channel, the huge Nazi army would have piled onto our shores and (theoretically) simply headed for the capital, where they would remove the politicians, occupy Whitehall and Parliament, and install their own men in every national institution, including the BBC and the armed services. Forty-seven million Britons would have had to put up with an occupying army.

But who exactly did the Nazis have waiting in the wings? Following the fall of France, the Duke and Duchess of Windsor, who had been living in Paris, headed to Portugal, where they stayed with Ricardo Espirito Santo Silva at his Cascaes villa. SIS (who, from 1939, were now using the designation MI6) believed that Santo Silva and his wife were in contact with the German Embassy in Lisbon, and cabled Sir Alexander Cadogan, the Permanent Under-Secretary at the Foreign Office, to this effect. From here on in, rumours of a German plot involving the Duke and Duchess flew thick and fast. David

Eccles, writing from the British Embassy in Lisbon, to Gladwyn Jebb, Private Secretary to the Head of the Diplomatic Service at the Foreign Office, reported:

MOST CONFIDENTIAL
4 July 1940
I had a conversation today with the Duke and Duchess of Windsor ... feel that we pushed France into a war she didn't want, and then let them down; and that the French Armistice was 'the best possible thing they could do'. When I asked H.R.H why he thought the French were right to stop fighting, he said 'because they would have got worse terms if they had gone on!'. 'Do you believe the Germans will keep any terms that have been made?' He wouldn't answer. So I asked him again, and he said, 'Why not?'

Three days later, Sir Alexander Cadogan received the following communiqué from C, the Chief of MI6, expressing the view that he should draw the following intelligence to the Prime Minister's attention:

MOST SECRET
7 July 1940
The Germans expect assistance from Duke and Duchess of Windsor, the latter desiring ... to become Queen. Germans have been negotiating with her since 27 June. Status quo in England except undertaking to form an anti-Russian alliance. Germans propose to form Opposition Government under Duke of Windsor having first changed public opinion by propaganda. Germans think King George will abdicate during the attack on London.

Whether the Duke would have accepted the throne following a German invasion remains one of the unanswered ifs of twentieth-century history. However, before any further trouble could brew in Lisbon, Churchill had the Duke appointed Governor of the Bahamas, and the couple were promptly put on a boat to the West Indies, where they remained for the duration, under the watchful eyes of the FBI and MI6. Whoever the Germans might have appointed as Britain's puppet head of state, one thing is clear – real power would have been in the hands of the Gestapo.

On 16 July 1940 Adolph Hitler told his generals, 'I have decided to prepare a landing operation against England, and if necessary, to carry it out.' The plan was code-named *Sea Lion* and the objective was to land 160,000 German soldiers along a 40-mile coastal stretch of the south-east of England from Ramsgate, Kent, in the east, to Selsey Bill, West Sussex, in the west, using Brighton as the main landing ground. The plan the generals eventually put to Hitler envisaged that the first wave of troops would be accompanied by 650 tanks and 4,500 horses. Once a bridgehead had been established, a further 500,000 troops would be landed to join the first wave fighting their way inland. German ships in the Dover Straits would fire powerful salvos at the coastline during the attack. *Sea Lion*'s first objective was to occupy south-east England, from the mouth of the Thames down to Southampton. Hitler approved the plan and believed that hostilities would lead to a rapid conclusion of the war. In the view of the generals, this was an achievable, if not a fool-proof plan; it had, however, one pre-condition, and that was that the Luftwaffe should first gain air superiority. By all accounts, no one worried too much about this, as Göring had already assured Hitler that this was as good as done, once the go-ahead was given.

The German blueprint for Britain included the establishment of regional headquarters and Gestapo regional offices in the cities of London, Birmingham, Newcastle, Liverpool, Glasgow and Belfast. They had also earmarked Bridgnorth in Shropshire as the site of a strategic military base as it was geographically in the heart of the country with good road and rail connections in all directions. Stately homes and other lavish piles were identified for top Nazis in the new regime. Hitler himself had his eye on Blenheim Palace, Churchill's birthplace, which was suitably near to Oxford, a location that he had told Göring was not to be bombed under any circumstances. London would more than likely have been replaced as Britain's capital city by Oxford, which was Hitler's preferred seat of government.

The great public schools had been a fascination for the Nazis for some time and the Nazis had been keen to discover more about their approach and what lessons could be learnt from them. National Political Education Institutes, or Napolas, had been set up in Germany aimed at training the future Nazi elite. In contrast to the British public school system, the German schools were open to boys of all social backgrounds, offering free and subsidised bursaries. The Napolas also provided pupils with the opportunity for foreign travel. In May 1936, for example, boys from the Naumburg Napola visited the Leys School in Cambridge. Exchange and sporting trips were arranged with a number of schools such as Eton, Harrow and Winchester.

One man who already had his eye on a place at Eton College for his son was Dr Franz Six. Few today have even heard his name. Had the Germans triumphed, it would no doubt have been a byword for loathing, fear and infamy, for not long after Hitler had given the order to prepare for an invasion, Six had been appointed by Reinhard Heydrich to direct state police operations in occupied Britain and to draw up plans for the elimination of all anti-Nazi elements. Heydrich was apparently impressed with Six's outstanding academic record and saw him as a great future prospect. Six's responsibilities would also include the arrest and detention of some 2,300 people in the days and weeks following a British surrender and the creation of a plan to quickly restore order to the vanquished enemy.

From Göring's point of view, Six was ideal since he knew a bit about art. Göring looked forward to having first dibs when the treasures of British galleries, abbeys and cathedrals were shipped over to the Fatherland. Hitler had personally ordered that Nelson and his column would also be transported to Berlin.

Like Himmler, Six was dogged – determined to shine at any job he was given, however cruel and vile, and work around the clock. His new job would start in September of 1940, as soon as the Luftwaffe's attacks on Britain's aerodromes and industries had achieved their objective of disabling the RAF. Six had never visited England but he read and wrote the language very well, an unusual talent in a Nazi. And he was a grafter; he got on top of things.

All British males aged between seventeen and forty-five would be interned on sight and deported. Food, gasoline, and all vehicles including horses and carts could be seized for use by the troops.

Factories must be left alone. Wehrmacht troops should speak as little as possible to British people and buy as little as possible from them, at an exchange rate which must not deviate from 9.6 Reichsmarks per £ sterling. (In France, in 1940, the compulsory rate was 1 Reichsmark per 20 francs, which robbed the French, who became desperately impoverished.)

Should any soldier try looting, he could be sentenced to death. Conversely, he must not dispose of his own necessities such as food and clothing. Nor must he destroy radio or phone or telegraph installations.

The British must not oppose the occupiers even passively. To do so would incur 'the most severe' punishment from a military court.

Active opposition would be punishable by death.

The British must keep all businesses open to trade.

They must not associate with Germans.

They must not assemble in groups.

They must not communicate with anyone outside Britain.

They must not publish or broadcast anything anti-Nazi.

They must immediately surrender all radios and firearms.

They must comply with a Requisition List of things the occupiers might need (for instance, blankets, food, fuel or hay for their horses).

There would be twelve regional Secret Intelligence centres each with their own Regional Leader. Everything possible would be organised into a hierarchy. There would always be a form to fill in and submit, and a permission required from someone at a higher level. Looting of valuable artefacts would be organised by thousands of 'economic staff', the transport of prisoners by another division, and so on.

One of the most important things Dr Six had to arrange before the planned invasion in September was the Einsatzgruppen. He would need squads of them to round up British men, transport them by freight train or forced march to interrogation centres, and maybe arrange mass shootings or alternatively, deportation to a concentration camp where they might be worked to death, tortured, starved, used and discarded for medical experimentation, or simply shot. In 1940 the Gestapo's immediate targets in Britain were prominent Jews, intellectuals of all kinds, politicians, diplomats, financiers, British secret agents and Freemasons. Their names were on a Blacklist, or to coin its official name, the Especially Most Wanted List – GB.

Most Germans simply called it the Black Book. With 144 pages, containing 2,820 names, it was not particularly well-informed or researched. Some people on the list had died before the war. Other names appeared twice. One of the Rothschilds was on the list, but not Victor, a keen scientist in MI5 who concentrated on industrial espionage; they didn't know about him. Another name on the list was the so-called 'Ace of Spies', Sidney Reilly. The former MI6 spy had been arrested and shot by the Russians in 1925. It had been headline news at the time, but possibly not in Berlin. The list included the names of writers, thinkers, and politicians. Virginia Woolf, H. G. Wells, Bertrand Russell and Sigmund Freud (who, like Sidney Reilly, was already dead). For many after the war, the list was almost a badge of honour. Rebecca West, the author and *Times* literary critic, sent Noel Coward a pithy telegram the day the list saw the public light of day: 'My dear, the people we should have been seen dead with.'

All these people were to be arrested as soon as the country was occupied. Each name on the list had been pre-assigned to a particular unit for interrogation, usually within the Gestapo. Those marked 'Emigrant' for men, or 'Emigrantin' for women – Jews or non-Jews who had fled the Nazis – were to be taken by the Gestapo.

There was also a Whitelist, of people who might prove to be friends, but it recorded fewer than fifty names, almost all of them obscure.

Beyond the blacklisted people, and the men of seventeen to forty-five, the camps would process millions of others, thanks to informants of the kind that the Gestapo had encouraged in Germany. Exposed: anyone on the political Left. Jews, people descended from them, people friendly with them. Intellectuals. Homosexuals. Criminals. Jehovah's Witnesses. Freemasons. Gypsy families. Disabled, blind, or entirely deaf people. Those with Down's syndrome or incurable diseases such as Parkinson's or epilepsy. Journalists or cartoonists who had published something disrespectful about the régime. In 1940 it was estimated that Britain's population included 420,000.

Twentieth-century historians were quick to point out that the Nazis knew very little about Britain before the planned invasion of 1940, and this was because Hitler had never been particularly interested in occupying it; and they never did succeed in knowing much, because of widespread patriotism among the British populace. This is only partly true.

When the Germans marched in, the officers at least would have a Gestapo Guide to Britain. *Informationsheft GB* was a handbook compiled with the aid of Ordnance Survey maps, the AA Guidebook, cuttings about grand houses from *Country Life*, and photographs of the British coastline obligingly provided by pre-war Lufthansa pilots. They would know where the airfields and arms factories were. They would not destroy factories. The assumption was that in due course, engineering, munitions or aeronautical industries would be directly or indirectly controlled by the Reich, as in Germany, and supplied with slave labour.

The Gestapo also showed a keen interest in the Metropolitan Police, going so far as to include a full and detailed organisational breakdown of the force. Gestapo researchers, with their usual insatiable fascination for trivia, had even included a list of building locations that held police records. As impressive as this looked, the information had been directly lifted from the publicly available Police Almanac (on sale for one shilling and sixpence) and a Metropolitan Police organisation chart that is hung in every police station for public information purposes. The Gestapo were also intrigued by Special Branch, who they saw as fellow political policemen and dwelled in the handbook on their responsibility for protecting the royal family and important overseas visitors.

It would be a mistake, however, to believe that the Gestapo would find themselves entirely without friends in Britain. MI5 files undermine the myth that everyone in Britain was loyal. Thanks to their network of spies, and the small underground British fascist movement, it would not have been impossible to trace some likely sympathisers.

The Abwehr had employed spies in Britain long before war was declared – men and women both German and English. One Baillie-Stewart, a British officer and proven vendor of British military information, was arrested as far back as 1932. He was identified as a spy by Colonel Hinchley-Cooke of MI5. Hinchley-Cooke had been brought up in Germany, sent to England in

1914, and promptly recruited to serve in the newly developed secret service. There he stayed through two world wars, and in 1933 he saw to it that Baillie-Stewart was jailed for five years for espionage.

Because DORA, the Defence of the Realm Act, had ceased to prevail after 1919, there was no legal basis for charging any *non-British* intelligence agent with treason. Nor could such a person be quietly 'interned'. According to judicial opinion, internment without trial was unthinkable. It would do away with *habeas corpus* and shake the foundations of English law. That attitude changed as late as August 1939 with the Emergency Powers (Defence) Act which permitted blanket, and sadly often unfair, despatch of thousands of non-nationalised immigrants to internment camps.

Around the time of Baillie-Stewart's release in 1937 (he fled to Austria, then Germany) another spy arrived in Scotland. She was Jessie Jordan, who had been born there over forty years ago but as a young woman had emigrated with her German husband. She had been schooled by an Abwehr handler about what to do when she went back home – essentially, draw sketch maps of naval and military installations. She did this, and posted the results to PO Box 629 in Hamburg. MI6 knew all about Box 629; it belonged to the Abwehr. They collected her mail and sent it to Hinchley-Cooke, who played a waiting game. There was at first no return address to connect these letters with anyone in Britain. By the time he knew who she was, her own address was acting as a dead-letter box for a German spy communicating from the US to Hamburg. In 1938 she was arrested by Hinchley-Cooke and the Dundee police, and the German in America was hauled in by the FBI.

Jordan was sentenced to four years' imprisonment but she was inadequately interrogated. The German spy's arrest by the FBI was not sufficiently exploited by the British to make even a dent in US isolationism before the war. It seems certain that before the mood changed in May 1940 some in the British secret service still assumed their antagonists in Nazi Germany valued fairness, honour and decency, so they behaved accordingly.

Before the war, Germany actually sent a Party official to live in England, where he founded the Nazi Landesgruppe (Country

Group) of Great Britain and Ireland, with its base – incredibly – in Parliament Street, from which he claimed to 'promote understanding'. He circulated Nazi news to supporters, the Conservative Party and Sir Oswald Mosley's BUF, which was very cosy with Berlin. To Adolf Hitler, he sent reports on opinions being voiced in England. He was hiding in plain sight.

A man called Arnold Littmann tried to pass himself off as a Jewish refugee. He had entered Britain in 1936 as a journalist to work with a German already established here, who acted as London Correspondent of various regional papers in Germany. British intelligence suspected that he was acting on behalf of the Gestapo and spying on refugees from Germany. When, after a year in London, Littmann applied to become a permanent resident, Hinchley-Cooke was even more interested and dropped a quiet word at Toynbee Hall, in Commercial Street in the East End. This charitable organisation was Littmann's base for his involvement with the German Jewish community. Littmann was to be interviewed by MI5 in connection with his application, but instead left the country. He did come back, but this time his cover was blown by another refugee who had known him as a Gestapo interrogator in Berlin. Even before that, Littmann had been the Cologne District leader of a youth group and a national official of the Hitler Youth movement. Such a promising start. Unfortunately, he was arrested as a homosexual and sentenced to suffer in a concentration camp, and finally, released on condition that he would work for the Gestapo.

In 1938 Littmann left Britain for good and set up a news agency in France, with support from German intelligence. This did not leave the field clear. Agents of German intelligence continued to arrive in Britain, and even to recruit British people to their cause, after war had begun.

In the event of an invasion, articulate British people who self-identified as friends of National Socialism would be of great value to Dr Six – and there were plenty of them. In the 1930s, German Ambassador von Ribbentrop became the darling of certain titled individuals and newspaper tycoons. Money flooded in, from Berlin and from home-grown fascists, to support violent anti-Semitism through far-right organisations.

Even MI6 had an in-house enthusiast for Hitler in Anthony Ludovici, who had been an enthralled visitor to Nazi rallies where, he wrote in the *English Review*:

> To watch [the crowd] was to learn what miracles can still be wrought with the ultra-civilised and often effete populations of modern Europe if only they are given a lofty purpose.

Ludovici was not sacked from MI6 until around the original date of the planned invasion in August 1940. MI5 had been a trifle shocked, when they came across plans for a fascist revolution in Britain, to find that Ludovici of MI6 would have a role in it.

Admiral Domvile, Director of Naval Intelligence in 1927–30, was another Hitler follower; he founded a notorious right-wing group in London, with regular speakers, a newspaper, money coming in from Germany… And then there was Beamish. One gasps at Beamish, a Conservative MP. The Board of Deputies of British Jews sent a spy to a meeting he addressed and heard him say that 'the [International Fascist League] knew of three remedies to the Jewish question: to kill them, to sterilize them or to segregate them.'

When, during the war, Eric Roberts (a former Mosley supporter) was employed by Victor Rothschild of MI5 to pose as a British Gestapo officer on the lookout for some help, he found seething nests of unashamed sympathisers in north London suburbs, provincial cities and English villages. Most of these fifth columnists were frankly eccentric, and others too ineffectual or conspicuous to be considered as spies even by the Germans; but some set off bombs or tried to start fires, and others – Rothschild was particularly interested in those working in factories such as Siemens – proved only too willing to pass on highly sensitive industrial secrets that could lose the war for Britain.

Maybe their names were not on the Whitelist. And it is easy to exaggerate the threat from some elderly person in Barnes or Tewkesbury who displayed a swastika on the mantelpiece. But would such people have flocked, right arm extended to the sky, to greet their new, German occupiers? Would they have informed on patriotic neighbours with glee? Almost certainly. The incoming Gestapo, and their putative leader Dr Six, would have received a welcome from this gaggle of small-time traitors in every city.

8

THE LAST DITCH

The Battle of Britain, in which the RAF defended airfields and shipping in the Channel, lasted from July to October 1940. It has left us with images of Spitfires firing at Messerschmitts over the sunlit fields of Kent, of little planes bursting into flames and tumbling to earth, of parachute landings and arrests by village policemen, of a vicar on a bicycle being dive-bombed as he pedalled along a country lane. Terrifying but somehow cosy; it was not cosy. At the time, children in school could study aeroplane silhouettes on posters on the wall, and they quickly learned to read the skies, if they dared. Göring's Luftwaffe were determined to smash British Bomber Command and they failed, but not before too many young pilots had died.

Trepidation and anger were well founded. On classroom walls there was also a map of the whole world and it showed, in the first years of war, exactly how isolated Britain was.

It was a time to learn geography and be very, very alarmed at the same time. Ten days after Hitler's announcement on 17 September that Britain would be invaded 'next year' rather than immediately, and about three weeks since relentless night-time bombing raids had begun to wreck London, Germany, Italy and Japan had officially formed the Axis.

The world war between Axis and Allies really was being fought across the globe. From 1939, any British twelve-year-old with a map to look at could plot the onward march of the Axis as they took more territory. Japan methodically invaded Cambodia, Thailand, Burma, Laos, Vietnam, Malaya and the Philippines having, before the war, already taken Manchuria and parts of China. You could colour the places in: black if they had been captured by Japan, brown for Germany, and green for Italy.

The brown stain of Germany would spread through the whole of northern Europe and parts of North Africa, through Iraq and into Turkey, Bulgaria and Romania, down to Greece and the Balkans. And while Italy, prewar, had controlled Libya, Ethiopia, Somalia and Eritrea, it would in the course of hostilities invade Egypt and Albania, Greece and Montenegro. The USSR was not a combatant on the Axis side, and its obvious expansionist tendencies were something Hitler would soon address.

Britain's ally had been France, which was overrun. America gave all kinds of practical support but was not a combatant at this point. Britain's active allies were not countries, but individuals: the devoted resistance fighters of Poland and France and Norway, and the fifteen million fighting men and women from the Commonwealth – Canada, Australia, India and Nepal, South Africa, the West Indies and numerous smaller colonies and dominions.

The big news was framed as Britain *vs* Germany and Italy. When you saw that the Axis powers were able to claim all the resources of a vast swathe of Europe and the near East, on the map, you were not encouraged; and when you forgot the Commonwealth, you wondered how a country with only 45 million inhabitants could defeat the massed forces of the Axis. Every one of the countries invaded by the Third Reich would have its Dr Six, its curfews and Gestapo-enforced rules about being executed for resistance.

At MI14, Kenneth Strong, aware of the fact that by the early spring of 1941, with better cross-channel weather, Britain would be back on invasion alert, began the search for an officer who would be able to monitor German railway movements and work alongside Harry Pickering and Peter Earle, the aerial photography specialists. According to Peter Earle, the officer originally given this post was 'devious, bone-idle and bad tempered'. Strong swiftly disposed of him by using the age-old military tactic of having him promoted to the rank of Captain and transferred to another War Office department. Earle noted with amusement that within months, the officer was again promoted, this time to Major, and despatched to yet another 'long-suffering department'.

Luckily for Strong, in Noel Annan he found an officer who was not only eminently suitable for the vacant post, but just as importantly, readily available. Annan had left Stowe School in 1935 and gone up to King's College, Cambridge, where he read History. When the Munich crisis blew up, he joined the Officer Cadet Corps. No doubt hoping to see front-line action when the war eventually came, he waited patiently to be assigned to a unit. Dining one day at the London club where he and his father were members, Annan was introduced to railway economist Carl Sherrington, the son of Nobel Prize-winning Cambridge physiologist Sir Charles Sherrington. Hearing that Annan was hoping for a front-line Intelligence Corps posting, Sherrington pipped up that 'Kenneth Strong is itching to get his hands on people like you.' Two days later Annan received a summons to the War Office and found himself in the subterranean broom cupboard of a room from where Captain 'Sandy' Sanderson oversaw 'invasion intelligence'. Annan later recalled that Sanderson's first question was how much he knew about railways.

> I replied I didn't, to which Sanderson retorted, 'well, then, your father does.' I recollected that at some time before 1914 my father had been associated with the Chesapeake & Ohio Railway. 'Ah, that must have been it,' said Sanderson, relieved that he now had a cast-iron case for getting me transferred to his department. 'Can you read German? Tell me what this means,' he said, thrusting into my hands a long report. At this point his phone rang, and while he answered it, I was able to get the gist of it. 'It's to do with transport in Europe,' I began. 'Excellent,' he said without troubling me further.

And so, in January 1941, at the age of twenty-four, Annan found himself a fully fledged member of MI14, assigned to 'C' section, covering German troop movements in occupied Europe.

Working closely with Gubby Allen's section, who, among other responsibilities, tracked the whereabouts and strength of the

German anti-aircraft or flak regiments, Annan's task was centred on the German army. In particular, Sanderson wanted regular estimates on the number and character of German divisions and whether they were stationary or on the move. If they were on the move, where were they heading? Annan soon developed a growing respect for Kenneth Strong and his unique insight so far as the German army was concerned.

Strong looked like a beaver – an eager beaver bursting out of his uniform, with dark hair, a fine forehead, clever, shifty eyes and so chinless that he came to be known as hangman's dilemma.

For Annan, the key figure in the tightly knit team that assessed invasion intelligence was Peter Earle, with whom he shared an office:

> If Strong made one think of a beaver, Earle had the air of a greyhound. He was lean and sensitive, with a quizzical expression. He was one of those Etonians who appear to be indolent, but in fact develop curious talents and interests. He disliked horses but knew a lot about fast cars. However squalid our conditions became, his own corner of the room somehow conveyed the calm of a country house.

It was Earle who assessed the most crucial evidence by counting the fluctuating numbers of barges and other craft assembled in the Channel Ports. Pickering might have had more aerial photography know-how, but it was Earle who seemed to have a second sense when it came to interpreting what the minute clues meant and drawing conclusions.

By May 1941 it was clear that nine months of almost nightly bombing raids over London, the near-destruction of other cities, and the huge loss of civilian lives as well as service personnel had only strengthened the country's resolve. The country was physically devastated, financially rocky, but united in defiance of Hitler.

At the War Office, with most personnel working around the clock, many of them ignored all but the closest bombing raids. The ARP roof spotters would alert War Office staff to such raids, at which point everyone would go to the shelters in the sub-basement, the deepest level of the building, 30 feet below street level, which also housed the night canteen. The nearest miss so far had been on the night of 8 October the previous year, when the War Office suffered a direct hit from a stick of four bombs. Fortunately, this caused only superficial damage and only one fatality. In the following eighteen months, the building suffered a further seven direct hits, with damage mainly confined to the upper floors. During the Blitz, as it came to be known, Lt. Colonel Strong would normally spend most nights at his club, the Caledonian, in nearby St James's Square. Fortunately, the night the Caledonian received a direct hit, Strong spent the night in MI14's basement, although he lost all his personal possessions, clothes and books.

For the family of Harry Pickering there had been no lucky escape. Southampton, Pickering's home town and the headquarters of his former employers Ordnance Survey, was the seventh heaviest-bombed city in Britain. It was a strategic target for the Germans as it contained both a large and busy dockyard and the Supermarine factory building Spitfires in Woolston. The riverside aircraft factory received a direct hit on the night of 24 September, destroying most of the factory and killing 110 people.

During the night of 30 November and 1 December 1940, the Southampton Blitz reached its climax as the city came under sustained aerial bombardment by the Luftwaffe. Hundreds of tons of bombs rained down across the city, leaving 634 properties ablaze, including the Ordnance Survey head office in London Road. Pickering's home, close by to London Road, was completely razed, along with most of the street – there were no survivors. The resulting carnage, although subject to censorship, was described as 'equalling anything so far in the aerial attack of this country'.

Was the Blitz a precursor to invasion? Invasion was still a very real possibility in the spring of 1941. How would civilians react? Captain Sanderson, as part of his invasion intelligence portfolio, was asked to consider how civilians might react in an invasion/occupation scenario. While he did his best to produce detailed observations and theories, he found that his ultimate conclusion was that we wouldn't know until it actually happened. In the meantime, he could be more precise about the theoretical plans and strategies that were already in place for such an eventuality.

The Home Guard were much better equipped and trained than in 1940, and in cities there were places to hide, but smaller communities could be virtually defenceless. Public information films and leaflets told people to resist as much as they could while avoiding any military manoeuvres or fighting. If they saw thousands of jackbooted Nazis marching down the road they were to hide in slit trenches in their gardens. Village organising committees made sure the trenches were dug and place names painted out. Would this be an adequate or effective defence? Probably not.

As far back as 1938, a British Resistance had been set up under the aegis of the War Office which then failed to supply any funds. John Holland, an ex-Royal Engineer who worked on the idea, had studied guerrilla successes all over the world. He knew that a secret army which knew the territory, was passionate about the cause, well-armed, well-disciplined, and able to communicate without intervention could overcome a conscripted force. In MI (Research) he even had a colleague who had invented a couple of brilliant bits of kit. But Holland was in poor health and lacked the authority to make anything happen. In the summer before the war, the British Resistance remained a non-entity because only in the event of an invasion would the Resistance be trained, armed and supplied.

Colonel Colin Gubbins changed all that. He had experience of guerrilla campaigns and joined MI(R) in 1939 to teach Resistance techniques within the occupied countries of Europe. He wrote three useful booklets: *The Partisan Leader's Handbook*, *The Art of Guerrilla Warfare*, and *How to Use High Explosives*. He had identified the skills that a Resistance movement would require of its members: absolute discretion, marksmanship, fitness, daring without recklessness, cool-headedness in a crisis, stoicism, authority, mental alertness, cunning, imagination, survival skills ... In the summer of 1940 he selected linguists, mountaineers, engineers, explorers and people in business who had contacts abroad, and organised private classes to discuss the possibilities. He also visited the Danube area (probably Romania) and the Baltic to look into the likelihood of initiating anti-Nazi movements there.

Less than a week before war began, he took up a post with the British Military Mission to the Polish army in Warsaw.

That lasted, unfortunately, just five days before Poland was invaded, and two days after that, the Embassy staff and the BMM had to flee the country. That autumn, as bombs rained down on London, he helped to train those members of the Polish army who had escaped to France, before being ordered to take British Territorials to Norway to teach them how to attack the Wehrmacht there.

At home, the vacillating government was still supporting the Foreign Office's 'Section D'. This predecessor of MI(R) had a similar aim (to construct a British Resistance) but insufficient expertise and poor leadership. Untrained operatives created havoc, confusion, and actual damage all over the country. Section D was dissolved.

Gubbins returned to London. He was told that his Territorials would become Commandos, under a different leader. His job from now on in would be to create and run a Resistance movement in Britain.

In MI (R), other 'bits of kit' had been invented within the department since he left. They included RAF trouser buttons that could be used as a compass and would therefore be useful to escapees from POW camps. MI(R) had also formed the Phantom Resistance, which had landed at Dunkirk and made their way towards the retreating lines of British troops, telling them where they might expect to find German units ahead.

Military Intelligence had quite a lot on, so the British Resistance would have to find another home. It duly became part of GHQ Home Forces and Gubbins, seeking a name that gave no clue to its function, called it the Auxiliary Units.

He reasoned that since, in consequence of the Battle of Britain, the Luftwaffe was badly weakened, any German invasion would be by sea. Auxiliary Units were therefore to be located within 30 miles of the whole coastline of Britain excluding Northern Ireland (the crossing of the Irish Sea by a Nazi force seeming highly unlikely).

The coastal strip would be divided into twelve sectors, each headed by an Intelligence Officer. These would be soldiers Gubbins had worked with or men who came recommended by someone he knew; they wouldn't be members of Military Intelligence.

An intelligence officer would usually recruit, as patrol leader, a member of the local Home Guard – often a man who had served in the First World War. This Patrol Leader would suggest men who might be suitable for his patrol and Military Intelligence would check their security status and ask the local police to investigate their background (and the police would never know why). Patrol Leaders would be tasked with creating cells of six hand-picked local men with local skills, such as knowledge of disused mineshafts or other little-known places of possible concealment. Poachers, gamekeepers, stalkers, miners, fishermen with expert knowledge of the coast – strong, silent, clever types in all these categories were useful. David Lampe, in his book about the resistance, adds 'In some areas they recruited parsons, physicians and local council officials, as well as blacksmiths, hoteliers and innkeepers.'

It is easy to see how their knowledge would be valuable. These carefully selected Unit members, all of whom came recommended by existing members, were given uniforms and told that they were now in a special battalion of the Home Guard. (Since the Auxiliary Units were unrecognised by the army or government, they were not protected by the Geneva Convention, a fact which nobody pointed out to them.)

The Auxiliary Units must never be seen. Each unit of six men would have access to a secret underground hideout. Some had bunks, chemical sanitation, artificial light, a water source and a communications capability, the whole thing dug and constructed by the Royal Engineers – or adapted, since disused mines and ice houses were used too. Some were less well-appointed but still useable. In Scotland, Pictish dwellings more than a thousand years old, stone-built, largely underground and entered from above by removal of a stone slab, were also used.

Elsewhere the entrance would be ingeniously concealed, the entrance carefully engineered and almost impossible to find, and known only to unit members. These hideouts didn't all have toilets and telephones, but they were never dirty or squalid. Some replaced badger setts – the badgers had to move out but the entrance looked undisturbed. Many were hollowed out underneath giant trees. One was big enough to house 120 people, and another was carefully concealed in a brickyard.

The units also worked in well-constructed and equally secret two-man observation posts. Montgomery himself was invited to enter one of them by sliding a nail which released a catch at the bottom of a sheep trough.

In the event of an invasion, Unit personnel would disappear from home and assemble in the hideout, which was furnished with arms, ammunition and food sufficient for a long stay. There they would live, emerging only when the Nazis had left the area or occupied it. If they had the opportunity to attack or sabotage, they must do so under cover of darkness and retreat to the hideout as rapidly as they had advanced.

Sabotage, of roads and bridges for instance, was among the guerrilla tactics taught at Coleshill, a large mansion in Wiltshire. Security was tight before they were allowed in, and they had to sign the Official Secrets Act. They learned about plastic explosives before anybody else in the British army, and were supplied with the very latest in weaponry including 'a special .22 rifle ... fitted with a powerful telescopic sight and a silencer [which] fired high velocity bullets capable of killing a man a mile away'.

Every man was issued with a rubber truncheon and a Fairbairn Commando dagger, and taught how to creep silently up on a German sentry and stab him before he squealed. Coleshill was surrounded by acres of woodland and fields.

Women as well as men were sought for hazardous home defence intelligence roles as well as being selected by the Special Operations Executive, the overseas sabotage and spying service, for what was, without doubt, extremely dangerous overseas operational service. Perhaps that was enough to prove that they could be discreet, brave and resourceful, because by 1942, more than ninety women were finally recruited to the British Resistance as well.

From the start no women had been allowed to join the Home Guard. A pressure group called the Amazons – led by a woman who had won the King's Medal in 1930 on the rifle range at Bisley – demanded admission to the Home Guard and an equal right to weapons training. It didn't happen, but until it did, they practised shooting anyway. Since they might also, in the event of an invasion, usefully lob hand grenades at the enemy, they practised by throwing half-bricks at buckets from 20 yards away.

If it did nothing else, this empowered them, improved morale and – had it ever received support from on high – would have doubled the number of effective resisters in the population.

Many women worked as bus drivers, train guards, bill-posters – anything that they could do to be useful. Others – although not conscripted until 1941 – were recruited into the services, or they could also choose to become Land Girls (farm and forestry workers) or work in factories. In the services they were not (with few exceptions) supposed to engage in armed combat, but they did act as decoders, non-combatant pilots who delivered planes to airfields, nurses, drivers, radar plotters, analysers of reconnaissance photographs, wireless telegraphists, electricians, plotters in operations rooms, and many other back-room jobs that helped win the war. This is not to say that they were valued at the same level. Their pay was lower than that of men of equivalent rank, although by working alongside men at military or airbases or a shore-based naval 'ship', they ran the same risk of being bombed.

Some joined the Auxiliary Territorial Service, the women's army. WRNS (Women's Royal Navy Service) – 'Wrens' – were told that by joining up they would 'free a man for the fleet', while the Women's Auxiliary Air Force tried to recruit with the message 'Serve in the WAAF – with the men who fly.' Abram Games' marvellous posters were a lot less sexist and supremely well designed. Unfortunately, his simple command 'Join the ATS' was accompanied by a head-and-shoulders profile of a blonde in scarlet lipstick and a perky ATS cap. She looked smart and determined. This was the limit! Mrs Thelma Cazalet-Keir, Conservative MP, was horrified. This girl on the poster was too glamorous by half. The formidable Mrs C-K got certain other MPs harrumphing in support while, over in the Ministry of War, senior army people muttered that it was the most effective recruitment poster so far. For three weeks in October 1941 the media were full of this controversy, while the Nazis drove determinedly deeper and deeper into Soviet territory. Perhaps, on reflection, the distraction was better for morale than endless reminders that Britain was running out of money and the Germans would soon reach Moscow.

The British Resistance, should an invasion succeed, would need people to spy on the Gestapo and communicate fast. 'Special

Duties' Intelligence officers visited areas near the Auxiliary units and recruited people whose jobs kept them on top of local gossip: farmers, doctors, midwives, postmen, vicars, bus drivers, ladies' hairdressers, barbers.

The Auxiliary Units were armed and operational, but 'Special Duties' Auxiliaries (of whom they would never hear) were the people who would actually spy. And spies needed to communicate with the operational units without either side knowing much about the other.

So, radio operators were required. In 1942 promising members of the ATS or certain voluntary services were – in conditions of strict confidentiality – invited one by one to meet a Miss Temple in the public lounge on the fourth floor of Harrods department store in Knightsbridge. Some never heard from her again; others were told to make a journey from Liverpool Street to Essex, strictly according to instructions which – a couple of train rides and an army car later – would land them at a farmhouse deep in the country. There, a Signals officer gave each of them a piece of paper and asked them to read its message aloud into a microphone. Having done so, they drank a cup of tea and were taken back to the railway station and told to return to their units.

For some, that was the end of the matter. For others, the whole rigmarole of a confusing journey was repeated, west from Paddington this time. When they reached their destination, a large house in the country, they signed the Official Secrets Act. They were told that they would work for a deeply secret entity – the Auxiliary Units, Special Duties section.

They would serve not far from their billets, near existing Auxiliary patrols, but they would never know that the patrols existed.

The women would operate a new short-range radio transmitter-receiver – small, well insulated against damp, working on a 6-volt car battery, and broadcasting voice-only. It had been designed to work underground from a dedicated outstation. The voice transmissions could be heard, in normal conditions, only within line of sight, although under certain atmospheric conditions the signals might reach France. Operators were taught how to recognise the signs of that happening and switch off. It is said that they were told their transmitters would resist location by Gestapo detector vans; this was untrue. They were certainly told that to be caught in their hideouts meant torture followed by death.

The aerials were flexible but 40 feet long, and disguised by Royal Corps of Signals staff in tree trunks or embedded in walls. The transmitting sets were concealed in rooms deep underground; entry was via a trapdoor and down a ladder, or through a cellar, or a privy in a yard. It could be cold down there.

They would work six-hour shifts around the clock. They would collect hidden messages, written by whom they had no idea, and transmit them by voice to somebody they didn't know either. Together, they would form a radio network for the Resistance.

By the end of 1941, with German bombers heading high across the blacked-out land towards London or Liverpool, there were more than 300 hideouts from Land's End to John O'Groats and all the way down the west coast of Britain.

As vital, ingenious and courageous as the Auxiliary Units might be in the last resort, MI14's view was that the best hope of avoiding invasion was by being at least one step ahead. An innocuous country house in Buckinghamshire would provide just that opportunity.

9

HOUSE IN THE COUNTRY

Codes transmitted by the German armed services and the Abwehr had proved impossible to break throughout the 1930s. British code-breakers tried without success to figure it out as a linguistic system. The major advance came in July 1939. Seven years before, a secret agent working for the French in Germany had explained it to his control in Paris, and Paris had passed this information to a group of three mathematicians within the Polish military's Cypher Bureau in Warsaw. In the summer before Poland was invaded, these men – foreseeing that war was inevitable – agreed to reveal their secrets to a couple of British code-breakers. To their surprise, the German code was not word-based at all, but relied on mathematical patterns; it changed daily. A computer generated it, and the Poles knew how it worked. The British called it the Enigma. To have any chance of breaking the code, you needed to build your own primitive computer.

Britain's Government Code and Cypher School at Bletchley Park in Buckinghamshire received this vital intelligence just in time. Alan Turing and others in the Bureau devised a suitable decoder, had a great many made, and called it the Bombe machine. It could trawl through, and select from, numerous options faster than a person could. Bombe machines were supplied at listening stations up and down the country. They were staffed mostly by 'Wrens' (Women's Royal Naval Service staff), who worked six-hour shifts taking down code transmitted from German military radio operators on land, sea and air. They fed the coded information from their listening stations into Bombe machines and sent it to Bletchley.

The people who worked there, many of them mathematicians, cryptographers and astute intellectuals not unlike those at Wood Norton, would be able to decrypt and translate some of the most sensitive intelligence of the war; they were 'fanatically loyal' and gave away nothing about what they did at any time and for almost thirty years afterwards. Theirs was what was known as the Ultra Project.

Commander Alastair Denniston was operational head of GC&CS from 1919 to 1942. On the day Britain declared war on Germany, Denniston wrote to the Foreign Office about recruiting 'men of the professor type'. Personal networking was one of the main recruitment tools and focussed on people such as solvers of cryptic crossword puzzles, as these individuals had strong and effective lateral thinking skills. Many early recruits were drawn from the universities of Cambridge and Oxford. Trustworthy women were similarly recruited for administrative and clerical jobs.

Denniston also recognised that Germany's use of electro-mechanical cipher machines meant that formally trained mathematicians would also be needed: Oxford's Peter Twinn joined GC&CS in February 1939; Cambridge's Alan Turing and Gordon Welchman began training in 1938 and reported to Bletchley the day after war was declared, along with John Jeffreys. Later recruited cryptanalysts included the mathematicians Derek Taunt, Jack Good, Bill Tutte, and Max Newman; historian Harry Hinsley; and chess champions Hugh Alexander and Stuart Milner-Barry. Joan Clarke was one of the few women employed at Bletchley as a fully fledged cryptanalyst.

After initial training at the Inter-Service Special Intelligence School set up by John Tiltman, staff moved to Bletchley Park on 15 August 1939. The Naval, Military, and Air Sections were on the ground floor of the mansion, together with a telephone exchange, teleprinter room, kitchen, and dining room; the top floor was allocated to MI6.

The size of the new operation dictated that additional accommodation in the way of huts would need to be speedily erected in the mansion grounds. According to MI14 records, Bletchley Park was effectively organised as follows:

Hut 1: used to house the Wireless Station and later used for administrative functions such as transport, typing, and Bombe maintenance.

Hut 2: A recreational hut.

Hut 3: Intelligence: translation and analysis of Army and Air Force decrypts.

Hut 4: Naval intelligence: analysis of Naval Enigma and Hagelin decrypts.

Hut 5: Military intelligence and German police codes.

Hut 6: Cryptanalysis of Army and Air Force Enigma.

Hut 7: Cryptanalysis of Japanese naval codes and intelligence.

Hut 8: Cryptanalysis of Naval Enigma.

Hut 9: ISOS Intelligence Section.

Hut 10: Secret Intelligence Service (MI6) codes, Air and Meteorological Sections.

Hut 11: Bombe building.

Hut 14: Communications Centre.

Hut 15: SIXTA (Signals Intelligence and Traffic Analysis).

Hut 16: ISK Abwehr ciphers.

Hut 18: ISOS Intelligence Section.

Hut 23: Engineering department.

In addition to the network of wooden huts that were erected, eight brick-built blocks were also commissioned:

- *Block A:* Naval Intelligence.
- *Block B:* Italian Air and Naval, and Japanese code-breaking.
- *Block C:* Store for punch-card indexes.
- *Block D:* From February 1943 it housed those from Hut 3, who synthesized intelligence from multiple sources, Huts 6 and 8 and SIXTA.
- *Block E:* Incoming and outgoing Radio Transmission and TypeX.
- *Block F:* Newmanry and Testery, and Japanese Military Air Section.
- *Block G:* Traffic, analysis and deception operations.
- *Block H:* Tunny and Colossus.

Most German messages decrypted at Bletchley were produced by one or another version of the Enigma cipher machine, but an important minority were produced by the even more complicated twelve-rotor Lorenz SZ42 on-line teleprinter cipher machine.

In August 1939, Warsaw's Cipher Bureau made contact with their British and French counterparts, revealing that they had succeeded in breaking Enigma to astonished French and British personnel. The British used the Poles' information and techniques, and the Enigma clone sent to them in August 1939, which greatly increased their (previously very limited) success in decrypting Enigma messages.

The bombe was an electromechanical device whose function was to discover some of the daily settings of the Enigma machines on the various German military networks. Its pioneering design was developed by Alan Turing (with an important contribution from Gordon Welchman) and the machine was engineered by Harold 'Doc' Keen of the British Tabulating Machine Company. Each machine was around 7 feet (2.1 m) high and wide, 2 feet (0.6 m) deep and weighed around a ton.

At its peak, GC&CS was reading approximately 4,000 messages per day. Luftwaffe messages were the first to be read in quantity. The German navy had much tighter procedures, and the capture of code books was needed before they could be broken.

When, in February 1942, the German navy introduced the four-rotor Enigma for communications with its Atlantic U-boats, this traffic became unreadable for a period of ten months. The British produced modified bombes, but it was the US Navy bombe that was the main source of reading messages from this version of Enigma for the rest of the war. Messages were sent to and fro across the Atlantic by enciphered teleprinter links.

The Lorenz messages were code-named *Tunny* at Bletchley Park. They were only sent in quantity from mid-1942. The Tunny networks were used for high-level messages between German High Command and field commanders. With the help of German operator errors, the cryptanalysts in the Testery (named after Ralph Tester, its head) worked out the logical structure of the machine. They devised automatic machinery to help with decryption, which culminated in Colossus, the world's first programmable digital electronic computer. This was designed and built by Tommy Flowers and his team at the Post Office Research Station at Dollis Hill.

Noel Annan's job at MI14 centred around the plotting of likely movements of enemy troops. This meant collating every scrap of information from aerial photography, interrogations, diplomatic reports, newspaper reports, MI6 agents abroad, Foreign Office briefings, and key facts and figures about the enemy's weaponry and transport from the Ministry of Economic Warfare.

Most intensely secret were the radio messages between German army units, as noted in the listening stations, decrypted at Bletchley Park and received at MI14 by teleprinter. These were at the heart of it. No other source could do more than confirm the intentions predicted in the radio messages. The fact that what they predicted *did* happen was proof enough that the Germans did not know the code had been cracked. And they must never know; nobody in MI14 could discuss their work with anyone, even those in other Military Intelligence departments. MI14 files reveal that confidential news was certainly passed at the highest levels.

In the first winter of the war, no amount of information seemed to have much effect on British defence planning. To influence it at all, Military Intelligence had to pass on its conclusions to an alert audience, but the Foreign Office and the Services were suspicious customers.

Faced with this Ultra-informed, fact-based analysis of what the Germans would do next, Sir Maurice Hankey set up a Joint Intelligence Committee in 1939 so that the leaders of the FO and the services would compare notes and come to a conclusion – but they didn't. They ignored the JIC until the shock invasion of France in June 1940. Kenneth Strong had forewarned the French about that too, but they didn't listen. Even then the British armed services were never entirely convinced by Ultra, and its evidence was sometimes dismissed.

In September of 1940 MI14 was able to update MI5 on the Gestapo 'as a result of our liaison with the Poles'. The Polish government in exile in London had received sensitive military information about Nazi Germany from agents and informants throughout Europe. After Germany conquered Poland in the autumn of 1939, Gestapo officials believed that they had neutralised Polish intelligence activities. However, certain Polish information about the movement of Gestapo and SS units to the East during the German invasion of the Soviet Union in the autumn of 1941 was similar to information British intelligence secretly obtained through intercepting and decoding messages sent by radio telegraphy.

In 1942, the Gestapo discovered a cache of Polish intelligence documents in Prague and were surprised to see that Polish agents and informants had been gathering detailed military information and smuggling it out to London via Budapest and Istanbul. The Poles identified and tracked the German military trains to the Eastern front and identified four Order Police battalions sent to occupied areas of the Soviet Union in October 1941 that engaged in war crimes and mass murder.

Polish agents also gathered detailed information about the morale of German soldiers in the East. After uncovering a sample of the information, Gestapo officials concluded that Polish intelligence activity represented a very serious danger to Germany. The intelligence on the Gestapo, for example, was exceptionally detailed, particularly in terms of organisational matters. Much of this found its way back to MI14's Brian Melland and John MacLaren-Clarke. The new instalment was soon weaved into their encyclopaedic 'Gestapo History'.

MI14 was, thanks to MacLaren-Clarke, already well versed in the early development of the Gestapo in the six years prior to the war. With its 1936 merging with KRIPO (National Criminal Police), to form sub-units of the *Sicherheitspolizei* (SiPo – Security Police), the Gestapo was now classified as a government agency. This reorganisation went a big step further on 27 September 1939 with the creation of the RSHA (the Reich Main Security Office), which was henceforth to be headed by Reinhard Heydrich. While MI14 had awareness of the RSHA merger, the new wealth of intelligence added considerably to the overall picture they had of the Gestapo and the other constituent parts of the RSHA.

The Gestapo now became known as RSHA *Amt IV* (Department or Office IV), with Heinrich Müeller as its chief. The cache of Polish and Bletchley Park intelligence gave, for the first time, specific information about the internal departments of *Amt IV*:

Department A (Political Opponents)

- Communists (A.1)
- Counter-sabotage (A.2)
- Reactionaries, liberals and opposition (A.3)
- Protective services (A.4)

Department B (Sects and Churches)

- Catholicism (B.1)
- Protestantism (B.2)
- Freemasons and other churches (B.3)
- Jewish affairs (B.4)

Department C (Administration and Party Affairs)

Central administrative office of the Gestapo, responsible for card files of all personnel including all officials.

- Files, card, indexes, information and administration (C.1)
- Protective custody (C.2)
- Press Office (C.3)
- NSDAP matters (C.4)

Administration for regions outside the *Reich*

- Protectorate affairs, Protectorate of Bohemia and Moravia regions of Yugoslavia, Greece (D.1)
  Ist Belgrade Special Combat detachment
- General Government (D.2)
- Confidential office – hostile foreigners, emigrants (D.3)
- Occupied territories – France, Belgium, Holland, Norway, Denmark (D.4)
- Occupied Eastern territories (D.5)

Department E (Security and Counter-intelligence)

- In the *Reich* (E.1)
- Policy and economic formation (E.2)
- West (E.3)
- Scandinavia (North) (E.4)
- East (E.5)
- South (E.6)

In addition to the myriad departments and sections, the Gestapo also maintained offices at all concentration camps, along with liaison offices at SS sections and KRPO divisions. Personnel assigned to these auxiliary duties were often removed from the Gestapo chain of command and fell under the authority of the SS.

During the course of 1941, MI14 created a series of detailed, illustrated booklets for the armed forces and for other intelligences branches. These included an analysis of the German army, with a guide to identifying the uniforms and insignia of each rank. The Gestapo booklet, prepared primarily for MI9, explained that the Gestapo maintained police detective ranks which were used for all officers, both those who were and were not concurrently SS members.

The booklet also focussed on the fact that the Gestapo placed great store on recruiting women. Female youth leaders, lawyers, and business administrators in the Bund Deutscher Mädel were hired as detectives after a one-year course. Nurses, kindergarten teachers and female commercial employees with an aptitude for police work were hired as female detectives after a two-year course. After two years as *Kariminaloberassistentin* promotion to *Kriminalsekretärin* could take place, and after another two or three years in that grade the female detective could be promoted to *Kriminalobersekretärin*.

As the Gestapo were a plainclothes organisation, their agents generally wore every-day suits. Illustrations were, however, provided for Leitstellung (district office) staff who wore grey SS service uniform, with police-pattern shoulderboards, and SS rank insignia on the left collar patch. The right collar patch was black without the SS runes. Uniforms were also worn by Gestapo men assigned to the *Einazgruppen* in occupied territories, in this case the Waffen-SS field uniform.

Whether or not in uniform, Gestapo officers, when asked for identification, were required only to present a warrant disc, not a photo identification card.

In 1941, MI14 began to deploy specially trained messengers between England and France. They were carrier pigeons, and they spied by proxy. These well-trained birds would set off from Cambridge carrying a tiny questionnaire. Arriving in northern France or Belgium, they would be found and answers would be returned, affixed to the same bird. The snag, of course, was that their messages could also be found by the German occupiers, as indeed some were, so that before long there was a reward for handing in a British pigeon and a penalty (death) for being in possession of one. An MI14 note on the Pigeon Service records:

> During the summer months around 20-25% of the despatched pigeons successfully made it back to England with messages from Europe, dropping to 10% to 15% in the winter. These messages were often very detailed and sometimes included sketch maps. Although the quality of intelligence could be rather good there was the inherent risk of deception by German counter intelligence.... During the three years the MI14 Pigeon Service operated, about 950 different messages were received from the continent.

We don't have a questionnaire, but it is clear that MI14, in 1941 and '42 at least, were anxious for clues about Hitler's intention to invade. Here is an answer from July 1941. The pigeon had been despatched two days earlier.

Dear Friends,

With this I inform you that on the railway Thielt to Meulebeke and to Inglemunster there are groups of trucks laden with munitions.... There are here hardly any soldiers but around Bruges there are many. At Pittem they are repairing the chateau for important people from Germany. There is some movement on the road from Bruges to Courtrai of motor cars with officers and on the aerodrome of Wevelghem there are many airmen.

I found this pigeon on the 6th early in the morning while I was cutting clover for the animals and I have looked after it well and given it food and drink and am now anxious to know if the little animal will reach its loft. And now I must finish. The soldiers become dissatisfied for their food had become much worse and they are covered in lice.

Hoping that I have possibly rendered you some service and if possible I am always ready and sign myself
Jules V, Meulebeke St Ath.

The good-heartedness of that man could never be acknowledged. Many others sent similarly useful letters:

There are no troops here at the Callouet aviation field at the moment but there are dummy aeroplanes made of wood on the ground... The Société MN (Société des Minéraux Nationales?) despatches 4 mineral trains per day... Between Lassy and St Jean le Blanc there is an aeroplane beacon ... The morale of the troops here is very bad... We hear the BBC very well on 373m and we always listen at 9.15hrs (Occupied France time) ... (signed) Group of True Frenchmen who wish for your victory which will also be ours. Vive la France! Vive l'Angleterre!

In addition to pigeon intelligence, MI14 also benefitted from the intelligence provided by a network of agents in occupied Europe, many of whom were railway workers and officials. They gave MI6 details of the number of trains, the equipment and troops carried in them, and occasionally the insignia of a division or military unit, as they passed through a station. Noel Annan, as the MI14 officer responsible for processing the MI6-sourced railway intelligence, tracked the trains and made regular daily reports to Captain Sanderson. As early as November 1940, MI14 was trying to second-guess Hitler's next move. Agents had warned that rail traffic to the Balkans was increasing, and during February–March of 1941 some sixty trains a day were crossing Hungary. Their reports may have been low-level intelligence, but Annan was convinced that they were high-grade in terms of reliability. The conclusion was soon drawn that Hitler was set on attacking Greece; however, there was great uncertainty as to whether this was to be an isolated objective or a tidying-up operation before mounting an invasion of Britain in the summer of 1941. Why, Sanderson asked, did Hitler require such overwhelming strength to defeat a small country like Greece? He could achieve his objective in Greece with a sixth of the forces he now had in the Balkans – why were so many German troops in Romania? To compound the conundrum further, intelligence suggested that some of the best divisions in the German army were being transported to Eastern Europe. While MI14 had not yet reached a view about Hitler's ultimate objective in the spring of 1941, aerial photographs taken over the Channel Ports showed no activity whatsoever in terms of German road or rail movements. Sanderson, Annan and Earle all agreed that the invasion of Britain had, most likely, been indefinitely postponed, and this view, via Kenneth Strong, was the one flagged up to Churchill.

With the aid of Ultra, more data over a period of a few weeks was to give a clearer view of Hitler's possible motives. In a corner of one room in the MI14 basement area of the War Office stood the latest 'new toy' at MI14's disposal: a teleprinter which loudly burst into life when officers in the room were least expecting it. Kenneth Strong had likened it to the 'explosive whirring sound of the red grouse on sudden take-off'. The section that most relied on it was MI14(b), who were expected to identify the whereabouts of every division and formation of the German army, in particular the number of motorised divisions. This meant Annan was, more often than not, the duty officer deputed to sit near it throughout the night:

> If you were night-duty officer, you waited for it to clatter into
> speech and at the end of the message you conveyed your thanks
> to the unseen operator by typing 'OK Tks'. Once, when it had

hardly spoken all night and I was reading for the first time Henry James's 'The Turn of the Screw', it suddenly went off at 3 a.m. and I nearly jumped out of my skin. Around six in the morning you had to make a summary of the most important communications, get it typed and ready to present to the Colonel before he arrived at 8.30 – then shave and work through the next day.

A series of Ultra messages (sent by 'Source Boniface') referred to movements of German air force units in Eastern Europe. Annan recalled that the first one he saw revealed the movement of a unit to Bulgaria, 'and I was told that they were of such secrecy that no word of their existence should be breathed outside MI14 – not even to other MI departments, let alone to any inter-service committee that one attended'.

This and a variety of other intelligence fitted the view within the War Office that Germany was clearly planning to invade the Soviet Union in the very near future, and several clandestine efforts were made to warn the Russians. While Germany's occupation of large tracts of western and central Europe had meant the loss of MI6 stations and their networks of agents across the continent, this setback was partly compensated by the fact that the intelligence services of several occupied nations relocated their intelligence services to London. This close-quarter liaison between MI6 and the various exiled intelligence services henceforth provided the War Office with a good deal of vital German intelligence. Czech Military Intelligence, headed by General Frantisek Moravec, were the first to move their intelligence operations to London. On the evening of 14 March 1939, he and ten senior Czech intelligence officers were flown out of Prague's Ruzyne Airport, with British assistance, and were met at London's Croydon Airport by Foreign Office and MI6 officials. Smuggled out with them were a host of files and archive intelligence that were handed over to MI6, who duplicated them and passed on relevant copies to MI14.

Moravec quickly established his new headquarters at Porchester Gate off London's Bayswater Road, from where he worked hand in glove with the various arms of British intelligence until he returned to Czechoslovakia at the end of the war. One of the most significant German intelligence sources that Moravec shared with British intelligence was a senior Abwehr officer by the name of Paul Thummel, who had offered his services to Czech intelligence back in 1936. Apart from payment for his services, Thummel also volunteered that he was motivated by the fact that his Slav fiancée was an anti-Nazi. Known henceforth as agent A54, Thummel provided nothing but top-grade intelligence. While his warnings about an attack on France through the Ardennes in the spring of 1940 were not taken too seriously, his stock soon rose after the German offensive. It was his information about the shelving of Operation *Sealion* that played a key part in MI14 concluding that there would be no invasion of Britain in spring 1941. This was followed by further accurate advance information about Germany's entry into Romania in October 1940 and the invasion of Greece in the spring of 1941.

MI6 also established a close working relationship with Polish intelligence, who maintained wireless communication with its significant network of agents in occupied Poland. Again, MI6 duplicated considerable numbers of Polish files and further benefited from being copied into all subsequent intelligence gathered by the Polish network. Within months, this would yield a series of reports on German preparations for Operation *Barbarossa*, the code name for the German invasion of Russia.

At MI14, Noel Annan received copies of reports from the Polish network relating to the number of sidings that were being built at frontier stations in Poland, including Malkinic, Lukow, Siedlce and Przemysl. Other reports gave information on ammunition dumps being established at Ostroleka and Ostrow, and bridges over the Pruth and the Dniester being surveyed by the Germans.

It seemed clear to virtually everyone surveying the reports that Hitler's next target would indeed be Russia. Lt. Colonel Strong, however, was still conflicted:

I found this difficult to believe. It would certainly be contrary to all orthodox German military thinking to embark on what would be essentially a two-front war, unless of course Hitler considered that the German victories in the West had eliminated one of the two fronts, at least for the time being. In all my talks with German officers (before the war) I had never discovered the slightest hint or intention that they regarded Russia as an immediate enemy ... practically no effort had been devoted to studying the Russian Army, its mobilisation plans and strategic intentions.

Putting his pre-war experience and theories to one side, Strong balanced this with

...reports that were beginning to reach us which suggested that the next German moves might well be in eastern Europe. Our own officers at the War Office who studied Russia knew that the Russian Army had been purged of many of its best officers, and had not been particularly successful against weak Finnish forces. They were convinced that Russia would offer an easy conquest for the Germans.

Among these officers was the wildly eccentric Michael Holroyd, an elderly ancient historian who had been Eric Birley's tutor at Oxford. He had the habit of clearing his mind by delivering a lecture, cigarette in mouth, on whatever problem was intriguing him at the time. He would compare the comparative reliability of different sources, driving all and sundry to distraction in the process. In this case, he had finally concluded that the course of the war was dictated by Hitler, and it was his writings and statements, past and present, that should be taken heed of rather than the German General Staff who, in his view, no longer counted.

The Russians were warned several times both informally by British intelligence and later directly by Churchill himself. Stalin, however, rejected each and every warning. Even the head of his own foreign intelligence service, Pavel Fitin, had presented evidence from a well-placed source in the Luftwaffe, giving details of the German invasion plans. Stalin apparently thought it was all a double bluff.

Whilst Kenneth Strong, with his personal knowledge of Russo-German army and intelligence co-operation in the 1920s, had long suspected that the Gestapo and their Russian opposite numbers, the much-feared NKVD, would have been liaising during the period of their 'non-aggression pact', even he would have been shocked at the extent of it when intelligence records began to surface after the war.

The Gestapo-NKVD conferences were a series of secret police meetings organised in late 1939 and early 1940 by German and Soviet officials following their joint invasion of Poland in accordance with the Nazi-Soviet non-aggression pact. The purpose of the meetings was to enable the German and Soviet security forces, including Gestapo and NKVD respectively, to share information regarding their parallel terror operations in occupied Poland. In spite of their differences on other issues, both Heinrich Himmler and Lavrentiy Beria had common goals as far as the fate of Poland was concerned. The known conferences were devoted to co-ordinating plans for joint destruction of Polish nationhood as well as discussing ways of dealing with the Polish resistance during the Second World War.

Out of four conferences, the third took place in the famous spa of Zakopane in the Tatra Mountains of southern Poland – it is the most remembered, as the Zakopane Conference. From the Soviet side, several higher officers of the NKVD secret police participated in the meeting, while the German host provided a group of experts from the Gestapo. After the signing of the Molotov-Ribbentrop Pact on 23 August 1939, Germany invaded Poland on 1 September and the Soviet Union invaded Poland on 17 September resulting in the occupation of the country by the Soviet Union and Nazi Germany.

The first Gestapo-NKVD meeting took place reportedly on 27 September 1939 in Bześć nad Bugiem, while some units of the Polish army were still fighting. Both the Gestapo and the NKVD expected the emergence of a Polish resistance movement and discussed ways of dealing with the expected clandestine activities of the Poles. In the immediate aftermath of the meeting, the Soviet NKVD began the collection of data leading to the Katyn massacre committed in the spring of 1940. The second conference between the two secret police organisations took place sometime at the end of November 1939, probably in Przemysl, divided into German and Soviet zones of occupation between September 1939 and June 1941. Apart from talks of fighting the Polish resistance, the Russians and Germans discussed ways of exchanging Polish POWs.

The third conference took place in Zakopane, on 20 February 1940 in the villa Pan Tadeusz, close to the Dolina Bialego valley. The German delegation was headed by Adolf Eichmann and the NKVD delegation was headed by Grigoriy Litvinov. The fourth and last meeting took place in March 1940 in Krakow.

The NKVD and the Gestapo, while being poles apart ideologically, were, in many ways, opposite sides of the same coin. Both had concluded long ago that cruelty and sadism would be their stock in trade.

10

THE TORTURER

February 1941:

Dear Sir,
My Department is particularly interested in obtaining information on Gestapo methods.

We do not require the general organization of the Gestapo, but information on how their agents are placed, what control they exercise, how 'round-ups' are conducted, in fact, how an individual, living as a normal member of his community may be affected by the activities of the Gestapo.

Also, we should like certain details of their methods of interrogation.

In 1941 the threat of invasion was real. Early that spring, with London being bombed night after night, MI14 enquired into the sort of thing Gestapo officers might inflict on British citizens if Hitler were to re-launch Operation *Sealion* and if, this time, it succeeded.

One fact was undeniable: the Gestapo could get away with murder. As another internal document pointed out,

A Hitler proclamation of 22 Oct 1938 removed even theoretical limitations, such as they were, by pointing at the 'unwritten law' of Germany as expressed in the will of the Party Leader ... every means adopted for the purpose of carrying out the will of the Leader is considered though it may conflict with existing statutes and legal precedent ... Since the Gestapo is in no way subject to veto, review or advice by the judiciary its powers are absolute and unlimited both in theory and in practice.

This in itself explains a lot. It explains how nearly seventy million Germans bowed to the will of only 50,000 Gestapo officers, and how, for decades after the war, citizens were unwilling to admit that they ever even suspected what went on in the extermination camps. They had seen the trains arriving, they had seen the lines of people marching under guard, they had seen tall chimneys that belched black smoke day and night, and they had smelled the stench of blood and guts from the mass shootings of tens of thousands; they even knew people who had worked in the camps. Perhaps they had never expressed horror because to do so was to suffer the same fate. Perhaps they said nothing after the war because the guilty people remained undiscovered in their community and were as dangerous as ever.

People near every single camp – and there were many in Germany and Poland – had known about violence of a type some dared not acknowledge even to themselves at the time. Yet children in the playground, nearer to places like Auschwitz, would warn one another 'You do that, and you'll go up the chimney like them over there.'

It also explains how, in Fresnes prison outside Paris, the Gestapo were able to torture Odette Sansom (of the British Special Operations Executive) by pulling out her toenails and prodding her spine with a hot iron. German law would not restrain them. She refused to inform on anyone in the Resistance and was sentenced to death but was finally sent to Ravensbrück. There she nearly died of starvation. She was kept in solitary confinement next to a crematorium, with heaters turned upon her until she passed out. Later she would see cannibalism among the starving prisoners. She was one of the 'lucky' ones who survived to bear witness at Nuremberg and send the camp Kommandant to his death.

If you were arrested and removed to the local Gestapo HQ, you would emerge – if at all – broken, telling stories of cruelty. Or you would be sent to a camp. Either way, your fate inspired fear. So everybody with a life to lose kept their heads down, even after the war ended, and internalised a kind of mass amnesia about the war.

The Gestapo used non-physical methods as well. An internal report from Norway describes how they might track a person down and harass and frighten him:

> They work by listening to rumours; when a rumour is connected with an individual, they look up his history and shadow him. They do not wait to produce a case against him before taking action, but satisfied that suspicions may be founded, they will make a domiciliary visit, examine all his rooms and effects and remove him at once.

After that they would interview the person again and again, asking the same questions, making him mistrust his own memory, hinting that he would soon be charged with a terrible crime, leaving him in confinement without charge, subtly undermining his sense of self for days on end and then leaving him to rot for a few weeks, alternately, so that his resolve would soften and when desperate he might say something, anything, to incriminate himself and have something happen.

If he resisted all this, he would still emerge psychologically traumatised. MI14 files report the case of a Norwegian taken by the Gestapo:

> Arrested at 06.00 hours at his home, placed in prison and completely isolated. Some days passed and one evening he was informed he was not to go to bed as he would be examined at 11pm. He waited until 2am when he was told it was postponed. Two days later the same thing happened. The day after, he was examined without warning. The line taken is indicated by the following scrap of dialogue:
> 'Well, then, you know surely how serious this is. We know all that you have undertaken, even inside four walls. You had better therefore confess everything. It would be very foolish of you to deny what we all know. But you must tell us everything without our being obliged to ask. We know all about your intelligence

service with England. If you do not tell everything, then you are finished' [descriptive movement across the throat].

'I have nothing to tell.'

'You are playing high stakes. I do not wish to sit and talk with you any longer. Here is pencil and paper. I am coming again on Monday and will fetch what you have written. You have probably played quite a subordinate role, so you will be able to get off cheaply if you tell us everything.'

This sort of thing went on without warning for weeks, examinations, accusations, re-examinations, the Gestapo talking about his neighbours and friends in great detail, attitude change from strongly accusatory to pleading to threatening.

His stay in prison and the waiting had a most depressing effect ... uncertainty as to what would happen and the constant variation of treatment in prison contributed to his wretchedness. For some time before an examination he was often cut off entirely from any occupation or reading. On one occasion this lasted ten days. The mental effect on this man – who was extremely strong minded – was such that his recollection of the later examinations is by no means so clear as that of the earlier ones.

An American resident of Berlin had a plan. She was Mildred Fish, a young university lecturer from Wisconsin who had married a liberal-minded German graduate student, Arvid Harnack. They lived in Berlin from 1929 onwards, and watched Hitler rise. In 1939 friends at the American Embassy pleaded with her to leave. She would not; she had always supported the Left, and she intended to stay with Arvid and work to subvert the horror of Nazism. For a long time they secretly helped Jews get out, translated speeches from Roosevelt and Churchill and fly-posted them all over town, and helped to smuggle Nazi secrets to the USA and the Soviet Union (which of course no longer supported the Axis after the summer of 1941).

In 1942 the Germans fell upon the Harnacks' clandestine short-wave radio broadcasts to and from the USSR. They immediately called them and their friends the 'Red Orchestra' – Red because of their politics, and Orchestra because they transmitted secrets via short-wave radio – 'pianos'– operated by 'musicians'. They were arrested and interrogated. Arvid was hanged. Mildred's interrogator was Walter Habecker, a Gestapo officer who had his own methods of extracting information. In Habecker's Berlin torture cell, two hooks in the ceiling were used to support ropes, by which prisoners were hoisted up and down. Directly below the hooks, a channel in the floor ran into a drain in which the blood of torture victims flowed. Sockets in the wall showed where plugs with electric cables had been extended to electrocute prisoners. In a locked wooden cupboard was housed a sinister range of tools and implements that Habecker used freely to extract the information he needed.

Habecker was born in 1893 in Berlin and according to Gestapo records, steadily advanced through the ranks, rising from a Kriminalsekretar in October 1934 to Kriminalobersekretar by February 1936. Early on he saw a niche for himself as an interrogator. Extracting information from prisoners and detainees in the quickest and most effective way was something he figured would enhance his reputation and career prospects. He very quickly acquired a reputation for brutal and sadistic methods of torture, beginning with fists and boots to extract information, and progressing from there to other more inventive methods. His ability as a torturer did indeed lead to his progressive promotion within the Gestapo. By April 1944 he was again promoted, this time to Kriminalkommissar. He gained further feathers in his cap by being called upon to torture many of those German officers implicated in the 20 July 1944 'Valkyrie' plot when Claus von Stauffenberg and other conspirators attempted to assassinate Hitler inside his Wolf's Lair field headquarters near Rastenburg in East Prussia. Hitler, by a stroke of luck, survived the bomb explosion, and the subsequent failure of the military coup that was to follow led to the Gestapo arresting more than 7,000, of whom 4,980 were later executed. This swollen number of conspirators was very much down to Himmler. As with the 'Night of the Long Knives' in 1934, he immediately saw the opportunity for widening the net to include anyone who was, in his view, less than 100 per cent committed to the regime. Many who had little or nothing to do with the plot were, as a result, rounded up in the melee. Himmler then went one sinister step further. At a conference in Posen on 3 August he addressed those assembled:

> All you have to do is to read up on old German sagas. When they proscribed a family and declared them outlaws, or when they had a vendetta, they went all the way. They had no mercy. If the family were outlawed and proscribed, they said, 'this man is a traitor, the blood is bad, there is bad blood in them, they will be eradicated.'

In this way, the families, friends and acquaintances of the conspirators and others considered anti-regime were added to the round-up. Those who survived interrogation and summary shootings were paraded at show trials conducted by the People's Court and presided over by Roland Freisler. These kangaroo court trials, at which the accused were harangued and insulted by Freisler, were filmed for public spectacle as well as for the pleasure of Hitler. The defendants were stripped of their uniforms and made to wear shabby old clothes to further humiliate them.

Under the direction of Standartenfuhrer Walter Huppenkothen, Habecker and a team of torturers employed a range of macabre methods to extract confessions that were then placed before the court. The torture routine consisted of chaining prisoner's arms behind their back, and at the same time fastening a device to their fingers, the inner side of which was studded with pins whose points pressed against the fingertips. The progressive turning of a screw pressed the pins into the fingers. If this failed to work, the second stage commenced. This involved the prisoner having a blanket placed over their head and being strapped down on a metal frame which resembled a bedstead. Cylinders studded with nails were rolled over the prisoner's bare legs, from ankle to thigh, using a screw mechanism to contract the tubes and puncture the flesh. The third stage consisted of using the metal-framed 'bedstead' as the main implement of torture in a similar way to a medieval rack, which progressively stretched their shackled bodies. The fourth and final stage, if required, was tying down the prisoner in a crouched position which did not allow any sideways or backwards movement. Habecker and his aids would then set about the prisoner with clubs, causing them to fall forwards, smashing their face on the stone floor.

Above left: Rudolf Diels, first commander of the Gestapo from 1933 to 1934.

Above right and below: MI14 officer Noel Annan.

Kenneth Strong, founding head of MI14.

Kristallnacht, or the Night of Broken Glass, 9/10 November 1938.

Reinhard Heydrich, head of the Bavarian Police, at Police HQ, Munich, 1934.

A 1939 photograph of Franz Josef Huber, Arthur Nebe, Heinrich Himmler, Reinhard Heydrich and Heinrich Müller (left to right) discussing the recent assassination attempt on Adolf Hitler.

Russian spy Leo Long (left) and Noel Annan (third from left).

Above left: Brian Melland, head of MI14's section D.

Above right: Captain Peter Earle of MI14 section H.

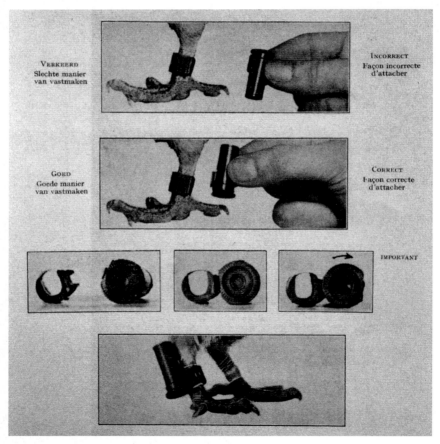

An MI14 leaflet explaining how to convey messages by carrier pigeon.

Above: The London Cage, an MI19 prisoner-of-war facility in Kensington Palace Gardens.

Right: Lt Col Alexander Scotland, commandant of the London Cage and a feared interrogator.

The War Office building in Whitehall, home of MI14.

Gestapo Headquarters on Prinz-Albrecht-Strasse in Berlin.

Heinrich Himmler, head of the SS and one of the chief architects of the Holocaust.

Heinrich Müeller, head of the Gestapo 1939–1945.

The photograph of Göring
in his MI14 file.

The photograph of Heydrich
in his MI14 file.

Sqn Ldr Roger Bushell, mastermind of the 'Great Escape' from Stalag Luft III, who was murdered by the Gestapo after his capture.

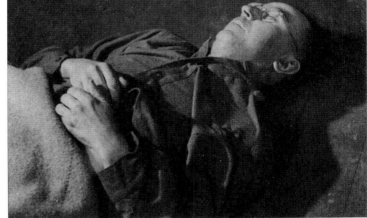

British Military Intelligence photograph of Himmler shortly after he had committed suicide on 23 May 1945.

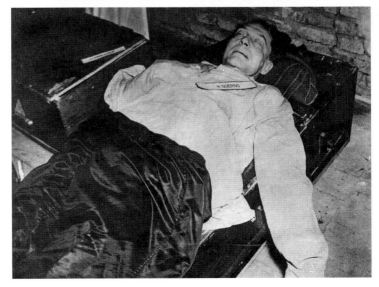

Göring was found dead in his cell, having taken cyanide.

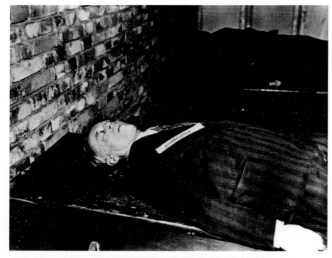

Joachim von Ribbentrop shortly after his execution.

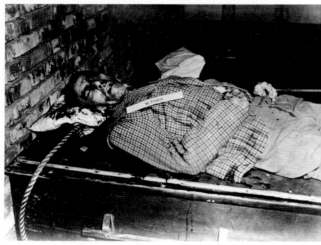

Wilhelm Frick, his head bloodied by a botched hanging.

Alfred Jodl photographed after being cut down from the gallows.

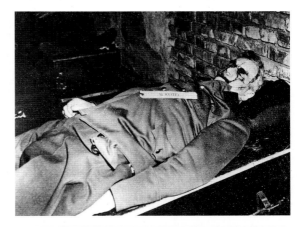

Like Frick, Wilhelm Ketel's head was disfigured by the hanging.

Alfred Rosenberg after his execution.

Executioner John Wood, hangman for the Nuremberg executions.

Above: German parachute troops pictured in the MI14 Great Britain invasion handbook.

Below: Cover page for the MI14 'most secret' document concerning Operation *Anthropoid.*

MOST SECRET

COPY NO: I.

DETAILED REPORT ON OPERATION

ANTHROPOID.

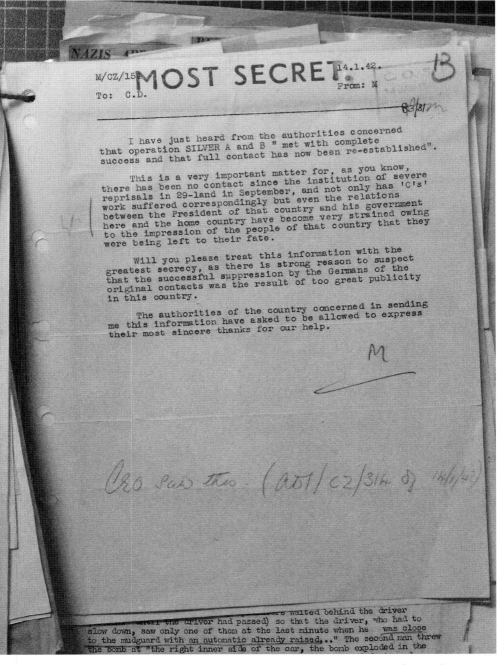

MOST SECRET. 14.1.42.

From: M

B

I have just heard from the authorities concerned that operation SILVER A and B " met with complete success and that full contact has now been re-established".

This is a very important matter for, as you know, there has been no contact since the institution of severe reprisals in 29-land in September, and not only has 'C's' work suffered correspondingly but even the relations between the President of that country and his government here and the home country have become very strained owing to the impression of the people of that country that they were being left to their fate.

Will you please treat this information with the greatest secrecy, as there is strong reason to suspect that the successful suppression by the Germans of the original contacts was the result of too great publicity in this country.

The authorities of the country concerned in sending me this information have asked to be allowed to express their most sincere thanks for our help.

M

CEO saw this. (AD1/CZ/314 of 14/1/42)

...waited behind the driver
...the driver had passed) so that the driver, who had to slow down, saw only one of them at the last minute when he was close to the mudguard with an automatic already raised..." The second man threw the bomb at "the right inner side of the car, the bomb exploded in the

A page of the MI14 'most secret' document concerning Operation *Anthropoid*.

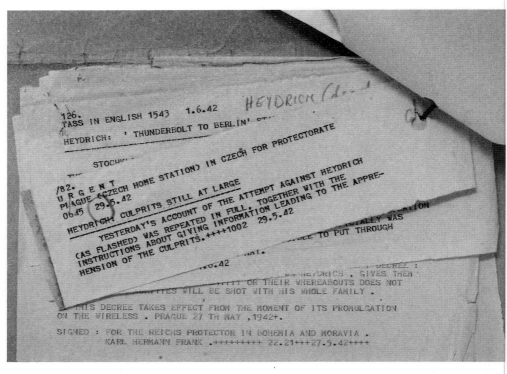

126.
TASS IN ENGLISH 1543   1.6.42   HEYDRICH (dead)

HEYDRICH: ' THUNDERBOLT TO BERLIN' ST..

STOCH...

/82.
U R G E N T
PRAGUE (CZECH HOME STATION) IN CZECH FOR PROTECTORATE
0645   29.5.42

HEYDRICH: CULPRITS STILL AT LARGE

YESTERDAY'S ACCOUNT OF THE ATTEMPT AGAINST HEYDRICH
(AS FLASHED) WAS REPEATED IN FULL, TOGETHER WITH THE
INSTRUCTIONS ABOUT GIVING INFORMATION LEADING TO THE APPRE-
HENSION OF THE CULPRITS.++++1002 29.5.42

....ALLY WAS
....EE TO PUT THROUGH

...0.42   ...AY.

.... HEYDRICH , GIVES THEM
....TT OR THEIR WHEREABOUTS DOES NOT
....TIES WILL BE SHOT WITH HIS WHOLE FAMILY .

.... THIS DECREE TAKES EFFECT FROM THE MOMENT OF ITS PROMULGATION
ON THE WIRELESS . PRAGUE 27 TH MAY ,1942+.

SIGNED : FOR THE REICHS PROTECTOR IN BOHEMIA AND MORAVIA .
KARL HERMANN FRANK .++++++++++ 22.21+++27.5.42++++

Above and below: MI14's English translations of cables regarding the assassination of Heydrich.

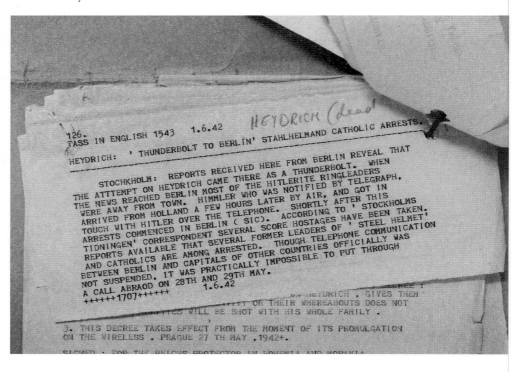

126.
TASS IN ENGLISH 1543   1.6.42   HEYDRICH (dead)

HEYDRICH: ' THUNDERBOLT TO BERLIN' STAHLHELMAND CATHOLIC ARRESTS.

STOCHKHOLM: REPORTS RECEIVED HERE FROM BERLIN REVEAL THAT
THE ATTTEMPT ON HEYDRICH CAME THERE AS A THUNDERBOLT. WHEN
THE NEWS REACHED BERLIN MOST OF THE HITLERITE RINGLEADERS
WERE AWAY FROM TOWN. HIMMLER WHO WAS NOTIFIED BY TELEGRAPH,
ARRIVED FROM HOLLAND A FEW HOURS LATER BY AIR, AND GOT IN
TOUCH WITH HITLER OVER THE TELEPHONE. SHORTLY AFTER THIS
ARRESTS COMMENCED IN BERLIN (SIC). ACCORDING TO ' STOCKHOLMS
TIDNINGEN' CORRESPONDENT SEVERAL SCORE HOSTAGES HAVE BEEN TAKEN;
REPORTS AVAILABLE THAT SEVERAL FORMER LEADERS OF ' STEEL HELMET'
AND CATHOLICS ARE AMONG ARRESTED. THOUGH TELEPHONE COMMUNICATION
BETWEEN BERLIN AND CAPITALS OF OTHER COUNTRIES OFFICIALLY WAS
NOT SUSPENDED, IT WAS PRACTICALLY IMPOSSIBLE TO PUT THROUGH
A CALL ABRAOD ON 28TH AND 29TH MAY.
++++++1707++++++   1.6.42

.... HEYDRICH , GIVES THEM
....TT OR THEIR WHEREABOUTS DOES NOT
....TIES WILL BE SHOT WITH HIS WHOLE FAMILY .

3. THIS DECREE TAKES EFFECT FROM THE MOMENT OF ITS PROMULGATION
ON THE WIRELESS . PRAGUE 27 TH MAY ,1942+.

SIGNED : FOR THE REICHS PROTECTOR IN BOHEMIA AND MORAVIA

NAME	RANK	DEPT	REMARKS
MAHN, Ernst	PS	IV A 4 a	
MERTIN, Wilhelm	Ostuf	IV A 5 b	
MEYER, Gerhard	Ustuf	IV A 1 a	
MEYER, Hermann	PGS	IV A 2 a	Southern Group.
MEYER, Walter	Hstuf	IV B 2	
MYK, Johannes	Ustuf	IV A 2 b	Southern Group.
MILLER, Friedrich	PS	IV A 6 b	
MILO, George	PS	IV C 1 d	November 1943.
MINNINGER, Hermann	Ustuf	IV A 4 b	
MISCHKE, Alexander	Rastn	IV A 4 b	
MITTELSDORF, Wilhelm	PS	IV A 6 a	
MOCHLER, Erich	Stubaf	IV A 3	November 1943, at Stapostelle Berlin 1945.
MOEHLER, Walter	Hstuf	IV B 1 a	
MOSS, Ernst	PGJ	IV A 4 b	
MOSIG, Eugen	Stubaf	IV C 4	Later VI B representative in Spain.
MOTZKUS, Max	KM	IV A 3 b	
MUELLER, Hans	Hstuf	IV A 2 b	Southern Group.
MUELLER, Heinrich	Gruf	Amtschef	Berlin 23.4.45.
MOEHLER	KR	IV A 5 b	
MUGGE, Paul	KOS	IV C 4 a	November 1943.
MULLER, Christoph	KS	IV A 5 a	Fahndungstrupp.
MULLER, Georg	Hstuf	IV C 4 a	November 1943; in Berlin beginning of 1945.
MILLER, Herbert	KOS	IV A 5 a	
M.CK, Kurt	PJ	IV A 6 a	
MUHRBERG, Dr Ludwig	Hstuf	IV C 4	Later VI B; arrested American Zone.
NEUENDORF, Franz	KS	IV C 4 b	November 1943.
NEUHAUS, Dr Karl	Stubaf	IV A 4 a	Went to Poznan Spring 1945, believed killed.
KONRADS, Herbert	KK	IV B 1 b	November 1943.
NILSSNG, Robert	KS	IV C 4 c	November 1943.
ACIVOS	Hstuf	IV C 5	1939-40.
KOSSMANN, Wilhelm	KS	IV B 4 c	November 1943.
Notghach, Hans	Ostuf	IV A 2 a	

NAME	RANK	DEPT	REMARKS
NOSSKE, Walter	Ostubaf	IV D	Arrested British Zone.
NOTHNAGEL, Wilhelm	KOS	IV A 2	
NOVAK	Hstuf	IV A 4 a	
OBERSTADT, Reinhold	PGJ	IV A 5 b	
COHN, Theodor	PS	IV A 6 a	
OETZEL, Eduard	Min Reg	IV B 6	November 1943.
OETZEL, Ewald	Ostuf	IV Gas	at Hof February 1945.
OETZEL, Gregor	KOS	IV B 6	November 1943.
OPITZ, Paul	Stubaf	IV C	Transferred IV G early 1945; formerly Referent IV A 3 b.
OPITZ		IV Gas	Courier April 1945.
OPPERMANN	H.stuf	IV B 2 b	
ORTLER, Kurt	POS	IV D	November 1943.
ORTMANN, Reinhold	Kischer	IV A 1 a	
PACHOW, Max	Ostuf	IV A 4 b	
PaHLKE, Franz	KS	IV B 5	November 1943.
PLNZINGER, Fritz	Staf	IV A	Gruppenleiter until august 1944; later Amtschef V.
PANZER, Hermann	KS	IV A 5 a	
PAPHLE, Paul	KOK	IV B 1	
EBERG, Willi	Ustuf	IV A 6 a	
PICH, Johannes	Stuschaf	IV A 2 b	Southern Group.
MICHLER, Johann	KS	IV C 4 b	November 1943.
PIEPER, Hans	Stubaf	IV C 4 b	at Schwerin 26.4.45.
PIETSCH	Hastuf	IV A 1 b	
PIEPFELDER, Achamer	Oberf	IV B	Gruppenleiter, killed April 1945.
PILLING	Hastuf	IV B 2 a	
PILLING, Alain	PGJ	IV D 3	November 1943.
PITZ	Schaf	IV A 1 a	
FLaTE, Emil	KS	IV B 4	November 1943.
POPISCHEL	KS	IV A 1 a	November 1943.
FABISCHER, Johann	KS	IV N	November 1943.
PREUSS, Paul	PJ	IV A 4 b	

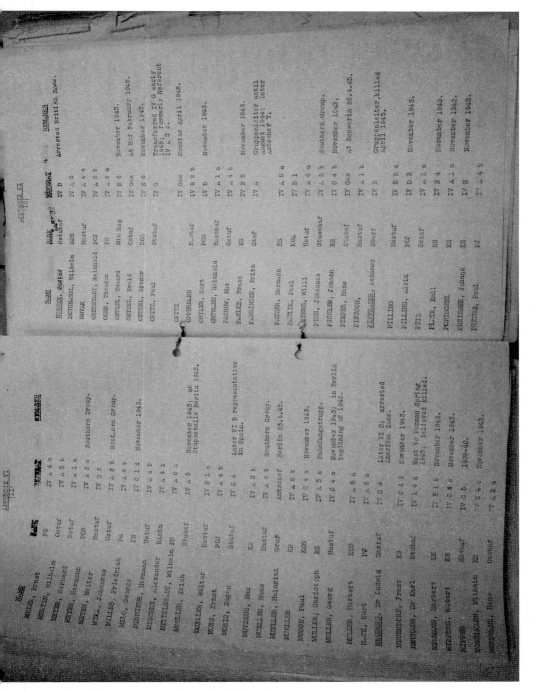

A list of Gestapo agents from the MI14 files.

Top: The Arisaig House Estate where Operation *Anthropoid* agents underwent training.

Above: Inverlair Lodge Estate, or the Cooler', a secret detention centre on the west coast of Scotland.

Left: Lt Alfred Fyffe, commandant of the 'Cooler'.

The first trials were held on 7 and 8 August 1944. All the defendants without exception were found guilty. Hitler had decreed that they were to be 'hanged like cattle', and Himmler did his best to ensure that they were by having the condemned men hung with piano wire. Hans Hoffmann, a warder at Plotzensee prison, later gave testimony to the Allies about the fate that awaited them:

> Imagine a room with a low ceiling and white-washed walls. Below the ceiling a rail was fixed. From it hung six big hooks, like those butchers use to hang meat. In one corner stood a movie camera. Reflectors cast a blinding light, like that of a studio. In this strange, small room were the Attorney General of the Reich, the hangman with two camera technicians, and myself with a second warder. At the wall was a small table with a bottle of cognac and glasses for all the witnesses of the execution. The convicted men were led in. They were all wearing their prison garb and were handcuffed. They were placed in a single row. Leering and making jokes, the hangman got busy. He was known in his circle for his 'humour'. No statement, no clergyman, no journalists. One after another, all faced their turn. All showed the same courage. It took, in all, 25 minutes. The hangman wore a permanent leer, and made jokes unceasingly. The camera worked uninterruptedly, for Hitler wanted to see and hear how his enemies had died.

By the end of 1944, when many Germans were beginning to stare defeat in the face, Habecker was still doggedly pursuing his mission with zeal and enthusiasm. In January 1945 he was sent to Mauthausen-Gusen concentration camp in Austria, which he apparently saw as a great honour and recognition of his skills.

The trouble with Habecker, as with all the torturers and killers of the Second World War, was that only at the end of the war was there a possibility of obtaining witness statements, and since victims tended to be conveniently dead, the facts of any given case could be lost forever. However, we do have the testimony of an interpreter who worked with Habecker early in 1945. This man had been sent from Berlin to Linz, and then around 20 kilometres east to the Mauthausen-Gusen camp – notorious for the hardest, most punishing labour, which in itself killed some people and made others kill themselves. There he was told that tomorrow he must translate during the interrogation of some English and American servicemen. Surprised to find POWs in a place like this, he asked why they were not in a detention camp, and was scornfully informed that these men were not prisoners of war but agents and partisans.

The POWs consisted of eighteen members of an Anglo-American military mission who were captured in Slovakia in December 1944. The Dawes mission, as it was known, was jointly organised by Major John Sehmer of SOE and Lieutenant Holt Green of the American OSS (the forerunner of the CIA), and had the objective of working with Slovakian partisan groups to locate Allied airmen who had been shot down over the Balkans. The aim was then to rescue as many of them as possible and equally to assist the partisans in any way they could to mount an uprising against Slovakia's pro-Nazi rulers; by September 1944 more than 1,900 airmen had been rescued. The planned uprising was, at the same time, gaining ground. The rebellion by partisans and deserting Slovak troops was led by General Jan Golian, and was centred around the city of Banska Bystrica, which became the de facto rebel capital. The Nazis responded by sending in large numbers of SS reinforcements to crush the revolt, and by 27 October 1944 they had taken the city after a fierce and protracted assault. This forced the British and Americans, along with the retreating Slovak troops and partisans, to flee into the mountains just as a bitterly cold winter was setting in.

Their plight was not only a desperate one but one that was ultimately doomed. The winter conditions were harsh in the extreme. Deep in the mountain forests they had to survive freezing rain, snowstorms, icy streams that froze boot leather to the skin and sleepless nights without food. At the same time, they had to stay on the move, knowing full well that they were being pursued by SS search squads. A number, led by Maria Gulovich, managed against the odds to escape the Nazis by passing through German lines and meeting up with advancing Russian army units. However, the others were finally tracked down and captured on 26 December 1944 after the SS had surrounded the hunters' hut in which they were found sheltering.

The captured men were then taken not to a POW camp but to the Mauthausen-Gusen concentration camp, where they were subjected to interrogation and torture to discover the details of their mission. The prisoners included Joe Morton, an American Associated Press correspondent who had apparently talked his way onto one of the planes taking off from Bari to Slovakia. Just before take-off, he'd cabled his boss at AP: 'I'm off on the biggest story of my life.' The biggest story of his life was to end with the loss of it. He, along with the majority of those captured on 26 December 1944, was executed after days of torture at Mauthausen-Gusen.

Gestapo chief Heinrich Müeller sent a specially selected team from Berlin, led by Dr Manfred Schoeneseiffen, to the concentration camp to carry out the interrogations. His torturer of choice was again Habecker, accompanied by several interpreters. One particular interpreter was later to reveal details of what occurred. Habecker was to interrogate a Scotsman called Wilson. The interpreter quickly realised that he was not Scottish at all, but spoke English with a Viennese accent. The man denied that he was anything except Scottish.

The interpreter took Habecker aside. He explained the issue, and said if he could just telephone Berlin, and talk to a German he knew who had lived in Scotland for more than twenty years, he'd get to the bottom of this at once.

Habecker told him that would not be necessary. He would make other arrangements. The interpreter stayed where he was. Habecker took Wilson by the hand and led him into another room.

Very soon afterwards the interpreter heard cries of pain. He ran into that room and saw that Habecker and two Gestapo men had hung Wilson from a ladder by his wrists. He was visibly suffering.

> I remarked to the Kriminal Kommissar my thoughts on this matter. He answered me by saying he had no further use for me in this case because 'the Jew speaks German very well'.

The interpreter walked out and left the building. That afternoon he returned to the camp when the Gestapo did. Habecker began again to interrogate 'Wilson', who had now confessed that he was called Wandorfer. Habecker was carrying a whip, and Wandorfer was plainly terrified of him.

During the other interrogations, which lasted four or five days, the British and American officers were slapped, hung by the wrists, or tortured with the Tibetan Prayer Windmill.

These were what the Gestapo called 'reinforced' interrogations. The 'windmill' may be an erroneous translation. He may have said a Tibetan prayer mill, which was a large cylinder balanced on a strong support, so that it could be spun around by a sharp push – if a person were strapped to such a thing in an odd position, such as upside down, and somebody spun it around very fast, over and over, then that would indeed be torture, and what's more, it would leave no physical scar.

The functionaries of the Gestapo did not torture the prisoners during fits of anger, but, on the contrary, very cold-bloodedly.

The interpreter saw many more instances of this kind, committed by others there. Some prisoners were strung up by handcuffs with spikes inside them and beaten with a rubber bar. Others were ordered to strip and get into a tub filled with ice-cold water. Their legs were tied to a bar which was used to pull them under water. Another prisoner was ordered to lie flat on a chair and was then struck on the back with a spiked ball, which was attached to a chain.

He also worked on interrogations where this kind of treatment did not occur. But Mauthausen-Gusen shocked him and he reported this and several other violent interrogations to his superior. The man replied sadly:

Persons more powerful than you or I have already lodged grievances against those dogs of the Amt. We can do nothing there, we risk all, as well as the danger of being interned in a concentration camp. Try to forget the thing. For the love of God, don't speak to anyone because neither Schellenberg nor myself will be able to save you if you do.

And so, things remained as they were, until the Americans and British took over. The interpreter then started to see photographs of the hundreds of thousands of skeletal people emerging from the camps, and the piles of corpses. Until he saw torture with his own eyes, he said, he had dismissed such stories as enemy propaganda.

'*Vernichtung durch Arbeit*' – 'extinction through work' – was in favour until 1941, partly because murder on a huge scale had not yet been perfected, but mainly because the SS could make money out of it. Jews and other sub-humans worked until they fell down, were injured or fell sick, and then shot. But more slave labour could be brought in from the occupied territories to replace them – for a fee. The SS therefore set itself up as a kind of giant recruitment consultancy under a man called Oswald Pohl, who was keen that the cost of labour should remain very low – which it would, so long as slave labour remained in abundance as a disposable resource with few overheads. The Gestapo were there to fulfil the 'disposable' part.

The judges at Nuremberg heard hundreds of witness reports of Jews being killed with an axe, shot because they were ill, poisoned in medical experiments, starved or simply locked in and burned to death. Many of the perpetrators were SS or Gestapo men. They could justify their acts as carrying out the Führer's intent to liquidate the Jewish 'race'. In countries other than Germany the difference was unclear, since the Gestapo wore SS uniform while back in Germany they were plainclothes men.

Steps were taken after the war to bring to justice the Gestapo team responsible for the torture and execution of the Anglo-American Dawes mission, but with mixed success. Dr Manfred Schoeneseiffen seems to have slipped through the net entirely. It was not until June 2001, two months before his death from natural causes in Cologne, that he was tracked down by a journalist, but had little or nothing to say about his Gestapo career. Walter Huppenkothen was arrested in Gmunden on 26 April 1945 and interned by US forces until 1949. During this time, he worked for the US army's counter-intelligence corps, who seem to have been particularly interested in his knowledge of communism and the Gestapo post he held, which focussed on searching out communist resistance members. In 1949, he was finally charged on several counts of torture and murder, but against the odds was found not guilty. He was later charged with other torture cases and this time found guilty and sentenced to five years' imprisonment. He died thirty years later in Lubeck, aged seventy-eight. Habecker was arrested by British troops in 1947 and sent to Bad Oeynhausen, where he escaped justice by hanging himself in his cell.

Joseph Kahane, who worked from 1942–44 at the Heinkel factory north of Berlin, lived to bear witness at the Nuremberg trials. Kahane, like hundreds of others, had been supplied to the factory direct from the Sachsenhausen camp in March 1942, as a Soviet prisoner of war. When workers began to grow faint or weak, he said, they would be beaten to death or if they were simply ill, the Gestapo would take them out and shoot them. At Nuremberg, he described sadistic treatment and named names; other survivors did the same. Heinkel, like IG Farben and others, did very well out of the camps, employing tens of thousands of people. They cleared redundant workers when necessary to restart with fresher, healthier ones.

As abhorrent as the record and methods of the Gestapo were, every barrel, as the old saying goes, has a rotten apple, and the Gestapo were always on the lookout for rotten apples, even ones wearing a British uniform.

11

THE MAN WITH NINE LIVES

The Gestapo were looking for people they could 'turn'. Harold Cole was one of them. That was his real name but he used at least ten others. He was described by the War Office as 'the worst traitor of the war'.

Born in poverty in an East End slum in January 1906, he grew up to be a thief, a con man and a housebreaker. By August 1939, with nine Metropolitan Police warrants out for his arrest, and having just been released from prison, he introduced himself and his blameless past to the Regimental Enlistment Officer, neglecting to mention his criminal career. He was assigned to the 18th Field Park Company, attached to the Royal Engineers. Six weeks later, he emerged from Basic Training and sailed to France as part of the British Expeditionary Force. Stationed in Loison-sous-Lens, he was quickly promoted to sergeant. In May, however, he was arrested for stealing money from the sergeants' mess. Kept in military custody, he became a prisoner of war when he was left behind when his unit pulled out during the retreat from Dunkirk.

Within a week he had escaped, stolen a black Peugeot 202 and made his way to Lille, where he morphed from being an East End sergeant in the Royal Engineers to a dapper, upper-class country gentleman by the name of Coulson. Decked out in plus fours, clipped moustache and Brylcreemed hair, Cole's new persona was that of a former Scotland Yard detective who was now an undercover captain in British intelligence. After making some money for himself trading in black market goods in Lille, he headed for Marseille in 1941, where he established contact with a French Resistance group who were working with SOE and MI9. It appears that he then aided the group who were providing safe houses, forged documents and couriers to enable RAF pilots who had been shot down to be collected and taken to Marseille, where they were shipped back to England. After nearly six months, the officers who ran this outfit noticed money was going missing. They suspected that Cole had been embezzling the money. He confessed. He hadn't picked up any downed fighters at all. He never even met them.

Lieutenant-Commander Patrick O'Leary, an MI9 agent working in the Marseille area, who was overseeing the 'O'Leary escape line', was called in to oversee Cole's questioning. On hearing Cole's admission, he immediately saw red and punched Cole so hard in the face that he broke his own hand. O'Leary was actually an MI9 cover name – he was, in reality Captain Albert-Marie Guerisse, a Belgian military doctor formerly attached to a Belgian cavalry. During the German invasion of Belgium, Guerisse escaped to England and volunteered for service in the SOE. In September 1940 he was assigned to HMS *Fidelity*, a 'Q ship' conducting sabotage operations along the French coast, and soon proved himself a brave and resourceful officer. On 26 April 1941 he was accidently left behind after a night landing operation at Collioure and was quickly arrested by the Vichy French, who put him in a camp for British POWs. On 4 July 1941 he escaped and headed for Marseilles, where he made contact with French Resistance fighters who were helping escaped RAF airmen passing through France. They had apparently been on the lookout for him for some time, and he was quickly passed down the line and recruited by MI9's Jimmy Langley. O'Leary was given responsibility for overseeing the escape line to Gibraltar, which is where he first came across Harold Cole.

O'Leary, perhaps unaware of how dangerous Cole was, had him locked in the bathroom while the rest of the group decided what to do with him. While the debate was going on, Cole forced open a lavatory window and made good his escape. O'Leary later made a statement to London about the incident:

In August I had been introduced to a man called Sgt. Harold COLE alias PAUL who was working for the organization in Northern France, his H.Q. being in Lille. Our organization had given COLE about 600,000 francs (six hundred thousand francs) and I began to get suspicious that he was not using it for the purpose for which it was provided as he was spending too much on women when he was in Marseilles. In September '41 COLE was given another 50,000 francs in order to make arrangements for a lorry to transport from Lille to Marseilles six or seven RAF. pilots. COLE told me he was going to Lille to make these arrangements but in fact I saw him in Marseilles spending this money on women. COLE knew that I had seen him and he disappeared. Ten or twelve days, later COLE reappeared and said he had brought the pilots in the lorry from Lille. I was not sure that this was true and I went to the flat where two of the Pilots were being hidden. They said they were French-Canadians and described their journey from Lille to Marseilles in the lorry. They could not speak English at all and I accused them of being French and of lying. They admitted that they were French and had been in Marseilles for a long time hoping to escape to England. PAUL, they said, had told them to tell me the false story about the journey from Lille. I reported the matter to my chief who ordered COLE to report to him but COLE did not appear. This was still in September '41. Two or three days later my chief sent me to Lille to find out what had happened to COLE as we wanted to check up on his activities. I contacted in Lille M. DUPREZ, a member of our organization, who told me that PAUL was spending his money on women and did nothing whatever for the British pilots. DUPREZ accused COE of misappropriation of funds and abuse of confidence. I asked DUPREZ to order Paul to go to Marseilles with DUPREZ to give an explanation to my chief. When I returned to Marseilles in October, I found that my chief had been arrested. 2.11.41 COLE and DUPREZ arrived in Marseilles and had a meeting at Dr. RODOCANACHI's flat at which the other members of our organization were present. DUPREZ, having accused COLE of misappropriation of funds and abuse of confidence, COLE broke down and admitted his guilt. I was present and COLE admitted that he had spent the money we gave him on women and high living. I was so annoyed that I hit COLE and broke my hand. I told COLE that in view of the fact that he had done good work for us, I would not report his misconduct to London on condition that he at once left France by the Pyrenees for U.K. I left him under guard but COLE escaped through the bathroom and lavatory. I never saw him again.

At the beginning of November, mixed reports were circulating. Some said Cole had been arrested by the Germans in Lille; others said he had turned himself in to them. One thing though seemed clear – he had returned to the Nazi-occupied sector knowing that he had information to sell.

Rumours began circulating in Lille that the Germans had a new inside source of intelligence, as the number of Resistance movement arrests in November and December of 1941 increased dramatically during a short period of time. Several Resistance fighters who had not been arrested in Lille fled to London, where they denounced Cole and voiced their suspicions that he had defected to the Germans.

Among those eventually arrested were Ian Garrow and later Tom Groome. As a result of Cole's information, the Gestapo had been monitoring their movements and radio transmissions. When the Gestapo finally tracked down the apartment where Groome was hiding, they crept up the stairs, opened his door and silently walked up behind him. Groome, with his back to the door and headphones on, was so engrossed with his wireless set that he heard not a sound. The first he knew of his unwelcome guests was when a revolver was put in his back, and a Gestapo officer told him, 'Finish that message. If you stop you will be shot.' He finished the message but deliberately left out the key letter to let MI9 know he was now in German hands.

He was then marched out of the building and driven to Gestapo headquarters where he was thoroughly interrogated. After some twenty minutes, Groome suddenly leaped to his feet, jumped onto the desk, kicking away all the papers on it. Then, using the desk as a springboard, he leapt through a large glass window and fell 30 feet to the street below. Covered in glass and having sustained a bad ankle he somehow managed to run up the street and hide among the crowds. Sadly, he was only at liberty for a short while, before he was given away to the pursuing Gestapo by a bystander. On 2 March O'Leary too was arrested in a café in Toulouse.

As a result of Cole's obvious treachery, the War Office liaising with SOE, MI6, MI9, and MI14, and MI5, the Security Service, opened a file on him. An investigation, headed by MI5 officer Dick White, was hastily put in place. White, who would, in the 1950s, make intelligence history by becoming the only man to head both MI5 and MI6, was a shrewd operator and a man with good connections throughout Whitehall. He quickly made contact with MI14's Brian Melland in order to tap into their flow of German intelligence, both from within the German-occupied zone of France and the southern Vichy sector, administered by the collaborationist Petain regime. White's call for intelligence on Cole soon yielded results:

> I am sending you herewith a copy of a report by Captain J.B. Oakes (U.S.A.), an officer of one of the American S.C.I. units in Paris. This speaks for itself. I shall be grateful if you could make enquiries with a view to identifying this man, and we shall then be able to brief our S.H.A.E.F. representative on the case and to desire him to make further enquiries.

Memo from Captain Oakes

> A captured agent has given us the following information.
> COLE: British subject: condemned to death by the court in Lyon. I saw him at the camp in Nexon. He was freed at Compiegne. Description: 1.85m approximately; tall, light red hair, thin elegant face, speaking French with an English accent. Signed: John B. Oakes, Capt. Inf.

MI5 correctly put two and two together, concluding that:

> COLE is, I think, almost certainly identical with Harold COLE who went to France with the BEF. and later became employed by SIS in the Lille area in connection with an escape organization. He is a man with a criminal record in this country, and he embezzled some of the funds supplied him by SIS. He seems to have gone over to the Germans some time in 1942. He was condemned to death by a military tribunal in July 1942, and it may be that he promised to work for the Germans in order to obtain commutation of this sentence.

COLE's description is as follows:

> Height: 1.80m.
> Very thin: narrow, bent shoulders.
> Reddish-fair hair, parted at side.
>   "   "   eyebrows
>   "   "   moustache (small)
> Blue-grey eyes, very short sighted.
> Small head, bony face.
> Rarely wears glasses; has to screw up eyes to read or
> look into distance
> Small mouth, all false teeth.
> Shifty glance.
> Long, bony hands, rather hairy (red-fair hair).
> Gait; very long thin legs; shoes size 41.
> Neck: Size 14 collar.
> Speaks very bad French with strong Cockney accent.
> He makes constant use of the expression 'old man'
> Speaks no German.
> Has a loud guffaw.
> Sticks out his tongue when writing or concentrating.
> Never wears hat.

Examination of Cole's Army Papers gave more of an insight into his criminal background and tendency to reinvent himself with different dates of birth:

L/Sgt. Harold COLE, Royal Engineers. Army No. 1877989
Born: 24.1.11. in London (Marylebone)
Nationality - British

Civil occupation – Driver Mechanic

Religion- Christian Scientist.

Record of Service.

15.8.39.   Enlisted at Hounslow.
 " " "   Attested – Driver.

18.8.39	Posted R.E. H.O.M.T.D.
8.9039	Posted A/U/L/Cpl. C.R.E. 4th Div, Colchester.
" " "	Posted 18 Fd Pk Coy R.E
29.9.39.	Proceeded overseas. L/Opl.
2.10.39	Appointed Cpl.
27.12.39	Granted paid acting appt of L/Sgt. having remained unpaid for a consecutive period of 21 days from 27.12.39.
10.1.40	Granted 10 days leave in U.K. from 18 Fd Pk Coy.
17.5.40	Escaped from Commiserate Prison, Lille, France whilst under close arrest – no further information available.
17.5.40.	Posted MISSING B.E.F.
15.11.41.	COURT OF INQUIRY held at Bishop Waltham declared that this soldier illegally absented himself without leave or other sufficient cause at Lille on 17.5.40. and that he is still so absent. The Court further declare that they are unable to find the accused deficient of public clothing or equipment as all records of issues to the accused were destroyed during the move into Belgium in May 1940. C.R.E. 4th Division.

Declared a DESERTER, with effect from 17.5.40.

Further damning evidence against Cole piled up:

S E C R E T.

Harold COLE, RE:
alias PAUL; alias Richard GODFREY; alias ROOKE; alias PRM.
CORSER; alias de LOBELLE; alias Paul ANDERSON; alias Joseph
DERAM; alias Capt. MASON; alias Captain COULSON

COLE has nine convictions recorded against him for stealing, false pretenses, embezzlement and desertion, including two terms of penal servitude. He is wanted for eleven cases of larceny in the Metropolitan Police District, two cases of larceny at Oldham, house breaking at Weymouth, and attempted flat breaking at Hove. He is posted as a deserter from the British Army. After working for a time (1940/41) for a British escape organization in France, he denounced his former colleagues to the Gestapo, causing the arrest and torture of many.

COLE enlisted on 15.8.39 and proceeded overseas with the BEF on 29 September 1939. On 5 May 1940 he escaped from custody in Lille whilst under close arrest and was posted missing. On 15 November 1941 he was declared a deserter with effect from 17 May 1940. After his escape from custody in 1940, COLE worked for a secret escape organization employed in passing to friendly territory, British airmen who had been shot down and who had evaded capture by the Germans. This organization was directed in France by Capt. Ian GARROW who had assisted by Lt. Commander O'Leary, RN. COLE's work was satisfactory for a time but in the summer of 1941 Capt. GARROW and Lt. Commander O'LEARY became suspicious that certain funds with which COLE had been supplied, were not being used for the purpose for which they had been provided and Lt. Commander O'LEARY subsequently was able to prove that COLE was spending large sums on women and high living and was doing nothing to help the organization. When accused by members of the organization of misappropriation of funds and abuse of confidence, COLE admitted that this was true. Because of his previous good work, he was told that he would not be reported to London on condition that he left France at the earliest opportunity. Lt. Commander O'LEARY left COLE under guard in Marseilles but COLE managed to escape on 2 November 1941. While working for the organization, COLE was known as 'PAUL' but he also used other aliases.

COLE then went to Lille and it was reported that he was arrested by the Germans on about 6 November 1941. He was released after a very short time and almost immediately several members of the escape organization were arrested. COLE admits that he caused the arrest of 10 members of the Resistance Movement but it is clear that he denounced many more including a woman who had been his mistress and a number of persons who had previously assisted him. Monsieur POSTEL-VINET, who was working for the organization, was denounced by COLE and arrested by the Gestapo who admitted to him that COLE was working for them. M.P.O TEL-VINET managed to escape and reach London. Other members of the organization were also able to escape from France and have testified as to COLE's treachery. A German who was interrogated in London, stated that when captured, 'Captain COULSON' betrayed all his British and French friends. It is known that COLE used the name of Coulson.

Dick White's MI5 investigation case notes concluded that while working for the Gestapo in Paris, Cole had denounced many key figures in the French Resistance movement, including Ian Garrow and Pat O'Leary. It was believed that he had betrayed at least 150 Resistance members, of whom fifty had been executed. While in the pay of the Gestapo, Cole had, according to his file, married a French girl, but had abandoned her when their newly born child died. The file also records several other mistresses he betrayed; and he stole the life savings of one.

In June 1942, Cole was arrested by French police in Lyon (in Vichy France) who condemned him to death as an informer and spy for Germany. He was still in jail awaiting execution when the Germans moved him to Fresnes (the prison in Paris) for interrogation by the SD. From there he was sent with an SD Kommando unit to Colmar, in Alsace, which was German-occupied at the time. Intelligence reports reaching London refer to reported sightings of Cole wearing a Wehrmacht NCO's uniform and acting as a chauffeur. His activities during 1943 are barely reported on. The next we hear of him is in the summer of 1944.

Following the Allied advance into France as a result of the D-Day landings on 6 June 1944, Cole vanished from Paris before the battle for the capital's liberation, which began on 19 August 1944. He headed into Germany and appears to have joined an SD unit heading south to Bavaria. In April 1945, with Hitler still in his bunker but approaching the end, the Americans were pushing the Nazis back into southern Germany. Still with his SD unit but now wearing civilian clothes, Cole and the rest of the unit were ambushed near Biberach, a fairy-tale town in south Germany disfigured by the presence of two large internment camps. The quick-witted Cole took his commanding officer and another soldier and they all presented themselves at the nearest US army squadron HQ. Cole posed as a British army Captain Mason (a British intelligence officer he had denounced to the Germans in France) and introduced his two SD friends as prison guards who had helped him escape to the Allied lines. The Americans not only swallowed the story but gave him a US lieutenant's uniform, a revolver, and military pass. Off went Cole, picking up an ex-mistress and three other French friends to conduct

> ...what he claims to be 'security enquiries'. These enquiries were very profitable and he accumulated six motor cars, 200 gallons of petrol, U.S Army rations, hams, some 500 bottles of wine, a considerable quantity of personal baggage, weapons and ammunition.

These 'security enquiries', he claimed, were part of a secret mission to root out high-ranking Nazis and Werwolf members who had fled to Bavaria. He also had a couple of CIS (Communications and Information, US military intelligence) stamps forged. Cole set up house in Grunbach and kept French and American officers entertained and happy, not least because he had a tidy sideline going in joints of ham, cars, and so on. He also confided to the Americans that a man called Hanft, a civilian who lived in Altshausen, was in fact an SD officer. He took a lieutenant over there and they arrested the man. Shortly afterwards, Cole and the lieutenant took Hanft into the woods outside Altshausen and shot him with sub-machine guns.

This charade might have continued for some time had Cole not let his self-confidence get the better of him. On 9 April 1945 he sent a postcard to a former girlfriend in Paris, confiding in her about his idyllic new life. Unsurprisingly, in light of the way Cole had previously treated her and other women in Paris, she immediately took the postcard to the authorities, and word quickly made its way to MI9 in London. As a result, Cole was arrested on 12 June 1945 and taken to the SHAEF (Supreme Commander's Allied Expeditionary Force) jail in Paris. Remarkably, five months later, on 18 November 1945, he again escaped from custody, or to be more precise, simply sauntered out through the gates in the uniform of an American serviceman, leaving a bubbling heap of blame, fury and court martials behind him. The flack this caused is very apparent from a report written by Major C. P. Hope from MI5 (Paris) liaison on 23 November to Major T Patterson in London:

CONFIDENTIAL

Harold COLE.

Last night 8,000 photographs of Harold COLE were distributed through S.I.B. channels to civilian and military authorities in Western Europe. I attach herewith a copy of the photographs you requested and also copies of the circulars. I am afraid I was unable to get more copies of the photographs as they had all been posted before I could obtain them.

Lt. Col. Luff of A. Branch, B.A.S., asked me to see him on the 20 November and we discussed COLE's escape. He pointed out that he felt that the man would not have got away had I, as a Field Officer, not instructed the D.A.P.M., a Captain, and Sergeant Carpenter, the N.C.O. in charge, that COLE should be given special facilities, such access to the guard room. Although Luff reluctantly withdrew this vote of censure when I informed him that Major Wake, the A.P.M., with my concurrence, had withdrawn these facilities some six weeks ago. I thought it wise to make a statement covering COLE's transfer and making our position in this matter entirely clear. Colonel Luff was at first unwilling to accept such a statement, pointing out that he was anyway going to court martial Carpenter and that I might make myself available as a witness for the defence. Nevertheless, he finally agreed, and I attach for your information a copy of a statement I am today sending him.

It is clear that whatever facilities I may have asked for in the past, subject always to the secure custody of COLE, there can be no suggestion that our interest in this case in any way facilitated COLE's escape, having regard to the fact that six weeks after Wake withdrew facilities, COLE was to be found typing on the Provost typewriter in the guard room at 11.30 p.m. I suspect myself that Wake did not make the position entirely clear to Sergeant Carpenter who is apparently to be court martialled and take the blame for the whole matter.

I am reporting this to you in some detail because, not unnaturally, British Army Staff are very sensitive about this escape and are making every effort to divert attention from themselves to outside bodies.

PARIS
<u>M.I.5 Liaison Section.</u>   C.P. Hope, Major.

As soon as he was clear of the jail, Cole riffled through his internal rolodex for useful girlfriends in Paris. One of them ran a bar in the Rue de Grenelle and – charmed, despite his ferrety face, bad teeth and sandy hair – was happy to let him hide in an apartment above it. He then went completely off both the French and British intelligence radar. Speculation had it that he may have managed to leave France and head for Africa or America.

He was, however, holed up in the same attic-like fourth-floor room he had been inhabiting since his escape. In the early evening of Tuesday 8 January 1946, Major Hope in Paris telephoned MI5 and told them that Cole had been shot dead by French police officers earlier that day, and promising a full written report to follow, which he despatched the next day:

<u>CONFIDENTIAL</u>
<u>Harold COLE.</u>

Confirming my telephone conversation yesterday, the above was shot dead by two police inspectors of the Police Judiciary in the Dixieme Arrondissement yesterday morning. The inspectors made a raid at an address in the rue de Grenelle on the instructions of Commissaire Metra who had received a denunciation to the effect that Germans were living clandestinely at the address.

The inspectors entered the bedroom were a man in civilian clothes immediately opened fire on them. The inspectors returned the fire and killed the man. They discovered on the body the military papers of Sergeant Carpenter, Provost Staff, and through these identified the corpse as that of COLE. I have myself seen the corpse and have confirmed the identification.

Curiously enough Commissaire Metra had been following a line on a man whom he believed to be COLE in the same area during the last few days and, with the aid of police informant, was hoping to identify an unknown British deserter whose appearance corresponded to COLE's and who was attempting to form a gang for robbery, having stated that he had a murder he wished to commit.

A garbled version of COLE's death appeared in the Paris press yesterday afternoon, and the Embassy and British Army Staff were bombarded with telephone calls from British and American correspondence asking for the full story. After obtaining your brief, I gave Donald Mallett the bones of the story and I attach two copies of the Continental Daily Mail for this morning showing the write-up. Part of this article has been obtained from other sources as I made no reference to the murder of HANFT, nor to the various aliases used by COLE. Furthermore, the last third of the article is a garbled version and this too was presumably obtained from other sources. I also enclose a copy of today's 'Allure', in which I have marked the column on COLE.

C.P. Hope, Major

Within days, MI5 had received a copy of a report from the Prefecture of Police:

<u>TRANSLATION.</u>

Prefecture of Police.
Judicial Police H.Q.
Director's Office.

Further to your request for information concerning the circumstances under which COLE, Harold, Sergeant, British

Deserter, was found, after being killed by Inspectors of the Judicial Police, upon whom COLE had fired, I have the honour to bring to your notice the following:

From confidential information received by Inspector COTTY, of the Commissariat of the St. Victor District, it was brought to his notice that the Manageress of 'Billy's Bar', 39, Rue de Grenelle, Paris, was hiding in one of her rooms on the third floor, an individual, thought to be of German nationality and who was said to be her lover.

This individual's position was all the more suspicious due to the fact that he but rarely left his room. Discreet enquiries made by Inspector Principal Adjoint LABERTY and Inspector COTTY round about No.36, Boulevard de la Bastille, abode of the Manageress of 'Billy's Bar', revealed the fact that the Manageress was hiding a deserter in her bar. They also learned that this woman, who was living apart from her husband, had a very bad character.

On 8 January 1946 at about 16.00 hrs. Inspector COTTY, accompanied by his colleague LEVY, of the Brigade du Centre, proceeded to the bar 39, Rue de Grenelle, Paris. They were admitted by the Manageress, whose particulars were obtained later on and identified as:

HERVEAU, Pauline Yvonne, born JUNGA, on 3 July 1904 at ARCACHON (Gironde) of Paul and ERD, Marie, saying to be living at 36, Boulevard de la Bastille. After having told who they were, they stated having come to verify the identity papers of the individual whom she was harbouring in a room on the third floor, and which room belonged to her.

Although she declared that there was nobody in that room, before the persistence of the Inspectors, she ended by admitting that she gave accommodation to a friend and asked 'that no harm be done to him as he had done no wrong.'

Accompanied by the Manageress, the Inspectors went upstairs to the room in question. According to the saying of the Inspectors, Mme HERVEAU knocked on the door in a pre-arranged fashion, then opened the door with her key and said: 'It's the Police'. It was then that the individual who was near the door leapt backwards, took a revolver out of his pocket and fired on Inspector COTTY who was first, wounding him on the left forearm and the right side. Inspector COTTY immediately fired back and killed the man.

Without any further ado or ceremony, Cole was buried in an unmarked pauper's grave the following day. For the man with nine names and nine lives, his luck had finally run out.

THE BUTCHER OF PRAGUE

The Battle of the Giants between Germany and Russia began in midsummer 1941 and ended in a Soviet victory in late January or early February 1943, by which time around eleven million combatants, and countless civilians, had been killed or maimed. It was the war within the war.

In December 1941, while the Wehrmacht was still in the ascendant and driving forward into Russia, Reinhard Heydrich was the Deputy Reichsprotector of Bohemia-Moravia, part of Czechoslovakia, which Hitler's troops had annexed in 1938. He wanted to make a mark *before* he took power out of the hands of his predecessor. He had to stage an event with impact that would put the fear of God into anyone who might be thinking of opposing him.

So, he arranged a kind of theatrical performance. He instructed someone else to organise the event, but it was done to his complete satisfaction. The wide snow-covered yard of the great Gothic Cathedral of St Vitus, high above the river in the centre of Prague, was his stage. It was roped off with black, red and white cord, punctuated at the corners with red and black banners emblazoned with an eagle atop a swastika, and guarded by armed SS men. A little pavilion adorned with a swastika flag stood with its back to the cathedral, and inside it was a dais on which stood five carved chairs arranged so that they were slightly above the snowy expanse of the forecourt. Over a hundred neat circles had been carved out of the snow, and were kept clear, revealing yellow discs painted beneath. A machine gun, manned by an SS soldier, had also been set up in front of the cathedral, aimed at the forecourt.

Himmler arrived in his Mercedes and was welcomed by Heydrich and other dignitaries. They took their seats in the pavilion and the show began. Wretched prisoners were led onto the scene and ordered to line up, shivering in sub-zero temperatures, on the yellow disks, one disk to each man or woman. They were housewives, factory workers, clerks, trembling students, older people – they looked ordinary. All had offended the Gestapo. Some had been tried and sentenced to death a year ago. Others had been kept in confinement without trial for a long time. None spoke. None made a run for it. A crowd of onlookers was kept at a distance by armed police.

At 12.15 p.m. the cathedral bell chimed and an Obergruppenführer bellowed 'Fire!' As Himmler's Mercedes swept away, soldiers rolled up the cordon and lorries drove in. Jewish prisoners, supervised by guards with guns, lifted the bodies into the lorries and were finally, themselves, taken away, to join them in death. Hatred of Heydrich, the Butcher, was immediate and universal in this Czech part of the Sudetenland. He had achieved his objective: Czechs now understood how far he would go in pursuit of authority. However, he would deal with them later, because he had another big event coming up: the Wannsee Conference in Berlin, which he had convened for the third week of January.

The Wannsee was a charming lake outside Berlin. 'Conference' it wasn't. It was hardly a discussion at all: rather an opportunity to set out Heydrich's plans for a 'Final Solution' to the 'Jewish Question'.

Göring had revised the instructions for liquidation the previous summer. Originally Hitler had advocated expelling the Jews – deliberately moving them as far east as possible and then working them to death, or allowing them to starve, or if necessary, shooting them. And in the summer of '41, the main methods of killing were still shooting (usually by Einsatzgruppen or Gestapo) and carbon monoxide poisoning (achieved by cramming as many people as possible into a mobile 'gas van' and pumping exhaust fumes into it).

Shooting people was quick but even machine-gunning was slow when you had a death target of at least 10,000 people per day per camp. And carbon monoxide could take an hour to work. It was a question of finding some faster method. Göring and other people around Hitler had heard estimates of twenty million Jews alive in this occupied country, thirty million in that – the numbers were staggering. There had to be faster ways to get rid of people. In September of 1941, a new solution was tested and found to be efficient. Crowds of prisoners were confined in a space where they had to breathe the toxic gases which were released by crystals of Zyklon B (an insecticide) upon exposure to air. It killed them in minutes.

Adolf Eichmann, who was in charge of herding Jews away from wherever they were and getting rid of them by any means possible, seized upon this new method and used it. At Wannsee, in the presence of all the senior Nazis including Eichmann and Heydrich, it became official policy. All Jews were to be exterminated mainly by a program of gassing, for which work had begun. Soon three camps with new and efficient gas chambers – at Belzec, near Lublin, at Sobibor, in eastern Poland, and at newly extended Treblinka – would be known as Reinhard Camps as a compliment to Heydrich's inspiration.

Back in Prague the Gestapo, under Heinrich Müeller's direct control, were busy with plans for Czech Jews, who would be herded into a ghetto at Theresienstadt before deportation to Poland. Jews in Slovakia were 'redefined' in September 1941 and made to wear the Star of David, which meant that at any time they could be evicted from their homes and/or taken east in cattle trucks. There was non-Jewish disapproval of this, more than in Poland; more discontent, less obedience

Heydrich decided not to encourage further resentment. This region of Czechoslovakia was its industrial heartland. Germany needed the Skoda factory to work flat out, not to be disabled by sabotage; it did not want to see freight lines sabotaged or bridges destroyed. So, from the beginning of 1942 he began a charm offensive at all levels. Industrial workers were allowed more fat in their rations. Pressure groups were given audiences with him and he promised to consider their concerns. He and his wife Lina entertained lavishly. The media published cosy pictures of the good-looking couple at home with their little girl.

In London, the Czech government-in-exile under Edvard Benes began to notice that the Czech resistance was less active. They were getting soft, placated, willing to ignore the iron fist hidden in the velvet glove. But there were plenty of Czechs in Britain who retained their hatred of the Nazis and ten of them undertook to train with the SOE for a special mission. The Czech resistance in Prague were appalled. Whatever offensive Benes was planning would be terrible for them; reprisals would be fierce. Already most of the arms they could ever hope to use had been confiscated by the Gestapo. They feared for themselves and their families.

Benes delegated the operation to Frantisek Moravec, head of the Czechoslovak intelligence services. Moravec liaised with Brigadier Colin Gubbins, the SOE Director of Operations who oversaw the Czech and Polish sections. Gubbins readily agreed to assist in carrying out the operation, although knowledge of it was restricted to a few of the SOE headquarters staff. The operation was code-named *Anthropoid*.

Preparations began on 20 October 1941. Moravec had personally selected two dozen of the most promising personnel from among the 2,000 exiled Czechoslovak soldiers based in Britain. They were sent to one of SOE's commando training centres at Arisaig in Scotland. Warrant Officer Jozef Gabcik and Staff Sergeant Karel Svoboda were chosen to carry out the operation on 28 October 1941 (Czechoslovakia's Independence Day), but Svoboda was replaced by Jan Kubis after he received a head injury during training.

Training was supervised by Major Alfgar Hesketh-Prichard, who turned to Cecil Clarke to develop the necessary weapons, light enough to throw but lethal enough against what they assumed would be an armour-plated Mercedes.

On 28 December 1941 Gabčík and Kubiš, along with nine other soldiers from Czechoslovakia's army in exile, were flown out from RAF Tangmere by 138 Squadron RAF and parachuted into their homeland in three separate areas. Some landed far from their intended targets and were subsequently arrested and shot by the Gestapo. Others lodged in safe houses and bided their time. On their covert arrival in Prague, Gabčík and Kubiš, neither familiar with the city, contacted several anti-Nazi families and lodged with them while laying their plans. They initially considered killing Heydrich on a train, but after examining the practicalities, they realised this was not a practical possibility. They finally settled on a plan to ambush Heydrich on his journey to Prague Castle on the morning of 27 May 1942. They would be informed when their target left home 14 kilometres north of Prague and would then be able to calculate his approximate arrival time at the spot they had chosen for the ambush at the junction between the road then known as *Kirchmayerova tčída* and *V Holešovičkách*. The tight curve at this point would force the car to slow down as it turned into *V Holešovičkách*.

When Heydrich's green, open-top Mercedes 320 came into view, Gabčík concealed his Sten sub-machine gun under the raincoat over his arm. As the car slowed, he dropped the raincoat and raised the gun, and at point-black range squeezed the trigger; however, the gun jammed. As the car passed him by, Heydrich made a fatal error. Instead of ordering his driver, Wolfgang Klein, to accelerate from the scene, he ordered him to stop. Heydrich then stood up in the car and drew his Luger. As the car braked sharply, Kubiš unexpectedly found himself at close quarters with Heydrich. With only a split second to think, he quickly threw a modified anti-tank grenade he was carrying in his briefcase. In the heat of the moment, he misjudged his throw and instead of it landing inside the car, the grenade fell on the road against the rear wheel, and exploded with an ear-shattering bang. Heydrich was severely wounded by the blast; shrapnel from the grenade had ripped through the right rear fender and embedded fragments and fibres from the car's upholstery into Heydrich, causing critical injuries to his left side, fracturing a rib and ripping into his diaphragm, spleen and lung.

The explosion also shattered the windows of an oncoming tram, striking several terrified passengers. Following the explosion, Heydrich and Klein leapt out of the Mercedes with pistols drawn. Klein instinctively ran towards Kubiš, who, momentarily dazed by the blast, was slumped against the railings.

Heydrich staggered after Gabčík, who for a moment stood frozen to the spot clutching his Sten gun.

As Klein came towards him, Kubiš recovered, fired into the air with a pistol, jumped on his bicycle and pedalled away at speed. Klein tried to fire at the departing cyclist, but, according to his later statement, pressed the magazine release catch and the gun jammed.

A staggering Heydrich moved towards Gabčík, who dropped his gun and tried to get to his bike. Heydrich managed to get a few shots off, which forced Gabčík to abandon his efforts to reach the bike and take cover behind a telegraph pole. Heydrich then took cover behind the tram, before moments later doubling over in pain and collapsing. As Gabčík made good his escape, Klein, having given up on his pursuit of Kubiš, ran over to Heydrich, who was now going into shock and muttering 'Get that bastard!'

As Klein dutifully ran off in pursuit, Heydrich made one last attempt to stand up before again collapsing against the bonnet of the wrecked Mercedes. Klein, a former sprinter, managed, against the odds, to catch up with Gabčík, who, in desperation, ran into a nearby butcher's shop. With Klein, only a few metres behind, shots were exchanged between the two men, before Gabčík miraculously managed to dodge Klein and jump on a tram passing the shop.

Back at the wreck of the Mercedes, a Czech woman and an off-duty police officer ran over to Heydrich. A passing van was flagged down. Heydrich was placed in the back and driven to Bulovka Hospital.

Within minutes of the explosion, the Gestapo were on the scene of the ambush and had found their evidence: an abandoned British Sten gun, cartridge cases, and a British-made briefcase containing an unexploded bomb. Later that day, a state of emergency was declared which placed Prague under curfew. Anyone, it was announced, who had given aid in any way to the attackers would be executed along with all members of their family. A search involving 21,000 German troops and Gestapo officers began, which resulted in the ransacking of 36,000 properties. At the hospital, Dr Slanina attended to Heydrich's wounds. Surgeons immediately operated on the collapsed left lung, removed the tip of the fractured eleventh rib and removed the spleen, which contained grenade fragments and upholstery. Himmler, on hearing of the incident, sent his personal physician, Karl Gebhardt, who was directed to fly immediately to Prague. On arrival he found Heydrich sitting up in bed, apparently making a slow but sure recovery following surgery. However, Heydrich soon developed a high fever of 38–39°C. Despite the fever, his recovery appeared to progress well. On 2 June, Himmler came to the hospital to visit Heydrich; shortly after he left, Heydrich slipped into a coma and never regained consciousness. He died two days later and an autopsy held soon after determined that he had died of sepsis.

Tragically, as the Czech resistance had predicted, there were reprisals. By 4 June, 157 people in Prague had been executed, but no information concerning the whereabouts of the assassins had been found or volunteered.

After an elaborate ceremony in Prague on 7 June, described in the British press as a 'gangster's funeral', Heydrich's coffin was taken by train to Berlin where a second ceremony took place on 9 June, the day Hitler gave the order that 'any village found to have harboured or aided' Heydrich's killers would suffer the following fate:

1. All adult men to be executed
2. Transport all women to a concentration camp
3. Gather all children suitable for Germanisation
4. Burn down the village and level it entirely

Under the mistaken belief in a Gestapo report that it had a connection with the assassins, SS and Gestapo men moved in on the village of Lidice in the early hours of the morning of 9 June 1942. All the men of the village were rounded up and taken to a farm on the edge of the village. There they were filed into the barn and stood up against mattresses that had been taken from the village and fixed to the walls to prevent ricochets. The firing began at 7.00 a.m.; at first the men were shot in groups of five, but this was increased to ten as Horst Bohme, the officer commanding, thought the executions were proceeding too slowly. By early afternoon 173 were left lying where they fell. 203 women and 105 children were taken to the village school and then moved to a neighbouring village where they were kept for three days. The children were separated from their mothers. Four of the women who were found to be pregnant were removed and forced to have abortions. On 12 June the women were loaded onto trucks and taken to Kladno railway station. There they were crowded into cattle wagons and sent by rail to the Ravensbrück concentration camp. The vast majority of the 203 women were thought to have been progressively worked to death on road building and ammunition manufacture. While investigators after the war were unable to find specific records relating to these deaths, a chilling record was found revealing the fate of the children. Of 105, twenty-three children thought suitable for Germanisation were taken away to orphanages. On 2 July, the remaining eighty-two children were handed over to the Lodz Gestapo office, where an order was received from Adolph Eichmann that they should be sent to the Chelmo extermination camp 43 miles away. It was here, on 2 July, that the children were gassed to death in Magirus gas vans. Investigators after the war concluded that of the twenty-three children sent to SS Lebensborn orphanages, six had died and seventeen were thought to have survived.

In the days following Lidice, no leads were found for those responsible for Heydrich's death. A deadline was issued for the assassins to be apprehended by 18 June 1942. If the assassins were not handed over by then, or information concerning their location not given, further reprisals would take place. By way of carrot and stick, the Germans also offered a reward of one million Reichsmarks. Gabčík and Kubiš initially hid with two Prague families, but were shortly afterwards offered refuge in the Orthodox Karel Boromejsky Church. Their location remained secret until Karel Curda, a member of a local sabotage group, walked into a Gestapo office to claim the reward. While he didn't know where the two assassins were holed up, he did reveal the locations of several safe houses and the names of several individuals who had shielded Gabčík and Kubiš. As a result of this tip-off, German troops and Gestapo men raided the flat of the Moravec family at 5.00 a.m. on 17 July. The family were dragged from their beds and lined up against a wall in the hallway while the flat was thoroughly searched. While the search was going on, Marie Moravec was allowed to go to the toilet. The moment she entered the toilet, she killed herself by biting on a cyanide capsule.

Although her husband Alois was unaware of his wife and son's involvement in the resistance, he was immediately dragged out of the flat along with his seventeen-year-old son Ata and taken to Gestapo headquarters at the Petschek Palace. Here they were systematically tortured for most of the day – Ata finally broke down after being shown his mother's severed head in a fish tank and being told that unless he confessed, his father would be decapitated in front of him. Ata Moravec, his father, his fiancée, her mother and brother were then taken to Mauthausen concentration camp where they were later executed.

With the identities and location of the assassins now in their possession, Waffen-SS troops descended on the church and surrounded it the next day. During the ensuing two-hour gunfight, they were unable to root out Gabčík and Kubiš and those with them and called in the fire brigade to pump water into the church vaults where the assassins were hiding. After repeated German assaults on the prayer loft and crypt, all those inside had either been killed or killed themselves. Karel Curda was then brought in by the SS to identify their bodies. Gabčík and Kubiš were brave men who gave their lives for the Czech cause. They had initially been among a highly able group of twenty-four men selected for the mission by Frantisek Moravec. Several of these men, however, didn't make it as far as Czechoslovakia; in fact, they didn't make it as far as RAF Tangmere, from where the *Anthropoid* team flew out on 28 December. They had been ordered to leave the Arisaig commando training centre and report to another training location where, they were told, further preparation for their role in *Anthropoid* would take place.

Their new destination was the Inverlair Lodge Estate, which lies in an un-signposted hamlet in Glen Spean, Inverness-shire, 2 miles off the main road between Spean Bridge and Newtonmore. Situated some 40 miles from Arisaig House, where the main group of *Anthropoid* agents were undergoing training, an entire area south-west of the Caledonian Canal was in effect a restricted area under Defence Regulations. On the surface, Inverlair too was officially designated as a training facility, but in reality, its function was anything but. In this hilly, rain-soaked, and desolate part of the Scottish Highlands, cut off from the rest of Scotland by the diagonal line created by the canal, strange rumours were already circulating among the locals.

In 1941, the lodge had been requisitioned by the War Office and became one of the secret facilities operated by the Inter-Services Research Bureau, the cover name for the Special Operations Executive. Known as No. 6 Special Workshop School, the white-painted Georgian manor house faced a huge conical hill that afforded an almost aerial view of the entire estate, which included a wood that shielded the lodge from the roadway. It was, in reality, more of a track than a road, that narrowed as it went on and eventually petered out altogether. Before reaching Inverlair, a deep gorge had to be crossed by means of a bridge. This small, wooden construction was the only way in and out of Inverlair. Without it, the estate was effectively cut off from the outside world.

Early on in the war, as undercover operations in occupied territories began apace, it was soon evident that there would inevitably be occasions when volunteers would refuse to take part in operations once they became aware of what they'd let themselves in for. Equally, there would be other agents who failed to make the grade during training, were injured during training, or flunked while on an actual operation. Whatever the situation, they were already in possession of highly classified, secret information. They knew too much to be permitted to return to their units and everyday lives, where an intentional or unintentional remark might compromise operations or endanger the lives of other agents in the field. There was, as a result, a clear need for such individuals to remain somewhere secure until the knowledge they held was valueless.

Inverlair Lodge therefore became a detention or internment camp where such individuals could be isolated and detained for the duration of the war or until the mission that had been trained for was carried out. The estate was, however, far from a prison; it was, in fact, a gilt-lined cage where living conditions were, according to some contemporary accounts, bordering on luxury. In addition to comfortable bedrooms, there was almost every kind of recreational facility available: fishing in the loch, a well-stocked library with a range of daily newspapers and magazines, billiards, table tennis, a music room with a gramophone and a small gym. In addition, the estate had all the facilities, equipment and activities of a normal training establishment, such as an assault course and a weapons range with pop-up targets to fool them into thinking they were still undergoing training. Indeed, some guests or inmates were apparently oblivious to the fact that it was not a genuine training facility.

One of the first group of arrivals at No. 6 Special Workshop School, Inverlair, were several members of the Norwegian Independent Company, NORIC1, who were formed to undertake sabotage operations on behalf SOE in their occupied homeland. The men, who had survived Operation *Archery* (also known as the Maloy Raid), in December 1941, had apparently created waves on their arrival back in the UK as the result of the unexpectedly high number of casualties suffered on the mission. Their leader, Captain Martin Linge, had been killed by a German sniper during the assault against German positions on the island of Vagsoy, along with seventeen other commandos. In addition, fifty-three men were wounded. The survivors were soon after assigned to Inverlair to 'train' for their next mission.

For security reasons, the only persons allowed across the canal into the restricted zones were local residents, staff and 'students' of the training schools. A good number of operatives who crossed the canal were under the delusion that they were to undergo a special training course to prepare them for an important mission. As the numerous training courses began, they would find the standards unexpectedly high.

When they had learned to transmit sixteen words a minute on the radio, they would be told to increase their speed to twenty-five words – 'it will be a very delicate mission you know.' Lectures on torture and interrogation techniques would likewise go into minute, irrelevant and seemingly endless detail. The duration of their training would stretch out and out while the war went on without them.

We know that at a host of training facilities there were a number of criteria and tests to weed out unsuitable agents. William Morgan, a psychiatrist who worked for SOE at this time, reveals once such ruse known as the 'train test'. This was simply a matter of planting an SOE officer on a train taking potential recruits to a training school. Any who couldn't 'keep their mouths shut on the train ride' were immediately noted and outwardly allowed to go through the four-day assessment. However, immediately afterwards, they received orders of an 'important assignment' that would require further training – at No. 6 Special Workshop School, Inverlair. Morgan recalled

> ...a lieutenant, a brazen young man with a loud voice and a hostile attitude. He hardly needed any probing from me to get him to talk. I tried to pipe him down but he was not even conscious of my wrinkled brow. He was a menace. I think he was sent to 'Siberia', an isolated post on the rainy west coast of Scotland.

At the same time as the repercussions of Operation *Archery* were being dealt with at Inverlair, preparation for Operation *Anthropoid* was just beginning. Unlike those involved in Operation *Archery*, who were sent to Inverlair as the result of their post-mission reactions, the Operation *Anthropoid* agents were posted there as a result of injury or shortcomings that became evident during initial training at Arisaig House.

When the idea for an establishment like Inverlair was first discussed at SOE's Baker Street headquarters in early 1941, it was clear that an exceptional officer would be required to create such an entity from scratch. Not only would the security arrangements need to be well thought out, but so too the regime for dealing psychologically with those sent there on a day-to-day and long-term basis. The man chosen by SOE Director Sir Frank Nelson (known as CD) to be the Commandant of 'the Cooler', as it was to become known, was Lieutenant Alfred Fyffe.

Fyffe was recruited from an Intelligence Corps posting at Fort William and joined SOE on 19 April 1941. Born in Dundee, he attended Harris Academy before going up to the University of St Andrews, where he had read Modern Languages. His SOE file describes him as:

> Dependable and resourceful. He combines to an unusual degree, intellectual qualifications with 'toughness'. He sets an excellent example of military smartness and has shown himself well qualified in dealing with foreign personnel and disciplinary cases.

It is clear from a memo dated 18 August 1941 that when the decision was made to give him command of the new Inverlair facility, the head of SOE's H. Section, where he was then posted, was not happy to let him go:

> I have tried to get in touch with you on the telephone today on the subject of our recent conversation regarding D/C.E.1's request for the transfer of Lieutenant Fyffe to this section with a view to his being put in charge of the new institution in Scotland. As I understood, the proposed appointment would involve immediate promotion for Fyffe and as he is keen to accept it, I felt that H. Section was not justified in standing in his way, particularly as there was no immediate prospect of promotion for him in H. Section. I have discussed the matter with Major Grayson, who shares this view and who feels that although Fyffe has been extremely useful and efficient at Thame he cannot be regarded as indispensable there.
>
> The matter has suddenly become one of urgency as D/C.E.1 tells me he is going to Scotland tomorrow and wishes to take Fyffe with him. In these circumstances, after a further talk with M.Z. and with Major Grayson, I have agreed that Fyffe should be released.

And so, the following day, Fyffe found himself on an Inverness-bound express train from King's Cross in the company of D.C. A car was waiting for them up at Inverness station to drive the two men directly to Inverlair. Having been a Spanish lecturer at the University of St Andrews before joining the army, Fyffe's unique experience of lecturing and intelligence work gave him a wealth of ideas for the new Cooler project. D.C's instincts had been right; Fyffe took to the job like a duck to water. Within weeks the new 'school' was up and running and welcoming its first students. Fyffe's instinct from the beginning was to engender at Inverlair a disorientating informality, while at the same time maintaining strict 'mission' secrecy and security rules. One of the cardinal rules, for example, was not asking other trainees personal questions or questions about their previous operations. On the other hand, apart from Fyffe himself and his staff, everyone else wore civilian clothes. Those sent to Inverlair were both men and women, which reflected the fact that SOE had a policy of proactively recruiting female agents, as well as male, as they believed they were less likely to attract attention or suspicion.

Fyffe's ability as a multi-linguist was a great asset in dealing with a wide international clientele. Not long after opening, it was the Norwegians, followed soon after by the Czechs. The following year a number of French officers were billeted at Inverlair at the request of General de Gaulle. There was, apparently, a strong suspicion that several of them might be security risks or even Gestapo informants. Fyffe's objective here was not only to isolate them from the outside world, but, more importantly, to discover whether any of them might be working for the enemy. No doubt a strong element of psychology and counter-espionage technique was used to discover whether de Gaulle's suspicions held any water or not. The use of 'femme fatale' tactics may also have come into play at Inverlair, where men and women mixed freely on the estate. Whatever the eventual verdict, the men were gone from Inverlair within six months. How many were returned to everyday life and how many, if any, were permanently disappeared can only be speculated upon.

While being sent to the Cooler was something that had little or no effect on those who thought it was simply a long and tedious training course, and were not there for any great length of time, for others, like the Norwegians and Czechs, the resulting resentment lasted a lifetime. As one former SOE agent put it decades after the war:

> The problem was that the agents in the holding school only had need-to-know knowledge of the organisation they served and its liaison with the Norwegian government in exile. The chaps did quarrel about something they ought not to have believed was an issue. My friend started to think in the Cooler that he had risked his life to go to the UK to do something worthwhile and now he was incarcerated. The animosity lasted the rest of their lives.

While no contemporary accounts now exist, it seems clear that several 'students' did try to escape from the Cooler. However, a combination of the wild and desolate terrain, the fact that the restricted area was hemmed in on all sides by natural obstacles, and a heavy military patrol presence, ensured that the facility gained an Alcatraz-like reputation within SOE. It is perhaps no surprise that two decades after it closed, the story and concept of the Cooler heavily influenced writer George Markstein and actor Patrick McGoohan in their creation of the 1960s cult TV series *The Prisoner*. Here in the Village, former spies who have now out-served their usefulness, been compromised or reached a stage in their careers where they now knew too many secrets are sent to an idyllic island on a permanent holiday from which there is no escape.

The Czechs who, from December 1941, had been training for *Anthropoid*, but instead found themselves undertaking 'further training', eventually found out a great deal more about the reprisals and the human cost of the mission on the Czech population. With over 5,000 lives lost in the reprisals, the wisdom of the Heydrich assassination is still debated today. While news of the reprisals was widely reported in the Allied press, it would take the murder of fifty Allied airmen who had escaped from a German POW camp to provoke, for the first time, the declared intention by an Allied government to pursue and bring to trial those responsible for war crimes.

13

TOM, DICK AND HARRY

On 5 January 1942, two Allied prisoners, Lieutenant Airey Neave and Dutch officer Anthony Luteyn, squeezed through a trapdoor, climbed a rusty ladder into a loft space, and from there quietly descended a stone spiral staircase past the German officers' mess. Dressed in home-made German officers' overcoats and caps, they then made a beeline for the main gate and freedom. Mistaking the two prisoners for visiting German officers, the duty guards saluted as Neave and Luteyn walked over the drawbridge, leaving behind them forever the Oflag IV-C POW camp, better known to posterity as Colditz Castle. From here, 24 miles south-east of Leipzig, they headed for the main railway station, taking an express train heading south to the city of Ulm, 100 miles from the Swiss border. From Ulm, they attempted to buy train tickets to Singen, a town close to the border. When asked to show their identity papers, they were promptly arrested by the railway police. Neave, however, managed to convince the police that they were genuine Dutch workers and they were then taken to the nearby office for foreign workers. Within minutes of arrival, they had given the police the slip and were on the run once again. Eventually arriving in Stockach near Ludwigshafen, they walked by moonlight, taking a little-used trail through cereal fields and two small copses of conifers, ending up on a farm track some 200 metres from Welschingen. It was exposed and snow covered the high ground there, but they had excellent views in all directions. From here the town of Singen was but a short distance away. With only the Singen Gestapo to avoid, they finally crossed the Swiss border on 9 January 1942, just south of the town.

From the border crossing they headed immediately for the British Legation in Berne and made contact with the minister there, Sir David Kelly, who provided accommodation in a small basement room at the Legation. Before too long Neave was contacted by the Military Attaché, Colonel Henry Cartwright, who cautioned him that the Gestapo had an active organisation in Switzerland, hunting for spies and escaped prisoners. He told Neave that a host of attractive girls were employed by the Gestapo to trap the unwary in bars and bedrooms. One of their principal tasks was to discover whether the British prisoners of war who had escaped from camps in Germany and Italy were being smuggled back to England. Neave spent some three months undercover in Berne before Cartwright briefed him on the plan to get him from Switzerland to Gibraltar through many hundreds of miles of enemy territory. Finally, on 5 May Neave sailed out of Gibraltar, arriving at Gourock on the River Clyde on 13 May, where he was given a message directing him to nearby Glasgow. Taking the overnight train to Euston, he was soon on his way to a second-floor room at the Grand Central Hotel in Marylebone:

> I climbed the wide stairs, with my cheap suitcase, still feeling I was a prisoner arriving at a new camp. The corridors were stripped and bleak. Everywhere I could hear the sound of typewriters and the bustle of troops in transit. I entered what had been a large double bedroom, which now served as an office for the interrogation of returned escapers by MI9. In place of the brass bedsteads were trestle tables and wire baskets ... an earnest Captain began to interrogate me. He was very interested in my 'Colditz story' and he would have kept me there much longer had I not shown my impatience.

After the interview, Neave was introduced to Captain Jimmy Langley of MI9, who he had last seen two years previously when they were both wounded at Dunkirk. Langley asked him if he'd like to go to lunch 'with someone important'. When asked who the important person was, Langley replied, 'Brigadier Crockatt, head of MI9 and Deputy Director of Military Intelligence. They met the brigadier at Rule's Restaurant in Covent Garden, where he was waiting for them by the bar. Wearing the uniform of the Royal Scots with the DSO and MC, he stood out in his red tabs and tartan from the rest of the officers who crowded the restaurant. Neave had half expected the chief of MI9 to be a crusty caricature from the pages of Somerset Maugham's *Ashenden* spy stories, but was pleasantly surprised to find that Crockatt was 'a real soldier and I liked him immediately'.

Crockatt was friendly and relaxed and keen to hear stories of life in prisoner of war camps. Neave eagerly told him that:

> In one camp, so it was said, the prisoners tunnelled and emerged by mistake in the Kommandant's wine cellar, which was full of rare and expensive wines. The Kommandant was a connoisseur and often asked the local nobility to dinner. The prisoners managed to extricate over a hundred bottles, drank them, put back the corks and labels after refilling them – I paused – with an unmentionable liquid.

Crockatt was highly amused and promised to tell Churchill the story. His mood then became suddenly more serious, and looking Neave in the eye, said:

> You've seen the people who work for us behind enemy lines. They need money and communications. Do you want to help them? Subject to you being cleared by the Security Service, I'm going to offer you a job; would you like to work in our secret escape section with Langley?

Neave gladly accepted and was told to report to Room 900 at the War Office on 26 May. Room 900, on the second floor, turned out to be Langley's own tiny office, which had apparently been a room reserved for making tea before the war. Two large filing cabinets almost obscured the daylight from the room's single window. Langley showed him an even smaller room next door which somehow housed two MI9 secretaries. Neave began to wonder if this could really be the nerve centre of MI9 that he'd heard so much about. MI9 was one of the relatively new intelligence departments that had proliferated in 1939 and 1940. Originally accommodated at the Metropole Hotel on Whitehall's Northumberland Avenue, it had since grown by leaps and bounds. Langley and Neave would somehow be squeezed into the same tiny room that had barely been big enough for Langley on his own. Langley went on to explain that Room 900 was the most top-secret part of the organisation and was kept separate from the rest of MI9, which was now based at Wilton Park in Beaconsfield.

Room 900's prime purpose was supporting prisoners of war, who were not only aided to escape from captivity but were also seen as a network of potential intelligence gatherers inside of Germany. The information garnered by MI9 from these sources was then channelled to other MI departments, including MI14, who wove it into the big picture of intelligence emanating from Germany. This theatre of espionage would, over the next year, see not only the biggest and best organised breakout from a German POW camp, but one of the worst and most shocking of crimes ever perpetrated by the Gestapo against Allied servicemen.

Neave's job was to look after secret communications with occupied Europe, training agents and building up an organisation in Belgium and Holland. This he did throughout 1942, with considerable success.

MI9 had five branches: Liaison (with other MI branches), Training, Planning, Codes and Tools. These MI9 sections reflected the fact that they had been tasked with several different objectives. For example, primary importance was initially placed on supporting European Resistance networks and utilizing these to aid Allied airmen shot down in enemy-held territory, whether they be prisoners of war or men who had thus far managed to evade capture. Getting airmen back to Britain not only helped maintain personnel but also enabled the men to be debriefed in terms of intelligence they could provide from spending time behind enemy lines. Even everyday observations about the mood of enemy civilians could be important.

In order to bring this about, MI9 needed to parachute agents into occupied Europe, who would then link up with local resistance groups. MI9 agents would be issued with a quantity of false papers, identity documents, ration coupons, money, maps and compasses to be passed on to Allied officers endeavouring to get back to London. Very soon, a third officer was recruited to MI9 to assist Neave – Lieutenant Michael Bentine, who had been seconded from RAF intelligence. Bentine acted as a liaison officer with the other intelligence services, principally, at this time, SIS and the Special Operations Executive, who were also working behind enemy lines with their own networks of agents, saboteurs, radio operators, couriers and escape organizers. Bentine also made regular reports to MI14, who effectively acted as a central clearing house for all German-based intelligence.

One of the first tasks for MI9 was to devise a code by which prisoners of war could communicate intelligence via their letters home to family and friends, which were read and censored by the Germans. In some instances, the simplest ideas can be the best. The answer in this case came by pure chance from Vera Hall, the wife of Graham Hall, a British bomber pilot held at Stalag Luft I near Barth, Western Pomerania.

Hall had developed his own method of communicating confidentially with his wife, based on a plan they had devised between them before he undertook his first flying sortie. Hall was notorious for using little or no punctuation in his letters and he told his wife that if he was ever taken prisoner and she received a letter from him, to look very carefully for any punctuation marks. Wherever she saw a full stop or a comma, for example, she should underline the first word following that punctuation mark. In this way, a brief message comprised of underlined words would make itself known to her.

Following receipt of the first letter from her husband using the punctuation code, Vera Hall had the good sense to take it to a friend of her husband who worked at the War Office. He, in turn, passed it on to MI9, who then recruited Vera Hall and kept her supplied with coded messages to insert into her letters to her husband. Following this initial success, other couples were recruited into the initiative, which became known as the 'dotty code'. MI9's intelligence requests might ask for a monthly report of how, when and where Allied aircraft had been shot down, or details of any troop movements prisoners might observe or hear about. As men moved and transferred from camp to camp, they took with them the 'dotty code' and new letter-writing teams set up accordingly. An intelligence-gathering officer was also appointed in each camp to oversee these operations. Very soon, MI9 devised new and more complex codes that were passed on to each camp intelligence officer.

At Stalag Luft III, near Sargan, Squadron Leader Roger Bushell, or 'Big X' as he came to be known, ran not only a first-class escape operation but a particularly effective intelligence-gathering unit that fed back directly to MI9 in London. Bushell, a thirty-two-year-old barrister, had joined the Royal Auxiliary Air Force at Cambridge University, where he read Law and represented the university at skiing, soon establishing himself as the fastest British downhill skier of the early 1930s. On arrival at Stalag Luft III, Bushell quickly built up the intelligence-gathering capability of the camp by introducing de-briefings for all new prisoners, quizzing them on what they had seen before, during and after capture, and on the location and circumstances of their aircraft being shot down.

Airey Neave's duties at MI9 also involved a good deal of procurement work on behalf of the POW camp intelligence centres, for which he very much depended on the ingenuity of quartermasters such as the 'in-house' Christopher Hutton and the Ministry of Supply's Charles Fraser-Smith. The Ministry of Supply, based in a Shell-Mex House in The Strand, had been set up in 1939 to co-ordinate the supply of equipment to the three armed services. The new ministry also took over all army research establishments. Fraser-Smith had been recruited directly from the Avro aviation company in Leeds by MOS director G. Ritchie Rice and given his own office, laboratory and workshop on the first floor of Portland House in Tothill Street, Westminster. From here he serviced a range of regular customers who included the Naval Intelligence Division (where he was on very good terms with one Ian Fleming, who later acknowledged Fraser-Smith as the template for Q in his James Bond novels), SIS, SOE and MI9.

Christopher Hutton (known to friends and War Office colleagues as 'Clutty'), had been a *Daily Chronicle* journalist before the war and had briefly worked in the publicity department for Gaumont Pictures. After a War Office interview in which he claimed some association with Houdini (he had briefly met the escapologist in 1912 when his uncle had made a wooden crate for his stage act), he was commissioned as a captain and assigned to MI9. Norman Crockatt gave him responsibility for evasion and escape devices. Eventually Hutton confined himself to working on maps and compasses that were hidden inside pens or tunic buttons, pioneering left-handed threads so that if the Germans' suspicions were aroused and they tried to unscrew them, they would simply tighten instead. Other Hutton devices included maps disguised as handkerchiefs hidden in canned goods, hollow heels that contained dried food, magnetized razor blades that would indicate north if placed in water and reversible uniform items that could easily be converted to civilian suits. Thought by some MI9 staff to be mad, Hutton eventually built himself an underground bunker in the middle of a field near Wilton Park, where he could work in peace.

Fraser-Smith was given a similar brief, although he tended to concentrate more on secretly commissioning work from UK manufacturers who were sworn to secrecy as a condition of receiving bespoke orders from the Ministry of Supply. Nestles had been tasked with producing highly nutritional concentrated food, but no suitable container could be found to conceal it. Fraser-Smith eventually had a brainwave when cleaning his teeth one morning – a squeezable toothpaste tube. Eventually Colgate toothpaste in Sheffield were contracted to supply empty toothpaste tubes, which were then sent to Nestles to fill them. He later pioneered the production of powered potatoes, which did not exist in 1941 and were manufactured in cube form by Chivers the jam makers, to Fraser-Smith's specifications. Other easily concealable cubes followed for dehydrated meat and vegetables.

Other Fraser-Smith inventions produced in secrecy by manufacturers included Slazenger golf balls and Parker fountain pens with compasses inside; miniature radios, complete with tiny earphones, in cigarette packets; miniature telescopes no more than 1½ inches long hidden inside a cigarette holder; silk maps concealed inside dominoes; shaving brushes and pipes; and flexible saws of interlaced wire concealed within shoelaces.

Two games manufacturers in particular were also taken into the War Office's confidence – Jacques of London and Waddington's. The popularity of chess in the Second World War had led to Jacques considerably upping production. Because chess sets were made of wood, they were ideal for concealment purposes. Jacques's directors assigned a team of craftsmen, all of whom had signed the Official Secrets Act, to produce chess sets that came in wooden boxes with hollowed-out walls, in which silk maps, currency, documents and hacksaw blades were inserted. The larger chessboard that came with the Staunton edition chess set was ideal for concealing maps. The chess pieces themselves were also hollowed out to hold compasses, dye and coins. A similar arrangement was struck with Waddington's who, from 1941, produced special sets of Monopoly which also concealed maps, compasses, money and other escape gizmos. Courtaulds Textile Ltd invented a system of disguising clothes as blankets dyed dark grey. When they were washed, the dye came out, revealing the pattern that the cloth should be cut along.

MI9 also took the high-risk strategy of creating fake charitable organisations that would send packages to POWs. The parcels were packed by a small team at MI9 which consisted of female relatives of MI9 officers and civilians. Each parcel had to be hand assembled and in some cases hand painted. This level of work required a workforce which could have been a very expensive overhead were it not for the free labour provided by relatives.

With the MI9-aided escape industry now firing on all cylinders, plans were afoot to execute the biggest ever intelligence-gathering mass breakout in history. Work went on around the camp with only a handful of the POWs having any idea of the grand scheme being hatched, or even the existence of an organization like MI9. Roger Bushell's scheme for the mass escape was set in motion in the spring of 1943 and created the need for a mammoth intelligence-gathering exercise in its own right. Acquiring information about train timetables would be done hand in hand with seeking intelligence on bomb damage.

Bushell's plan involved a considerable number of men, over 600 in fact, who would be involved in planning and organizing the escape. However, only a small proportion, around 200, would actually make the break. Most of the men went about their work on behalf of the plan as their way of making a contribution. Only a relatively small number of POWs were aware of the intelligence-gathering element. The camp was close to a military airfield, and some of the POWs were assigned to regularly observe the comings and goings. Reports were then sent back Britain to enable the RAF's radar team to track the development of the Luftwaffe's own night-fighter radar system.

At Stalag Luft III there had been many escape attempts in the past. The breakout in March 1944 was extraordinarily clever and almost unimaginably difficult to organise but it partly succeeded. In Bushell's own words, 'three bloody deep, bloody long tunnels will be dug – Tom, Dick and Harry. One will succeed!' Tom was started next to a stove-chimney in Hut 123. Dick was dug in the shower room of Hut 122, and under the stove in Hut 104 was to be found Harry.

The camp was considered to be one of the hardest to escape from due to the sandy nature of the soil, which made tunnelling hazardous. The prisoners' huts were also elevated on stilts to expose tunnels. Bushell calculated that going down 30 feet would minimise tunnel collapse so long as they were shored up by some 4,000 wooden boards, which were ultimately taken from prisoners' bunk beds. An estimated 100 tons of soil were eventually dug largely with the aid of home-made tools. Electric lights were rigged up and a pulley system installed to move the prisoners along the 2-foot-wide tunnel. Of the three tunnels started, Tom was discovered by the Germans, Dick was abandoned, leaving Harry as the only operative tunnel.

And so at 8.45 p.m. sharp, on the night of 24 March 1944, the first men began to make their way along the tunnel. Thirty feet above them the temperature was below zero; the ground was frozen and covered in several inches of snow. When they eventually reached the end of the tunnel, they found, to their horror, that the exit hatch above them was frozen shut. It was a further hour later that they finally succeeded in opening it, during which they lost valuable time. They discovered yet another setback when the first man out of the hatch realised that instead of surfacing just inside the nearby woods, the tunnel exit was, in fact, only yards away from the sentry tower in open ground.

Due to the fact that all their fake ID papers were date-stamped, they had no option other than to go through with the operation. The delay in effecting an exit from the tunnel and a further hold-up caused by a temporary cut in electricity, due to a nearby air raid, meant a big reduction in the number of men they could get out. Instead of their original plan of getting thirty men out per hour, this was now reduced to ten men per hour. By 5.00 a.m., the seventy-sixth man exited the tunnel and made a dash across the open ground in the direction of the trees – unfortunately, the seventy-seventh man was spotted by the sentry tower and the alarms were sounded. All hell was then let loose as the men waiting their turn in the tunnel had to make an about-turn in order to get safely back up the tunnel, change out of their escape clothes into their uniforms, destroy their fake papers and gobble down their smuggled rations before the Germans found the source of the tunnel in Hut 104.

Within thirty minutes the camp was swarming with hundreds of Gestapo men who, together with the 800 Luftwaffe camp guards, took the camp apart, searching every hut and every outbuilding.

The camp Kommandant, Friedrich von Lindeiner-Wildau, ordered a round-up of every prisoner left in the camp and paraded them in the freezing cold for a roll call, at which point it was discovered that eighty prisoners had escaped. Four had quickly been recaptured close by to the camp, which meant that seventy-six were currently on the run.

Within the hour not only was Dr Gunther Absalon of the Breslau Gestapo at the camp in person, but the head of the Gestapo, Heinrich Müeller, and half a dozen acolytes had arrived at the main gate, having driven directly from Berlin the moment the news of the breakout was phoned through to 8 Prinz-Albrechtstrasse. An immediate manhunt was ordered by the Gestapo, who pulled in reserves from neighbouring regions to set up roadblocks, searches of homes, farms and outbuildings, as well as checks on all trains out of the immediate area. It is clear from Gestapo messages and issued orders that day that they feared that with so many Allied officers on the loose, sabotage was a possibility.

Within two weeks of the breakout, a total of seventy-three escapees were eventually caught and were being detained at police stations and Gestapo offices in the Sargan area.

Hitler had been at the Berghof, his mountain retreat in Bavaria, at the time news of the escape had broken. The day after the escape, Himmler's report to Hitler had provoked an ugly outburst of temper from the Führer, who immediately summoned Himmler,

Göring, General von Graevenitz (head of the Prisoner of War Department), and the Supreme Commander of the German Armed Forces, Field Marshal Wilhelm Keitel.

Hitler apparently screamed that an example should be set and that all the recaptured prisoners should be shot. Göring pointed out that this could be counter-productive, since the British had German prisoners and there could be reprisals. A 'compromise' was therefore arrived at which Hitler reluctantly agreed to, whereby a token few would be returned to captivity. Although Himmler fixed the total of executions at fifty and set up the arrangements for carrying them out, it was Arthur Nebe, head of the Kripo, who apparently was deputed with the task of selecting the fifty names.

The fifty were to be picked off in pairs or small groups 'attempting to escape' as they made their way back to Sagan through the countryside. When one of the escapees was captured, his captor would receive a form letter from Heinrich Müeller, which would serve as order of the day. It read (with the appropriate names and places inserted):

REICH TOP SECRET. RHSA TO Chief of Gestapo Office, [town], or his Deputy:

By order of the Führer, the Reichsführer S.S [Himmler] has ordered that the [nationality, rank] who escaped from Sagan and is now held by the Kripo at [town] will be taken over by the officials of your office and during transport in the direction of [town 2] will be shot while trying to escape. The shooting will be done in such a way that the prisoner concerned will be unaware of what is going to happen. The corpse is to remain on the spot until inspected by the local gendarmerie and a death certificate has been issued. The body is to be cremated in the nearest crematorium. The urn is to be kept by the Gestapo Office. Further instructions about the urn will be issued at a given time.

Müeller knew this was a terrible act. His guilt shows in the fear that underlies the rest of his instruction:

The death certificate is to be returned to me with a description of the spot where the shooting took place. Only persons strictly concerned with this matter will be allowed to know of this teleprint. These persons must be pledged to special secrecy. The teleprint must be destroyed after the order is carried out. Destruction of the teleprint must be notified to me by teleprint. The Kripo [town] have been given relevant instructions.

And so it came to pass. Typically, three armed Gestapo men would collect one or two captive escapees from a Kripo jail. They would drive around 30 miles before stopping somewhere remote 'to relieve themselves'. The driver would stand outside the car. The escapees would be escorted from the car by two armed Gestapo men for the same purpose and told to use the bushes. They would be shot in the back where they stood.

Officially, it was the Swiss government who communicated with London, informing them of the killings. Word about the shootings had, however, filtered through from MI9 channels, who had shared this information with SIS and MI14 prior to the Swiss communique. On 19 May, the British Foreign Secretary, Sir Anthony Eden, made a statement to the House of Commons informing them that he had received information from the Protecting Power (Switzerland) that forty-six officers of the RAF, Dominion and Allied air forces had been shot after a mass escape from Stalag Luft III. He made a supplementary statement on 23 June revising the number of men shot to fifty. He concluded by telling the House:

> It is abundantly clear that none of these officers met his death in the course of making his escape from Stalag Luft III or while resisting arrest. His Majesty's Government are firmly resolved that these foul criminals should be tracked down and brought to exemplary justice.

Ironically, within months of the escape, Arthur Nebe, the man who had personally selected those to be shot, would find himself a Gestapo victim. By this time, a number of German army officers had decided that Hitler was leading the country to defeat and destruction. As Allied forces started pouring through France following the D-Day landings on 6 June 1944, dissent within Germany was in flower. People no longer expressed enthusiasm about Hitler. And there had been several attempts on his life, but none came quite so close to success as that of 20 July, mentioned in chapter 10. Hitler's base was far from Berlin, which had been ravaged by RAF bombing raids the previous winter. He now operated out of the Wolf's Lair, a complex near Rastenberg, in the far east of today's Poland. The site was a minefield, camouflaged, barbed-wired and protected by the SS. Important meetings were held in a large fortified hut above ground. On 20 July 1944, he was due to confer with members of the General Staff including General Count Claus von Stauffenberg, Field Marshal Keitel, General Heusinger and a Colonel Brandt. The party, including the Führer, made their way to the hut, carrying their notes.

Stauffenberg nipped back to the main building 'to collect his cap' and set a fuse. He then followed the rest of them to the hut. Reports were presented. He had to present one himself, but before the second speaker began, he murmured that he had to make a call and left 'for a minute'.

Outside, away from the hut, he departed in his staff car for the airport. Field Marshal Keitel, knowing that Stauffenberg's paper would be presented next, wondered where he was and slipped out. A telephonist told him that Obergruppenführer Graf Stauffenberg had left. Keitel returned and sat down as General Heusinger was explaining the situation on the eastern front on a map. When Colonel Brandt stood up to get a better look at the map, his feet were obstructed by Stauffenberg's briefcase, so he leant down to shift it. The blast brought down the ceiling and shattered the windows; four of those present were killed. Hitler suffered only minor injuries.

Von Stauffenberg was soon in the air, heading for Berlin. He knew the explosion had taken place, and should before leaving have received confirmation that Hitler was dead. He had not. He decided to go ahead with the putsch anyway. But other conspirators of the Wehrmacht got cold feet. They didn't act. The rest, in Berlin, was a shambles. Around midnight, the known conspirators – including Stauffenberg – were shot dead in the yard of the Wehrmacht's Bendlerstrasse headquarters. Keitel played an important role in the failed coup. He took an active part in handing over many army officers who were involved or suspected of being involved to Roland Freisler's notorious 'kangaroo court'. Around 7,000 people were arrested, many of them interrogated and tortured by the Gestapo. Five thousand of those were thought to have been executed.

There were other conspirators, all over the place. Within a month Hitler must have decided he could only trust Kaltenbrunner, the brutal Governor of Austria, because he got the job of finding every last one. He was fearsomely nasty, drunk or sober; a very tall man with a deeply scarred face. At his trial after the war, he would be pointed out as the only Nazi who actually looked like a war criminal.

14

TURNING THE TABLES

The British interrogators of MI19, an offshoot of MI9, were well trained and disciplined. This does not mean that their pursuit of information was always polite and considerate or within the rules of the Geneva Convention.

They came from all three of the Services and found out whatever they could from prisoners of war at dedicated locations up and down the country. They had to be able to speak German fluently. Also, they must be observant, emotionally intelligent, excellent listeners and accurate interpreters of what the prisoners were trying to say or to hide, and why.

Patience was not necessarily a virtue. The information they wanted could be of vital importance but if they received it a day late, lives could have been lost.

Lieutenant-Colonel Scotland OBE trained many interrogation officers. He had fought in the German army in South Africa between 1903 and 1907; he had been a spy; he had been an interrogator; and he had been a civilian with a civilian job. He liked to explain his impressions of a typical German mindset – 'German' because not all the prisoners of war were convinced Nazis. Luftwaffe pilots even at the start of the war were less likely to be true believers than, say, SS men. All, however, were more likely to talk freely to an authority figure than to someone of their own rank. The Mr Nice and Mr Nasty technique of interrogation also worked well, but one must never lose one's temper. Calm authority would nearly always achieve the best results.

Which was true only up to a point.

Two of the London interrogation centres are still well known: Latchmere House in Richmond and the short row of stucco-fronted Italianate mid-Victorian mansions at the north end of Kensington Palace Gardens that became The London Cage. Interrogators could go abroad to do their work. Some accompanied British night raids in Norway and in France in 1941 and 1942, and went with the troops on D-Day in 1944.

The idea was that in the first hours of capture, the enemy would be tired and fearful and therefore more likely to confide something that with more time, he might have edited out. It seemed to work.

All interrogators were well prepared with daily briefings from MI14, aerial reconnaissance photographs, the latest news of U-boats sunk, and so on. They knew the German order of battle and what every Nazi uniform badge and insignia meant. If an interrogator correctly combined selected snippets to arrive at a supposition of German intent and in passing, happened to refer to it as fact, captives would be unnerved. There seemed little point in keeping secrets if these people knew so much already.

Once softened up, a prisoner might be escorted by an officer and driven in style to one of the smarter restaurants in the West End for lunch. He expected to see people starving in the streets, as the German media had so often reported. Instead, yes, the terraces of white stucco-fronted mansions along the Bayswater Road had sandbags by the door and blast tape on the windows, but he could see that London was still going about its business. In the park, smart nannies pushed babies in huge Silver Cross prams. Young women still wore hats. Not everyone was in uniform, and certainly nobody was starving. Were he to be taken out to dinner, he would see men and women, some of them in uniform, queueing in Leicester Square to go to the Empire Cinema. There was fillet steak at Quaglino's, late, and dancing to the band. If the news in Germany was all lies, then ... was he on the right side of the war?

Dedicated Nazis would give nothing away, and could find themselves in solitary confinement. The adjoining houses formed an enormous complex, with basement kitchens, scullery, wine cellar and pantries, coal cellars and a warren of other small rooms once familiar only to the servants. For the purposes of Military Intelligence in wartime, these were soundproofed. The coal cellars in particular had extremely thick walls.

Perhaps the most useful means of extracting information was the microphone. Prisoners' rooms were bugged and their conversations with fellow prisoners recorded, as were their interviews. This was the case in every interrogation centre. High-ranking prisoners would, after interrogation at the London Cage, be moved to Trent Park, a magnificent neo-Georgian pile where in its comfortable rooms generals might talk among themselves and feel secure and entitled. All such conversations were recorded. The confidence of these people would be shattered later, at the Nuremberg trials.

At Latchmere House, MI5's Guy Liddell and Robin 'tin-eye' Stephens were strongly opposed to exerting physical pressure, believing it could be counter-productive. However, they did clandestinely dose prisoners with 'truth' drugs, as did Major Frank Foley and others in MI6.

Rudolf Hess, the much-promoted friend of Hitler's early days, having famously parachuted down to Scotland and spent some time in the Tower, was sent to a Cage near Aldershot. Nobody was quite sure what his arrival was all about (he claimed to be seeking peace), so both MI6 and MI5 at different times secretly administered mescalin and various mood-enhancing disinhibitors. He still didn't reveal much.

According to MI6, Hess was a dull fellow. Nonetheless he was astute enough to notice that there might be 'something in the food'. The inevitable comedown arrived; he suffered from mood swings, depression, paranoia and suicidal tendencies and was eventually wheeled off to a hospital near Abergavenny, where he remained for the rest of the war.

MI5 at Latchmere House specialised in 'turning' Nazis into double agents. Eddie Chapman pretty well turned himself. Having made his living as a safe-cracker before the war, he was in Jersey behind bars when it started. Upon release, seeing no way to leave the island he offered his services as a spy to the German occupiers. He persuaded them that he was genuine and they were tempted. His understanding of explosives was a big plus. Also, the Abwehr was short of good information. These days their spies in Britain never told them much they didn't already know. (This was because, unknown to the Abwehr, most of their spies had been caught, interrogated and kept in custody, and their messages from Britain had been written by MI5.)

The Nazis spent a year training Chapman in France, parachuted him into Britain with orders to blow up a De Havilland aircraft factory, and were delighted when their overflying planes photographed the result – the whole plant apparently in ruins with every sign of a recent, massive blast. What they did not know was that as soon as Chapman had rolled up his parachute he set off to a meeting with MI5, who were expecting him. They expertly disguised the 'bombed-out' factory so that from the air it would look wrecked. Colonel Robin 'tin-eye' Stephens (who always wore a monocle) debriefed Chapman at Latchmere House and sent him back to France as Agent Zigzag to pursue his career as a double agent with the Abwehr. Very good at it he was too; the Germans thought he was a regular marvel, and gave him the Iron Cross.

Chapman had picked the British side in the Second World War and stuck to it. Cole was too much of an opportunist ever to be trusted. It was that ability to tell the difference between two shifty characters which made British MI5 officers better than their counterparts in the Gestapo at selecting double agents.

The Allies won a significant victory when the Americans and British drove the Wehrmacht out of North Africa in the summer of 1943. Most of the prisoners they brought back to the interrogation centres after El Alamein were sullen, fed up and disillusioned. But the fanatical kind still existed and were hardest to break.

Polish prisoners were of particular value. They willingly talked about the camps and the horrors within, the Krupp arms factories in Poland and Germany, and IG Farben's production of Zyklon B and its effects. The full horror was in the numbers of people being starved, shot and gassed and no single participant could know what those numbers were. Babi Yar, where 33,000 people had been shot dead or buried alive in two days in 1941, was one of many massacres, some of which may never be known.

It was partly to relieve the mental distress of the Einsatzgruppen shooting parties that gas vans and, eventually, gas ovens were deployed; they could simply kill more people more quickly and with less psychological damage to the perpetrators, who did not even have to clear away the bodies. They made camp inmates do that.

When Noel Annan, formerly of MI14 and now working for SHAEF, drove into Germany with the Allied forces in 1945, he wrote:

> In Intelligence we knew of the gas ovens but not of the scale, the thoroughness, the bureaucratic efficiency with which Jews had been hunted down and slaughtered. No one at the end of the war, I recollect, realised that the figure of Jewish dead ran into millions.

The Nuremberg trials might have sent more Nazis to their death had the Nazis' lawyers not complained time and time again that 'confessions' elicited in London were untrue and made in response to threats. In some cases, they were probably right, because the kind of threats they described were so subtly delivered that only a good interrogator would make them. In one, a Pioneer Corps interrogator asked a prisoner where his family lived. Upon hearing the name of the town, he remarked that the Soviets were about to take it, if they hadn't already. They went on talking until the interrogator closed the file, ostentatiously marking it 'NR'. This meant 'Not Required' (interrogation finished). As he expected, the prisoner was horrified. To him it meant Nach Russland – (to be sent to Russia). All German soldiers knew that the Russians wanted revenge for German atrocities and any captured Nazi would be finished. The prisoner suddenly changed his mind about talking.

When the investigations into the Stalag Luft III murders began, the initial focus was on Breslau and Sagan, the two regions where the majority of Allied officers had been shot. Although the investigation, which began seventeen months after the 'Great Escape', was very much a 'cold case', in many ways this was the least of the problems faced by those seeking out the perpetrators. Military Intelligence at the War Office had known almost from day one that the Gestapo was responsible, as word had come through to Whitehall from the Swiss government within days of the shootings. It was also known from intelligence sources that the Gestapo had already raked over the tracks by providing many of its members with false identity papers, and had ordered them to go on the run as the Nazi state collapsed in the dying days of the war. This would therefore be no ordinary investigation.

The task of investigating the murders lay with Wing Commander Wilfred Bowes of the Special Investigation Branch (SIB) of the RAF Police, due to the fact that most of the victims had been British airmen. Bowes was ably assisted by Squadron Leader Frank McKenna, a former detective sergeant in the Blackpool Borough Constabulary, and Flight Lieutenant Arthur Lyon, formerly a detective inspector in London's Metropolitan Police. They in turn were assisted by fourteen SIB NCOs and the services of the Military and Air Intelligence. Arthur Lyon, who had joined RAF intelligence at the beginning of the war, and the only SIB officer with an intelligence background, was the main liaison with the various Military Intelligence sections such as MI5, MI6, MI9, MI14 and MI19, who were all involved in different capacities with the SIB lead investigation.

The first arrests were made in October 1944. One of those arrested was Major Hans Thiede, who had been attached to the No. 17 Inspection Centre, which was responsible for six POW camps, and where a number of recaptured RAF pilots had been detained before being shot. He was taken to London for questioning, and on 19 October told Captain Kettler that he was an anti-Nazi who had not witnessed any of the alleged events in Sagan. His only knowledge of events, he claimed, came from seeing a telegram about British airmen who had been shot while resisting arrest.

Thiede told his interrogators about the range of security measures employed in the six camps, and asserted that the Allies should be addressing their questions to Lieutenant-General Walther Grosch (the commanding officer of No. 17 Inspection Centre) and Colonel Richard Waelde, who he claimed were directly involved. Walter Grosch and Richard Waelde were, as a result, brought to London for questioning. Grosch was interrogated by Lieutenant-Colonel Alexander Scotland on 7 December 1945. For several days he refused to answer questions. Scotland informed Grosch that 'sufficient evidence to warrant a charge against you' existed and that if he could prove that he was innocent of a murder charge, he should make a full written statement covering his actions following the escapes.

An hour later Grosch relented and asked for a pencil and paper to write down his account. From this, Colonel Scotland eventually came to the conclusion that Grosch had actually taken no part in the Sagan crimes, and no charge was therefore preferred against him. On 6 September 1945, Breslau Kripo chief Max Wielen was interrogated at the London Cage by Major Riedel and Colonel William Hinchley Cooke. They were keen to question him about Gorlitz prison, where most of the officers who were shot had been held after their recapture. They wanted to know about his role in the search and recapture of the escapees and the suggestion by others that he had participated both in the preparation and the concealment of the crime, and along with Arthur Nebe in the execution of the order to shoot the fifty officers.

Johannes Post, the Gestapo officer who had been in charge of a correction camp at Kiel, was, according to all the assembled evidence, an out-and-out sadist. At the camp near Kiel, he had overseen a regime where labourers were beaten to death for not working hard enough. During questioning in London, he had been nonchalant and arrogant and, in the words of report on his interrogation, 'putting on an act'.

He tried the patience of Alexander Scotland to such a degree that Scotland turned to the guard, instructing him to 'take care of this man – he is one of the worst bastards of the whole lot.' This was apparently a pre-arranged signal for the guard to give Post a beating. The details of this incident are not contained in the report of Post's questioning, although Scotland later commented that with the exception of SS officer Reinhold Bruchardt, Post was the most cruel and brutal Nazi he had the misfortune to interrogate.

Bruchardt had been arrested in Germany after a concerted manhunt led by Wing Commander Bowes, who finally received a tip-off as to where Bruchardt might be hiding. During the questioning of former Danzig Gestapo officer Kurt Achterberg, he revealed that Bruchardt had had an affair with his wife. He described Bruchardt as 'a dangerous brute of a man' and was more than happy to give chapter and verse about Bruchardt and where he might be found. As a result, a team of four arresting officers were immediately despatched to the town of Kempten. In the early hours of the morning, the detachment forced their way into the small apartment where they had been told Bruchardt was living, finding him sound asleep in bed. Despite the advantage of surprise, it took all four men to subdue the 6′3″, barrel-chested Bruchardt after a struggle that lasted for several minutes. This melee had apparently been prolonged by the fact that when they had tried to handcuff him, his wrists were found to be too large for the cuffs. He was then sent immediately to London, under a larger than usual guard. The detachment guarding him carried a message from Bowes to Scotland, warning that Bruchardt was considered a high-risk, dangerous prisoner.

The investigation team had already pieced together a range of evidence that mapped out in detail the role Bruchardt had played in the murders. Unlike a number of previous inmates, Bruchardt showed no reluctance to commit his account to paper. MI19 officers were singularly unimpressed with this obvious work of fiction. The following day Scotland told Bruchardt directly, 'We know you were the man in charge of the special duty squad. You, and you only, were responsible for the murders. We already have all the evidence we want.'

In the early days of his incarceration at the London Cage, Bruchardt took great delight in showing off his physical strength. Lieutenant-Colonel Scotland met this challenge head-on by calling in Sergeant Prion, a giant of a man, who set Bruchardt to work for long stretches, scrubbing floors and subjecting him to sand-bucket lifting competitions. According to London Cage prisoner records, this combination of physical activity pretty soon exhausted him.

Another detained Gestapo officer brought into Scotland's custody was Erwin Wieczorek, a member of the Breslau Gestapo and a man who had played a direct role in the shootings. Wieczorek made a statement to the effect that when the shootings began, he had raised the bonnet of the truck that was carrying the RAF officers and pretended to be searching for an engine fault, so that he did not have to witness events. He listed in his statement the names of the Gestapo squad that had carried out the shooting, the principal role played by Wilhelm Scharpwinkel and the name of the truck driver, Robert Schroeder. He recorded the details of the journey back from the shooting and told Scotland, 'Hardly anyone spoke because we were tired and depressed by what had taken place.' Wieczorek claimed that he had made a number of excuses for not accompanying the squad on subsequent shootings. Investigation officers and prosecutors later decided not to charge Wieczorek and he was later released.

It took some time to track down Robert Schroeder, the driver named in Wieczorek's statement. When he was taken to London and interrogated by Scotland, he confirmed Schroeder's account, the part taken by Scharpwinkel in the killings, and named the men in the firing squad. In mitigation he argued that he was simply the driver and had taken no part in the murders. His version of events was corroborated by Hans Schumacher, who had been a member of the Kripo in Breslau. He pointed the finger at Wilhelm Scharpwinkel as the man at the centre of the web. He told interrogating officers that such was the degree of secrecy surrounding the killings, that hardly anything leaked out. The focus of attention was, without doubt, whittling down to Scharpwinkel, as the man in charge of the firing squads. A high-profile search for Scharpwinkel was already underway throughout Germany. As the weeks became months, not even the slightest lead was uncovered. Eventually, he was finally located in Moscow of all places, where he was being held a prisoner. While the Russians refused point-blank to hand him over to Wilfred Bowes, they were prepared to negotiate with the British Ambassador and the Foreign Office in London. While they began by arguing that Scharpwinkel was too ill to answer questions, let alone travel, they eventually relented. The eventual agreement led to the Russians agreeing to grant an entry visa and permission for Captain Maurice Cornish to visit Moscow and question Scharpwinkel under Russian supervision.

Over a period of three weeks, Cornish closely questioned Scharpwinkel; the Russians insisted on making a Russian interrogation transcript. However, they soon tired of the translation work involved, and compromised by agreeing to a German transcript being provided. During the questioning, Scharpwinkel told Cornish, 'I would have preferred that the order to shoot prisoners had not reached my office; but if it had not been carried out there would have been a court martial.' He blamed the shootings on Max Wielen, a man called Lux and others, saying that he had only received news of the shootings after they had happened. He claimed that the order to shoot had come not from him but had been received by Lux from Berlin. Lux, however, could never be brought to justice by Britain as he had been killed in the siege of Breslau during the closing weeks of the war.

In his statement of 31 August, Scharpwinkel admitted that he had been at the headquarters in Görlitz with Lux. Displaying no emotion, he calmly explained to Captain Cornish how he had witnessed Lux telling the captured pilots that they would be shot. The pilots were driven in a convoy towards Sagan. When they reached the main highway, they were ordered out of the vehicles. He told Cornish:

> The prisoners were placed in position and it was revealed to them that the sentence was about to be carried out. The prisoners showed considerable calm, which surprised me very much. The six prisoners stood next to one another in the wood. Lux gave the order to fire and the detachment fired. Lux shot with them. By the second salvo the prisoners were dead.

It is clear from his report that Cornish didn't believe a word of this lame attempt to shift the blame onto the now dead Lux among others. Unfortunately, the Russians were in no mood to transfer Scharpwinkel to British custody. They were right about his state of health though; he died within weeks of Cornish's return to London.

The hunt was still on for two Gestapo men – Hans Ziegler, who had issued orders for the Stalag Luft III prisoners to be taken into the countryside and shot, and police officer Erich Zacharias, who had already admitted his guilt to fellow officer Friedrich Kiowsky that he had personally shot two British prisoners. Ziegler had ordered Zacharias to take the prisoners out into the countryside at 2 a.m., telling him that it was 'a nice quiet time when you won't be disturbed, order them out of the truck for a pee and then shoot them'. Their bodies were to be swiftly cremated. The excuse given in the official report was 'attempting to escape'.

Wilfred Bowes eventually tracked down Zacharias to Bremen where he arrested him, personally escorting him from Germany to London. However, it would take the best part of two years before Ziegler was found. Zacharias already had his story worked out. He was described in MI19 reports as 'a brutal man, who readily obeyed orders'. Major Roger Mortimer described Zacharias as 'one of the most appalling men I have ever met'.

The interrogators had already heard from other witnesses how Zacharias' men had brutally beaten up two escapees, Squadron Leader Tom Kirby-Green of the RAF and Flying Officer Gordon Kidder, and had driven them out of town to be shot. Their bodies were cremated in Moravská Ostrava.

Captain Cornish led the interrogation of Zacharias, who stubbornly refused to make any statement, written or otherwise. It was Scotland, apparently, who decided, as a result, to take the unorthodox step of making Zacharias re-enact the last interrogation of Kidder and Kirby-Green, which he had undertaken with Hans Ziegler at Zlín. During the interrogation, Kidder's handcuffs had been ripped off, breaking his wrist in the process; he was then dragged to his knees. Alexander Scotland described this re-enactment in his unpublished memoirs:

> We knew that there had (originally) been four men in the room. We prepared a room for Zacharias; the blinds were drawn, the lights were on, and on the table we placed a microphone to record anything Zacharias might say. There were four of us in the room, two behind the table, and one on either side of the front. We had Zacharias brought in with handcuffs. He was made to kneel in front of the table, just as we imagined Kidder had done. A statement was read to Zacharias which gave the facts about his part in the murders. Once it had been read out, I moved over to Zacharias and put my hand on his shoulder, and said: 'What is the truth?' Whether the atmosphere and his memories of Zlín affected Zacharias, or whatever the bit of showmanship appealed to him, he admitted shooting Kidder. The whole incident took less than five minutes to obtain the confession.

Zacharias then made a full written statement that, along with other prisoner statements, was filed with the case prosecutors and in War Office records:

> I made the prisoner get out of the car and go to the kerb to pass water there. I took up position about one metre obliquely left behind him ... I drew my service pistol, which was all ready for firing, from the side pocket of my coat and fired obliquely in the left side of my prisoner in order to hit his heart. In order to make quite sure, I fired a second shot at the prisoner as he was collapsing ... I convinced myself of the death of the prisoner by feeling his pulse and looking at his eye.

Another man implicated in the murders was the head of the Karlsruhe Gestapo, Josef Gmeiner, who was arrested after an exhaustive search, and was found living under a false name. Gmeiner asserted that he had been serving in France at the time of the shootings, but changed his tune when confronted with his Gestapo ID records. On his arrival at the London Cage, he spent several days writing up a detailed statement that was immediately rejected by Scotland as 'utter nonsense'. In his statement, Gmeiner naively quoted the Sagan Order word for word. When it came to the part stating that escapees were to be executed, he was challenged by Scotland that the prisoners had not been tried by any court in Germany, and therefore it was an order to commit murder. 'Didn't your natural sense of justice revolt against that?' Gmeiner came out with the now stock answer that 'It was an order from the Fuhrer; therefore, it was legal and binding on me.' Scotland cautioned him: 'That statement will hang you, Gmeiner.'

By the time the first Sagan trials opened in July 1947, MI14 had been subsumed by MI3. However, records show that the now renamed 'German Section' of MI3 continued to monitor and record the proceedings and outcomes of the proceedings. The second series of trials commenced in October 1948, and by this time the methods allegedly employed by the London Cage came under the scrutiny of the lawyers representing the former Gestapo men, many of whom now argued that the confessions were false and obtained by torture. Alexander Scotland now found himself subject on the witness stand to answer accusations of brutality, and using starvation, sleep deprivation, beatings, drugs and electric shock treatment to entice confessions.

Many at the War Office feared that months and years of careful investigation and case preparation could be on the line if the defence lawyers succeeded in this tactic, let alone the appalling prospect that cold-blooded murderers could walk free. It was not to be – Scotland remained calm under close questioning, calling the accusations 'nonsense' and the military court overruled the objections. The court sat for forty-nine days, resulting in thirteen of those found guilty receiving death sentences on 3 September 1947. The sentences were carried out on 27 February 1948 by Britain's Chief Executioner, Albert Pierrepoint, who was flown to Hamelin by the RAF. The thirteen men on Pierrepoint's list that morning were as follows:

Eduard Geith
Josef Gmeiner
Walter Herberg
Walter Jacobs
Hans Kahler
Johannes Post
Otto Preiss
Alfred Schmidt
Johann Schneider
Emil Shultz
Emil Weil
Eric Zacharias

From the moment that each man was marched from his cell to the moment Pierrepoint pulled the trapdoor lever on the scaffold, all of twelve seconds elapsed. Although one of the most sadistic of the Gestapo killers, Reinhold Bruchardt, was condemned to death, his sentence was later commuted to life imprisonment. The War Office were enraged when, in 1956, after serving only eight years of his life sentence, Bruchardt was released by the West German authorities.

15

AN UNSATISFACTORY CONCLUSION

For a long time there had been whispers from Germany about a super-weapon. In 1943 Matthew Pryor of MI14 deduced from RAF reconnaissance photographs that at Peenemünde, an inshore island in the Baltic, Germany was building a long-range rocket. So, in August, RAF Bomber Command dropped 1,800 tons of bombs on it. Development stalled, but did not stop. Hitler thought rockets would destroy British resistance once and for all.

V1s started to hit London from June 1944 onwards. A V1 was a winged rocket 27 feet long that flew straight and low over the city, its loud growl approaching steadily above the rooftops until it stopped. Silence. Then it fell, detonating 1,000 kilos of explosive.

Thousands landed on London in the following months. Launched from occupied ports on the French side of the Channel, they terrified people and sparked an exodus from London. But V1s were flawed. Their range was too short to launch from Germany, and they were vulnerable to enemy defences: Bofors guns, shots from RAF planes, even entanglement by barrage balloons destroyed more than 2,000 of them before they landed.

Then came the V2s. These were the super-weapons – big rockets that stood 14 metres high on the launching pad. In London, they were a silent killer, for a V2 descended vertically from the sky, creating a massive crater and killing hundreds.

They were controlled and launched from Peenemünde, as ballistic missiles that shot up to the stratosphere before whistling down to earth – another triumph for their designer, Wernher von Braun.

One of the most remarkable intelligence officers in MI14 was the Oxford philosopher John Austin. His brain was unclouded by passion, vanity or caution, and his integrity matched his ability. He smiled rarely, and when he did it resembled the sun in winter. In a remarkably short space of time he worked out the composition of the Afrika Korps from the first lot of captured documents. He soon left Birley's section to become the order of battle chief at GHQ Home Forces where he produced an admirable intelligence report called 'Martian' that covered France and the Low Countries. He and Matthew Pryor in MI14 were alone in taking the flying-bomb threat seriously, and Pryor discovered numbers of launching sites that had been passed out as negative at Medmenham, the centre of air photo intelligence. Later he moved to Eisenhower's Supreme Headquarters Allied Expeditionary Forces (SHAEF). He held most of his fellow workers in pitying contempt. Once a junior officer advocated a certain course of action in a memorandum, saying it would leave the enemy surprised; Austin wrote in the margin 'very surprised'. When Montgomery arrived from Italy to command 21 Army Group, Austin had to contend with his intelligence chiefs Brigadier Bill Williams and Major Anthony Part. He summed them up: 'Williams, a lightweight: Part, a feather brain'.

This was unjust to Bill Williams, who was in a class by himself among intelligence officers in the field, and had gifts of a high order that Austin did not possess. Austin's capacity for work was extraordinary. At one time some 2,000 CX reports a week passed through his tray. No detail escaped him. Colleagues recall him discussing flying-bomb sites and suddenly reminding a passing corporal that there was no Lifebuoy soap in the lavatory. However, he occasionally made mistakes. He became hypnotised by some train movements just before D-Day and, despite the fact that all German armoured divisions had been reported beneath strength, conjured up an alarming estimate of 3,000 tanks in or near Normandy.

Germany was almost finished by then. Since August 1944 Hitler had lost the territory won in the early years, often to underground communist resistance fighters – in Slovakia, Bulgaria, Romania, Yugoslavia … Finland signed an Armistice with Russia; most of France, Belgium and the Netherlands were liberated; the Soviets took back Belarus and by 1945 they were also in Poland and Austria and Hungary.

On 28 April 1945, Mussolini met a humiliating end. On 30 April, Hitler killed himself and Eva Braun. Their dogs, including five new puppies, were shot dead.

The Nazis were running for their lives. On 1 May, Göbbels sacked Himmler and sustained the fiction of a new régime for just one day before killing himself. On 15 May, RHSA chief Ernst Kaltenbrunner was arrested by a US patrol, followed a week later by his boss, Heinrich Himmler, who was picked up by British troops. But where was Heinrich Müeller, the erstwhile head of the Gestapo? He had been in operational command of the Gestapo for years, since long before Heydrich's time. Never a member of the Party, which was slightly unusual. West German and Israeli secret services, and Simon Wiesenthal, hunted down Nazi war criminals of high and low rank for many decades. Müeller they couldn't trace.

He was last seen in the bunker on the evening of 1 May 1945, the day after Hitler's suicide. Hans Baur, Hitler's pilot, later quoted Müeller as saying, 'I haven't the faintest intention of being taken prisoner by the Russians.' From that day onwards, no trace of him has ever been found. While being one of the lesser-known war criminals, Müeller was from the earliest years of the Nazi regime, at the very centre of events. He oversaw Hitler's policies against the Jews and other groups and organisations deemed a threat to the state. The notorious implementor of the 'Final Solution', Adolf Eichmann, who headed the Gestapo's Office of Jewish Affairs, was Müeller's immediate subordinate. Back in August 1939, Müeller had been instrumental in orchestrating the faked and fictitious Polish army attack on Gleiwitz radio station, which Hitler used as the excuse to invade Poland. He had played a key role in initiating the torture and murder of escaping prisoners of war, signing the so-called Bullet Order in March 1944. He was in the thick of the revenge and reprisals that followed the failed plot to assassinate Hitler in July 1944, and his zeal and blood lust earned him

Hitler's gratitude in the form of the rarely awarded Knight's Cross, presented personally by the Führer in October 1944. On the surface at least, Müeller's fanaticism knew no bounds. In December 1944 he told his counter-espionage officers that Hitler's Ardennes counter-offensive was not only destined to succeed, but would ultimately lead to the recapture of Paris and Germany winning the war. He effectively used double agents against the Russians, which resulted in some of the greatest Russian intelligence setbacks of the war. There were, however, those within the Gestapo and the RHSA who believed that Müeller himself had either been turned by the Russians during this operation, or had, in fact, been working for the Russians from his earliest days in the Bavarian police service.

US President Roosevelt had taken a particular interest in apprehending Nazi war criminals and was keen to work with the Russians to bring them to trial.

On 12 April Roosevelt was at Warm Spring, his retreat in Georgia, discussing his plans to travel to the founding conference of the United Nations Organisation in San Francisco later in the month, with Dewey Long, the White House Travel Officer. At 10.50 a.m. he began work on his papers. In addition to the briefings that day about the United Nations conference were copies of material from the Allies' Counter-intelligence War Room (a combined operation under the umbrella of SHAEF, and led by America's OSS and Britain's MI5 and MI6). Their report contained a list of Nazi war criminals to be sought out by advancing Allied troops and included a list of standard questions to be asked of any arrested. One of the first questions on the list was 'where is Heinrich Müeller'?

Roosevelt was keen to keep the Russians onside in terms of the agreement reached at Yalta two months previously that such men would face trial, not summary and immediate execution. He feared that this and other aspects of the agreements reached with the Russians now appeared in jeopardy and wanted to contact Stalin directly reassuring him of America's good intentions. He therefore set about rewording a cable to Stalin that had been drafted for him by Averell Harriman, the US Ambassador in Moscow, that he considered a touch too hard-line. Shortly after approving the new wording at 1.06 p.m., Roosevelt complained of 'a terrific pain in the back of my head'. He lost consciousness moments later and was declared dead, as the result of a cerebral haemorrhage, at 3.30 p.m.

Vice President Harry Truman was sworn in as President two hours and twenty-four minutes later by the Chief Justice in the Oval Office. He was then extensively briefed on a range of critical issues, which included attempts by Himmler and Walter Schellenberg, the head of the RHSA's Foreign Intelligence Branch, to barter an agreement with the British and Americans through intermediaries in Switzerland. Truman, like Roosevelt, concurred with the policy reconfirmed with the Russians at Yalta, that there would be no separate negotiations with the Nazis. However, Schellenberg's contacts with the Allies since 1943 were referred to at length. Before too long, his name would reappear in White House briefing documents following his arrest in Denmark by British troops. He had been taken immediately to the London Cage to be interrogated, but MI19 had allowed the OSS (forerunner of the CIA) to question him too. Of particular interest to OSS and British intelligence was what Schellenberg had to say about Müeller. He was to prove the primary source of the school of thought that Müeller had possibly defected to the Russians. Schellenberg made a statement that Müeller had been in radio contact with Moscow during the final months of the war and was probably a double agent.

Müeller's immediate superior, RHSA chief Ernst Kaltenbrunner, however, fervently denied that Müeller could have been consorting with the Soviets when he was interrogated by MI19 in London the following year.

Müeller is, to this day, the most senior member of the Nazi regime whose fate remains a mystery. Possible explanations and scenarios include that he was killed, or killed himself, during the chaos of the fall of Berlin, and that his body was never found, or that he escaped from Berlin and made his way to a safe location, possibly in South America or even Russia.

He was ultimately to be the only one on the wanted list who was never located or interrogated. By the autumn of 1945 the OSS and their British counterparts had jointly gathered intelligence on a multitude of Heinrich Müellers (a very common German name), all with different dates of births and physical descriptions. Information reached the OSS that Müeller had taken the assumed name of Schwartz or Schwatzer and had escaped from Berlin with another Gestapo officer, Christian Scholz. However, neither OSS nor their British counterparts were ever able to find any trace of the two men, if indeed they had ever existed. On 20 September 1945, President Truman signed Executive Order 9621, dissolving the OSS by 1 October and splitting their responsibilities between the State Department and the War Department. Due to increasing tension with Russia and fears that they were embarking on a policy of communist expansion, Truman reversed his decision on 26 July 1947 and created a successor intelligence agency to follow in the footsteps of the OSS – the Central Intelligence Agency.

The CIA resumed the search for Müeller within weeks of its creation, sending its agents to search the home of his wartime mistress Anna Schmid. They found nothing there suggesting that he was still in contact with Schmid, nor did their renewed enquiries turn up a shred of evidence as to whether he was dead or alive. With the Cold War now hotting up, and the CIA shifting its priorities to meeting the challenge of the Soviet Union, interest in pursuing Müeller and other German war criminals declined. By this stage the conclusion seems to have been reached that Müeller was most likely dead.

British Intelligence and the Royal Air Force Special Investigation Branch also had an interest in Müeller in relation to the Stalag Luft III murders, for which he was presumed to have responsibility given his position in the Gestapo.

In 1960 Israel's Mossad intelligence agency lifted Adolf Eichmann from Argentina, and flew him to face trial in Jerusalem. It was here, during interrogation, that he sparked new interest in Müeller's whereabouts by telling the Israelis that he believed Müeller was still alive. This prompted the West German federal authorities to launch a new investigation into Müeller and his fate. The West Germans investigated the possibility that Müeller was working for the Soviet Union, but gained no corroborative information. They placed surveillance measures on his family and his former secretary in case he was communicating with them.

In 1967 in Panama City, Francis William Keith was accused of being Heinrich Müeller. West German diplomats pressed Panama to extradite him to Berlin for trial. German prosecutors said

Mrs Sophie Müeller, sixty-four, identified the man as her husband. However, he was released once fingerprints revealed he was in fact not Müeller.

The West Germans investigated several reports of Müeller's body being found and buried in the days after the fall of Berlin. None of the sources for these reports were wholly reliable; the reports were contradictory, and it was not possible to confirm any of them. The most interesting of these came from Walter Luders, a former member of the Volkssturm, who said that he had been part of a burial unit which had found the body of an SS general in the garden of the Reich Chancellery, with the identity papers of Heinrich Müeller. The body had been buried, Luders said, in a mass grave at the old Jewish Cemetery on Grosse Hamburger Strasse in the Soviet Sector. Since this location was in East Berlin in 1961, this gravesite could not be investigated, nor has there been any attempt to excavate this gravesite since the reunification of Germany in 1990.

The CIA also conducted an investigation into Müeller's disappearance in the 1960s, prompted by the defection to the West of Lieutenant-Colonel Michael Goleniewski, the Deputy Chief of Polish Military Counterintelligence. Goleniewski had worked as an interrogator of captured German officials from 1948 to 1952. He did not claim to have met Müeller, but said he had heard from his Soviet supervisors that sometime between 1950 and 1952 the Soviets had picked up Müeller and taken him to Moscow. The CIA tried to track down the men Goleniewski named as having worked with Müeller in Moscow, but were unable to confirm his story, which was in any case no more than hearsay. Israel also continued to pursue Müeller: in 1967 two Israeli operatives were caught by West German police attempting to break into the Munich apartment of Müeller's wife.

The CIA investigation concluded 'There is little room for doubt that the Soviet and Czech intelligence services circulated rumours to the effect that Muller had escaped to the West ... to offset the charges that the Soviets had sheltered the criminal ... There are strong indications but no proof that Müeller collaborated with the Russians. There are also strong indications but no proof that Muller died in Berlin.' The CIA apparently remained convinced at that time that if Müeller had survived the war, he was being harboured within the Soviet Union. But when the Soviet Union collapsed in 1991 and the Soviet archives were opened, no evidence to support this contention emerged. By the 1990s it was in any case increasingly unlikely that Müeller, who was born in 1900, was alive even if he had survived.

A secret CIA counter-intelligence briefing in 1971 called 'The Hunt for Gestapo Müeller' points out that Müeller 'would have been immensely valuable to Soviet counterintelligence' and goes on to assemble some clues. Müeller's mistress since 1940 said that on 20 April Müeller, knowing Germany was defeated, told her 'the best people are winning' – specifically the Russians.

In his 1951 book *The Labyrinth*, Schellenberg recounted his recollection of a brandy-fuelled Müeller in 1943, after the Rote Kapelle pursuit, talking passionately about the 'global aim of spiritual and material world revolution which offers a sort of positive electrical charge to Western negativism'. He talked of Harnack and others having had a *faith* in Communism that National Socialism could not inspire. That faith could win the war for the other side, he said. 'I am forced more and more to the conclusion that Stalin does these things better.'

Schellenberg's impression was that Müeller had switched sides in 1943, had been seen in Moscow in 1948, and had died shortly afterwards.

But really, nobody knows.

EPILOGUE

When the war in Europe finally came to an end on 8 May 1945, the process of justice – or more to the point, a hasty, compromise consensus of justice, agreed by the British, Americans and Russians – began to turn its wheels. According to this loose and reluctant agreement, to be proved guilty of war crimes an individual had to know that the organization which he joined was engaged in criminal activities, and was a criminal organization. This inevitably meant that a number of hardcore Nazis, many with vast quantities of blood on their hands, would, by accident or design, evade justice.

When the subject was first discussed in passing at the February 1945 Yalta Conference between Churchill, Roosevelt and Stalin, Churchill had proposed that a certain number of senior Nazi leaders would be summarily executed and other Nazis imprisoned without trial. At a dinner between the 'Big Three' prior to the official discussions, Stalin had made a proposal of his own that the Allies should 'shoot fifty thousand officers and technical experts'. Bearing in mind Stalin's dry sense of humour and his habit of provocatively testing his guests' reactions, Roosevelt pretended to play along and replied that forty-nine thousand would be quite sufficient. Churchill, at this point, apparently growled, pushed back his chair and made for the door. He was quickly brought back to the table by Stalin and Molotov, who apologised for what they claimed was a joke.

Roosevelt, timing his moment a little later in the proceedings, ventured the view that the American public would demand proper trials, and besides, they would forever pin the responsibility for the war on Hitler and place on the historical record the Nazis' infamy. Despite Stalin's semi-serious fifty thousand joke, he readily agreed with Roosevelt's proposal of a war crimes tribunal, as 'public trials possess excellent propaganda value'.

According to Guy Liddell, head of counter-espionage at MI5, it would seem that Churchill's ideas about executing key Nazis was something more than an off-the-cuff idea voiced at Yalta. Apparently, Britain's Director of Public Prosecutions, Sir Theobald Mathew, had, at some point before the Yalta Conference, made recommendations that:

> A fact finding committee should come to the conclusion that certain people should be bumped-off and that others should receive varying terms of imprisonment, that this should be put to the House of Commons and that the authority should be given to any military body finding individuals in their area to arrest them and inflict whatever punishment had been decided on.

Liddell also lamented the fact that Churchill's proposal had been rejected by Roosevelt and Stalin, and expressed the view that 'we are just being dragged down to the level of the travesties of justice that have been taking place in the USSR for the past 20 years.' A fierce anti-communist who had spent two decades at MI5 countering 'the red peril', Liddell felt that Hitler and Stalin were merely two sides of the same coin. Later the following year, he and MI5 Deputy Director Oswald Harker went to Nuremberg to watch the trial proceedings. This did nothing to alter his view that:

> Tribunals are little better than show trials. One cannot escape the feeling that most of the things the 21 are accused of having done over a period of 14 years, the Russians have done over a period of 28 years. This adds considerably to the somewhat phoney atmosphere of the whole proceedings and leads me to the point which in a way worries me most, namely that that the court is one of the victors who have framed their own charter,

their own procedure and their own rules in order to deal with the vanquished ... a dangerous precedent is being created.

Supreme Allied Commander (and later US President) Dwight D. Eisenhower may have had some degree of sympathy with Churchill's view if recent document disclosures are anything to go by. On 12 April 1945, Eisenhower, along with Generals Patten and Bradley, made his only recorded visit to a Nazi concentration camp, at Ohrdruf Nord. While Patten vomited and Bradley went mute, Eisenhower apparently forced himself to inspect the entire Buchenwald sub-camp. He then ordered that every available army unit not at the front should visit the camp. If they have any doubt what they are fighting for, he declared, the camp would show them what it was they were fighting against. One Seventh Army soldier who, as a result of Eisenhower's edict, visited Buchenwald was moved to write to his commanding officer that, 'if Reich Marshall Hermann Göring is to be shot, I would like to do the shooting.' This request was sent to Eisenhower by the Commander of the Seventh Army, General Patch. Eisenhower replied that, 'if ever we have the duty of shooting the fat bastard, this man's request should be granted if possible.'

The delusional Göring, who was allegedly taking even more morphine than ever by this point, had fled from Berlin to Bavaria. On arrival there, he learnt that Hitler had stripped him of his office and rank, and that Martin Bormann had issued a death warrant. With the Russians approaching from the east, and the American seventh army from the west, Göring, unlike his partners in crime, decided to make a beeline for the Americans and hand himself in. On 7 May, at a predetermined time, Göring, with a retinue of seventy-five others, including his wife, daughter, sister-in-law, chef, valet, and butcher, surrendered himself along with sixteen monogrammed suitcases, a red hatbox, two cyanide tablets and 20,000 paracodeine pills.

The notion of a fair trial, played out against the rule of law and judicial prudence, enabled a number of defendants to wriggle off the hook. Some were acquitted, others given prison sentences, while the likes of Göring and Himmler cheated the hangman by committing suicide. Himmler had managed to evade capture on several occasions until he was finally arrested trying to pass through Meinstedt in northern Germany on 22 May 1945. His fake documents identified him as a sergeant named Heinrich Hitzinger. What gave the game away was the fact that his documents displayed a unique stamp that British military intelligence had been briefed to keep an eye open for. This stamp identified him as an escaping member of the SS, and standing orders were to arrest anyone using this type of document. MI5 officers were immediately alerted to Himmler's arrest and sent officers to assist with his interrogation. Before much progress could be made, an army doctor was called in as it was suspected that Himmler could be concealing a cyanide capsule in his mouth. While the doctor was searching Himmler's mouth for the capsule, which was hidden between two teeth, Himmler bit on it and died within minutes. Lieutenant Colonel Sidney Noakes was one of the MI5 officers present. Prior to the outbreak of war, he had been a lawyer, before joining MI5 in 1943. His superiors apparently allowed him to keep Himmler's fake documents, while other officers present shared out between them Himmler's braces and other personal effects. Seventy-five years later in 2020, Noakes' great-niece revealed the ID documents and made them available to researchers.

As the trials moved on to prosecute members of the Gestapo, it seemed, for a moment, to be touch-and-go as to whether the prosecution case that the Gestapo was indeed a criminal organization would stick.

The defence, on behalf of the former Gestapo officers, was put by an exceptionally able German lawyer, Dr Rudolf Merkel. He called a range of witnesses such as Dr Werner Best, the former head of administration and personnel at Gestapo HQ until 1940. On the witness stand, Best asserted that the Gestapo were little different from the regular criminal police. Most Gestapo officers were not Nazi Party members, were poorly paid and transferred into the organization from divisional police departments, often without their consent. If any officer had refused the transfer, he would have been dismissed from the service without a pension. Best denied that the Gestapo was a sinister network of spies who kept an all-seeing eye on the civil population. Instead, it was run on a shoestring, with few officers who were mostly engaged in administrative duties. It relied mostly on reports coming in from the general public, most of which were personally motivated and groundless. Yes, of course, the Gestapo dealt with matters of alleged treason, but these were always handed over to the prosecutor's office following an investigation. It was a decision from the prosecutor's office as to whether the case would proceed and up to the criminal courts to decide on guilt and sentencing. Responding to the issue of the concentration camps, Best replied that the Gestapo did not run the camps and never thought that the 'life and health of inmates were being endangered in them'.

Best continued his rose-tinted evidence by adding for good measure that Gestapo officers were there to advise families of camp inmates on welfare payments they were entitled to while their relatives were in custody. Pressed about Gestapo interrogations, Best answered that 'enhanced interrogations' were very rare and were only carried out in a small number of serious treason cases – 'confessions were in no way extorted' from prisoners. While the Tribunal no doubt took Best's evidence with a very large dose of salt, Merkel very skilfully translated a number of the points Best had made into ostensibly logical legal arguments. Best himself was later sentenced to death in 1948 for war crimes in Denmark, only to have this reduced to twelve years imprisonment on appeal. In fact, Best was back on the street by 1951 after completing just under three years of his sentence due to a war crimes amnesty introduced that year. He was, however, rearrested in 1969 when West German police raided his luxury home in Mulheim. The authorities had documented a substantial case of new evidence again Best. His legal team, however, claimed that he was in ill health, too old and frail to face trial and would not, in any event, live for much longer. Finally, after three years of legal argument, the West German courts halted proceedings. The 'frail' Best was to die in 1989.

Merkel's case that the Gestapo were not a criminal organization rested partly on pre-Nazi German statutes. He argued that under German law, dating back prior to 1933, only individuals could be found guilty of specific crimes, not organizations. To establish corporate or collective guilt, he argued, the prosecution needed to prove beyond doubt that Gestapo officers and employees were not acting legally in accordance with German law that pre-dated the Nazi state and was still in force at the time of these alleged actions. He then went into greater and significant detail, following on from Best's assertion that Gestapo officers were merely civil servants, no different to regular police officers. The organization, said Merkel, was a non-political, non-Nazi state institution which carried out orders from higher authorities without question. This was, he said, a distinctly German characteristic which the Tribunal needed to appreciate and understand. Only now getting into his stride, Merkel spent a considerable amount of time explaining that the Gestapo had only approximately 16,000 officers. It was therefore far too small to be able to carry out many of the measures and actions that the prosecution had alleged. He dismissed 'the myth' that the Gestapo was staffed by committed Nazis. The reality, he said, was that the agency was staffed by individuals who were members of the pre-existing political and criminal police departments. At the outbreak of the war, only 3,000 Gestapo employees were members of the SS – less than 20 per cent of the total.

Merkel then moved on to attack a 'further myth' that Gestapo officers arrested individuals using 'protective custody orders', sending them to concentration camps without trial or judicial process of any kind. Merkel then produced boxes of documents to demonstrate that 'protective custody orders were governed by specific regulations that had been adjudicated upon by higher legal authorities, including the public prosecutor's office and the courts.'

Addressing directly accusations of torture and murder, Merkel told the tribunal that 'enhanced interrogations' were barely used and in fact, never used within Germany, particularly before the outbreak of war. Yes, there were a few exceptional cases that had been ordered by higher authorities, but even in these cases, Gestapo officers were repeatedly instructed by their superiors that 'any ill treatment during interrogations was absolutely prohibited'. With respect to Gestapo personnel taking part in the Einsatzgruppen mass murders in Poland and Russia, Merkel was at pains to underline that these men were not acting as members of the Gestapo or under Gestapo orders when they carried out these crimes. Yes, the Gestapo had participated in the preparations for community evacuations in liaison with Jewish community groups, but maintained that these were done 'under decrees and documentation emanating from higher legal authorities' such as the Office of Jewish Affairs in Berlin, who gave no details to Gestapo officers as to the ultimate purpose of these community evacuations. He ended his lengthy and detailed case by submitting that, 'It is not my duty to excuse or deny the crimes of the Nazi regime, or to whitewash individual officers within the ranks of the Gestapo who committed war crimes … however, on the basis of the evidence I have put before this Tribunal, the Gestapo as an organization cannot be deemed to be a criminal organization.'

The verdict of the tribunal on the matter of the Gestapo's culpability was equally considered, lengthy and detailed. To the great relief of the prosecution and indeed the countless victims of Gestapo and Nazi tyranny, it was ruled that the organization was indeed a criminal one. The judgement set out that it had performed its functions together with the SD and SS. It had arrested and interrogated the individuals who had been confined to concentration camps. It had directly persecuted Jewish, communist, social democratic, religious and other groups designated as enemies of the state. It had actively participated in the mass deportations and transportations of Jews to death and labour camps in Germany and throughout occupied Europe. Gestapo officials had taken part in mass murders in Russia. In light of this, all Gestapo officers and executive officials were collectively responsible for the criminal acts of the organization. The only exceptions would, the tribunal decreed, be Gestapo employees whose employment had ceased before 1 December 1939. This last section of the decision in itself raised eyebrows in a number of legal and intelligence circles, as it effectively meant that any crimes committed before this date, and there were a considerable number, were now beyond the reach of the courts.

Of the first wave of twenty-two front rank Nazis, twelve received the death penalty, although Göring cheated the hangman by biting on a cyanide pill hours before he was due to hang. Unlike many other Nazis condemned to death, including the Gestapo officers who shot the Great Escapers, it was decided that the Americans, rather than the British, would be responsible for carrying out the executions. It was therefore the inexperienced Master Sergeant John C. Woods, and not Albert Pierrepoint, who presided over what can only be described as a series of botched and incompetent executions. Woods had little knowledge of hangings, and had misled his superiors about the extent of his previous experience. He had apparently only volunteered for the post of army hangman as a means of escaping the front line. Unlike a professional hangman, such as Albert Pierrepoint, who tailored the length of the drop from the scaffold to the height, weight and physical condition of each prisoner, to ensure the neck vertebrae was severed on the 'jerk' of the rope, Woods used the same standard drop of 6 feet for each and every one of the men he hanged that day. Woods also used a 'cowboy' hangman's knot, rather than the conventional 'slip-knot'. It is now clear from contemporary records that because of these miscalculations and errors, many of those Nazis hanged that day fell from the gallows with insufficient force to snap their necks, resulting in a macabre, suffocating death. Ribbentrop and Sauckel, for example, appear to have taken fourteen minutes to die, while Keitel took twenty-eight minutes.

Furthermore, the scaffold constructed to Wood's specification added to the fiasco. Instead of a conventional scaffold, which has a double trapdoor that is caught and held open, the single trapdoor on the Nuremberg scaffold had no such mechanism, which meant that some of the condemned men were hit in the face by the rebounding trapdoor. This resulted in a number of notable head and facial injuries that are clearly evident in the post-execution photographs taken by the US army.

Despite the verdict of 'collective' guilt and its designation as a criminal organization, the anticipated Gestapo trials never materialized. Although the ruling cleared the way for the prosecution of all key Gestapo officials, the tide was turning. By 1949, the four Allied occupation zones of Germany had become two sovereign states; the Federal German Republic (or West Germany) was an amalgam of the American, British and French sectors, while the Democratic German Republic (East Germany) was effectively the former Russian sector. In 1949, during its first months of existence, the West German parliament passed a series of Immunity Laws. Under Article 131, any person who had worked for the public service between 1933 and 1945 could apply to the courts for a 'professional rehabilitation order'.

While, at first glance, this Article excluded former Gestapo and SS members, the small print stated that if individuals could prove they were police employees before 1933 and then transferred to the Gestapo, they were exempted and could apply for the professional rehabilitation order. As this applied to over 50 per cent of former Gestapo officers, the vast majority jumped through the loophole with little problem. Anecdotally, it is also believed that the threshold for providing evidence of pre-1933 employment was pretty low, and the minority of post-1933 Gestapo officers would therefore have had little difficulty in obtaining the rehabilitation order.

By 1950, the American, British and French authorities had agreed that the West German government and its courts should be given total responsibility for investigating and prosecuting war criminals. The now declassified records show that the courts were hardly overburdened by such cases. As late as 1965, a book published in East Germany called *War and Nazi War Criminals in West Germany* claimed to list the names of 1,800 former key Nazis who still held positions of rank and responsibility in West Germany. The list included fifteen government ministers, 100 generals and admirals, 828 senior judges and public prosecutors, 245 diplomats, and 297 police officials. The West German government issued an immediate statement denying the book's claims, and calling the book 'pure falsification'. A copy of the book that found its way into the hands of MI5 was read in detail by an unnamed officer, who wrote a scribbled note that concluded the lists were undoubtedly genuine, although the number of ex-Nazis holding key posts in West Germany was vastly underestimated by whoever had compiled the lists.

In a sense, Merkel, Best and the host of other deniers and apologists had been correct in that the Gestapo, and indeed the Nazi state apparatus, could not have acted to the extent that it did without the active connivance of the civil population, not only in Germany but in the occupied territories where many of these crimes and atrocities took place. Virtually all formerly occupied countries were conflicted by the fact that high-ranking officials and a significant number of everyday people had collaborated with the Nazis. In France, for example, between D-Day and the end of the war, at least 9,000 French citizens were murdered as the result of accusations of being collaborators. A total of 58,000 cases of collaboration were dealt with by French courts. Despite the number of cases taken to court, it is clear that the French state avoided punishing those who had played an active part in assisting the Gestapo in rounding up French Jewish communities. Around a quarter of France's Jews had been murdered by 1945. Even this token judicial effort did not last beyond 1953 when an amnesty law was passed and it actually became a criminal offence to name and accuse anyone of a war crime.

Jean Leguay, the senior French civil servant who organized the deportations with, it has to be said, much enthusiasm and zeal, never stood trial. He became an executive in an American firm in New York.

In the final analysis, as the former MI14 officer Noel Annan (or Lord Annan as he was by this time) observed, 'The desire to torture and kill those who are different lies deep in the human race and has erupted in every continent since 1945. But to do so on the scale and with the efficiency that occurred in Germany required a man and an ideology.'

Appendix 1

MI14 FILE ON REINHARD HEYDRICH

M.I.14 (b)
Report 1

H. was born on 7th March, 1904 in Halle (Province of Saxony) as son of the Director of a private musical academy. His mother also descends from a family of musicians. H. was educated at a Halle High School and at an early age (1918) became a member of some ultra-national youth organisation. Later in his life, H. used to brag about legendary feats of heroism (and terrorism) which he claimed to have performed at the time. In 1922 H. joined the German Navy, was commissioned as Sub-Lieutenant in 1926 and was posted to the ill-fated training ship "Niobe". During the last journey of this ship, from which it never returned, he was, however, not on board. Later Heydrich, promoted to the rank of Lieutenant in 1928, became Intelligence Officer in the Baltic Command of the German Navy ('Admiralstabsleitung der Marinestation Ostsee'). It was probably in this position that Heydrich got into contact with Admiral Canaris, the famous Chief of German Military Intelligence, a connection which, rumours contend, has never been cut. In 1931, Heydrich left the Navy, apparently owing to some scandal, the most current rumour being that this scandal was a homosexual one. In the same year H. joined the Nazi Party in Hamburg and made a rapid career: The end of the same year saw him already 'Sturmfuhrer' of the SS, attached to the SS High

Command in Munich, and in 1932, after a short spell of duty in East Prussia, Heydrich rose to the rank of 'Standartenfuhrer' (approximately Regimental Commander). Heydrich's job in the SS was the re-organisation of the existing spying and information services of the SS (the so-called 'S.D.' = Security Service of the SS) and he did this job so thoroughly that the mopping up of political opponents in 1933 was done with a thoroughness and swiftness which was decisive for the continuation of Hitler's regime. Thus, in the second half of September 1941 special difficulties were encountered by the German authorities in Czecho-Slovakia. Apparently Neurath, the Reichsprotektor, was considered too weak or the trouble was too strong. Therefore, Heydrich was kept on the spot as Deputy Reichsprotektor and the usual mass executions and phoney trials took place for several weeks.

His position as Deputy Reichsprotektor, however, did not prevent Heydrich from remaining Security Chief of German-occupied Europe. Thus, towards the middle of this month of May, Heydrich went again 'on tour', this time to the Western-occupied territories which had shown considerable unrest following upon British air and commando attacks. On the 7th May H. installed Oberg, the most 'capable' of the terrorist SS, Police and Gestapo Leaders in Poland, as Senior SS & Police Leader for occupied France. On the 7th, H. was reported to be in The Hague (mass shootings of former Dutch officers) and on the 26th he was reported back in Prague and received the heads of the Czech puppet government and administration, announcing to them the measures to be taken for the simplification' of administration in the Protectorate.

If Heydrich should not survive the attempt or if he is invalided for some appreciable time, the loss for the Nazi regime would be very serious indeed. It can safely be said that next to Himmler Heydrich is the soul of the terror machinery from which depends the fate of the inner front in Germany. The Gestapo machine, certainly exceedingly well organised, is already – and admittedly – heavily taxed by the lack of man-power and the rising unrest. The loss of the 'master mind' will have serious consequences. Another point worth noting is that Heydrich was one of the most important members of the Himmler group within the Nazi Party, all the more important as he controlled the Gestapo, the most important instrument of power in Germany.

PEOPLE ROUND HEYDRICH

The following personalities in the Protectorate were among Heydrich's closest collaborators and may be rather prominent in the coming days:

(1) Karl Hermann FRANK,   Senior SS & Police Leader in the Protectorate, Under-Secretary of State and as such permanent Deputy to the Reichsprotektor. (He issued the Proclamations and warrants after the attempt!)

(2) [Paul] RIEGE,   Chief of the (uniformed) "Ordnungspolizei" in The Protectorate, Major-General of the Police.

(3) Horst BOHME,   SS-Standartenführer, Chief of the Security Police in the Protectorate.

(4) Dr. GESCHKE,   SS-Standartenführer, Gestapo Chief in Prauge.

(5) v.TREUENFELD,   SS-Brigade Leader, Major-General of the Police and chief of Armed SS in the Protectorate.

(6) v.TOUSSAINT,   Major-General, Military Commander in the Protectorate.

Appendix 2

MI14 FILE ON HERMANN GÖRING

MI14 (b)

Born at Rosenheim in Upper Bavaria in January 1893. After attending Gymnasia in Furth and Ansbach and cadet schools, he obtained his lieutenant's commission in 1912 in the 112th Infantry Regiment in Mulhausen in Alsace. An aerial observer in October 1914, he became successively a pilot, a fighting pilot and squadron-leader, received the order 'pour le merite' in June 1918, and was the last commander of the famous Richthofen squadron.

After demobilisation he retired with the rank of captain and went to Denmark as a flying instructor in 1919. In 1920-21 he was chief instructor at the Svenska Luft Trafik in Stockholm. In 1922 and 1923 he attended Munich University and studied history, national economy and the party system. He took a prominent part in the Hitler "Putsch" in 1923, was wounded, and smuggled over into Austria by his friends. He subsequently went to Rome, where in 1924-25 he studied local conditions and established relations with Mussolini. 1925-26 he again spent time in Sweden, working as a journalist in Stockholm: then for a period he took to drink and other things, and rather went to seed.

After the amnesty in 1927 he returned to Germany and settled in Berlin as a journalist, writing mainly about air questions. Elected as a National Socialist Deputy in 1928, he first attracted attention by a stormy speech at the University of Munich; was re-elected to the Reichstag in September 1930. Göring had the confidence of Hitler, and accompanied the latter when he visited the President in the autumn of 1931, and during the subsequent negotiations with General von Schleicher regarding the possibility of a coalition between the Centre and Nazis.

After the elections in July 1932 Göring was elected Speaker of the Reichstag, and began to play a big role in the Nazi party. On the formation on the 30th January, 1933, of the Hitler Government, Göring was appointed Minister without portfolio, Commissioner for Aviation in the Reich and Commissioner for the Ministry of the Interior in Prussia.

As a result of his violent action against the Marxist parties before and particularly after the Reichstag fire, the elections of March gave a majority to the Nazi-Nationalist alliance. Göring continued by wild speeches to whip up feeling against Marxists and Jews, and must be partly responsible for the excesses which occurred in Prussia. At the same time, he began to agitate for the restoration to Germany of her place in the air. As a result of the decree of the 7th April establishing Statthalter in the various States, Göring was appointed Prime Minister of Prussia and the Deputy of the Statthalter.

Appendix 3

MI14 FILE ON
ERNST KALTENBRUNNER

MI14 (b)/MI19/020
Statement made by ERNST KALTENBRUNNER, 8.8.45

KALTENBRUNNER said regarding Eva BRAUN:

As far as I know, HITLER made the acquaintance of Miss Eva BRAUN during the years 1926/29 in Munich. At that time she may have been around 20 years of age. She was medium sized, slender, of somewhat delicate appearance, with blonde hair and dark eyes, a very pleasant voice and could be called pretty, but not a striking beauty.

Miss BRAUN comes from the low-middle class, and worked in Munich. She may have been employed with a firm of editors as she was a brilliant photographer. She was the only person besides the editor and photographer, HOFFMANN, who had the privilege to reproduce and sell pictures of HITLER. This was also her economical foundation, apart from her insignificant working income. Her income out of the picture sales was very high, due to HITLER's intention to make her financially independent and to avoid the necessity for either of them to speak about material things in their relationship with each other. She was, moreover, very unpretentious as far as I could see, and enjoyed HITLER's closest attention.

I had the impression that she loved HITLER humanly and sincerely and that the erotic factor played in their relationship a very secondary role. In return for that their spiritual comprehension was all the more profound.

In the presence of Miss BRAUN, one never talked about politics as HITLER deliberately avoided the subject and saw to it that others did the same. Miss BRAUN had, in my belief, little interest in such conversations, but was an excellent discussion partner for HITLER on all domains of art and belletristic [belles-lettres]. Miss BRAUN was an excellent dancer, which profession, according to my knowledge, she has studied. She was very erudite, and often discussed books with HITLER. A mutual passion existed for old pictures and she took a large part in such discussions before purchases were made and investments undertaken for one of the Galleries.

She devoted herself moderately to sport, liked ski-ing, skating and tennis and did an hour's exercise every day, always in ladies' company, never with gentlemen. She had her permanent flat in Munich but often visited Berchtesgaden or Berlin. HITLER worried with paternal anxiety about her health, his physicians also looked after her. She was not allowed to fly or to drive a car more than 60 kilometres an hour.

On the other hand, I could see that Miss BRAUN took great pains to look after HITLER's personal needs. She made efforts to see that HITLER could get his vegetarian diet in spite of living up to all food orders by the physicians, and she was anxious that he could get more sleep. She made his whole abnormal daily schedule fit her own. Accordingly, she directed HITLER's permanent entourage without getting the reputation of becoming a 'Commanderess', and she remained always a perfect lady and inconspicuous housewife ['Hausfrau']. I deem it quite possible that HITLER married Miss BRAUN, as it was stated by one of the surviving witnesses of the last days. I don't think that any other woman stood closer to HITLER, just as her exclusive sympathy for HITLER must be assumed. A suggestion that Miss BRAUN had any relation with other men I consider absolutely false. If there were found in her photo-album pictures of other men or even several snapshots of one certain man, this cannot be considered as proof. If the man in question belonged temporarily to the Adjutantur (HITLER's personal staff) it may be pointed out that HITLER's closer 'entourage' (here I mean Adjutantur) including Miss BRAUN, considered themselves as one family, and it is quite possible that confidential friendships were formed. To every member of this 'entourage', though, the true and affectionate liaison between HITLER and Eva BRAUN was known, and their relationship respected. The result of this was in fact that nobody, not even many of the highest placed men in Germany, knew anything about the intimate relationship existing between them.

Appendix 4

GESTAPO OFFICERS INVOLVED IN THE STALAG LUFT III MURDERS

Name	Office	Fate
Absalon, Gunther	Breslau	Died in Soviet prison May 1948
Baatz	Reichenberg	Prematurely released from Red Army Camp
Boschert Heinrich	Karlsruhe	Sentenced to death 3 September 1947, commuted to life imprisonment
Breithaupt Walter	Saarbrücken	Sentenced to life imprisonment 3 September 1947, released October 24 1952
Bruchardt, Reinhold	Danzig	Sentenced to death 6 November 1948, commuted to life imprisonment upon Britain abandoning the death sentence experimentally, released 1956
Dankert	Breslau	Untraced
Denkmann, Artur	Kiel	Sentenced to ten years' imprisonment 3 September 1947
Dissner, Max	Strasbourg	Suicide 11 May 1948
Ganninger, Otto	Karlsruhe	Suicide 26 April 1946
Geith, Eduard	München	Executed at Hamlin 27 February 1948
Gmeiner, Josef	Karlsruhe	Executed at Hamlin 27 February 1948

Name	Office	Fate
Hampel, Walter	Breslau	Arrested 1 September 1948, charge not proceeded with in accordance with British government's new war crimes policy
Hänsel, Richard	Breslau	Acquitted 6 November 1948
Herberg, Walter	Karlsruhe	Executed at Hamlin 27 February 1948
Hiker, Heinrich	Strasbourg	Prematurely released from French custody, charged but case dismissed 23 December 1966
Hug, Julius	Danzig	Untraced
Isselhorst, Erich	Strasbourg	Executed at Strasbourg 23 February 1948 for other atrocities
Jacobs, Walter	Kiel	Executed at Hamlin 27 February 1948
Kahler, Hans	Kiel	Executed at Hamlin 27 February 1948
Kilpe, Max	Danzig	Arrested 27 August 1948, charges not proceeded with
Kiske, Paul	Breslau	Killed during Siege of Breslau
Kiowsky, Friedrich	Brno/Zlin	Executed in Czechoslovakia 1947
Knappe,	Breslau	Killed during Siege of Breslau
Knippelberg, Adolf	Brno/Zlin	Prematurely released from Red Army Camp 1945
Koslowsky, Otto	Brno/Zlin	Executed in Czechoslovakia 1947
Kreuzer,	Breslau	Untraced, probably killed 1945
Kuhnel,	Breslau	Killed during Siege of Breslau
Lang,	Breslau	Untraced, probably killed 1945
Läuffer,	Breslau	Suicide reported, not confirmed
Lux,	Breslau	Killed during Siege of Breslau
Nölle, Wilhelm	Brno/Zlin	Arrested 10 June 1948, charge not proceeded with
Pattke, Walter	Breslau	Untraced, probably killed 1945
Post, Johannes	Kiel	Executed at Hamlin 27 February 1948

Name	Office	Fate
Preiss, Otto	Karlsruhe	Executed at Hamlin 27 February 1948
Prosse,	Breslau	Died 1944
Romer, Hugo	Brno/Zlin	Untraced
Sasse, Walter	Danzig	Escaped from internment camp
Schäfer, Oswald	München	Acquitted 11 December 1968
Schauschütz, Franz	Brno/Zlin	Executed in Czechoslovakia 1947
Schemer, Martin	München	Suicide 25 April 1945
Schimmel, Alfred	Strasbourg	Executed at Hamlin 27 February 1948
Schmauser, Ernst	Breslau	Captured by Red Army
Schmdt, Franz	Kiel	Suicide 27 October 1946
Schmidt, Friedrich (Fritz)	Kiel	Sentenced to two years' imprisonment May 1968
Schmidt, Oskar	Kiel	Executed at Hamlin 27 February 1948
Schneidere, Johann	München	Executed at Hamlin 27 February 1948
Schröder, Robert	Breslau	Not charged, used as material witness
Schulz, Emil	Saarbrücken	Executed at Hameln 27 February 1948
Schwartzer, Friedrich	Brno/Zlin	Executed in Czechoslovakia 1947
Seetzen, Heinrich	Breslau	Suicide 28 September 1945
Spann, Leopold	Saarbrücken	Killed in air raid Linz, 25 April 1945
Struve, Wilhelm	Kiel	Sentenced to ten years' imprisonment 3 September 1947
Venediger, Günther	Danzig	Sentenced to two years' imprisonment after four years of appeals, 17 December 1957

Name	Office	Fate
Voeiz, Walter	Danzig	Untraced, believed killed
Weil, Emil	Műnchen	Executed at Hamlin 27 February 1948
Weissman, Robert	Reichenberg	Held by French authorities but not transferred
Wenzler, Herbert	Danzig	Arrested 1948, charge not proceeded with
Weyland, Robert	Reichenberg	Refuge in Soviet zone
Wieczorek, Erwin	Breslau	Sentenced to death 6 November 1948, conviction quashed on review
Wielen, Max	Breslau	Sentenced to life imprisonment 3 September 1947
Witt, Hary	Danzig	Arrested September 1948, charge not proceeded with

Appendix 5

MI14 FILE ON GESTAPO (PRAGUE OFFICE)

MI14 (b)
The German Secret Police: Prague Section

THE GERMAN SECRET POLICE: PRAGUE SECTION

The German Secret Police of ill fame and known everywhere by the abbreviation 'Gestapo' have their quarters in the palace of the Petschek Bank in Prague II, Bredovska Ulice. In this palace are more that 250 officers and also private dwellings for leading officials and members of the staff.

As far as can be established, the staff of the Prague Section numbers about 274. In this number is included legal assistants and clerical and executive sections. Beyond these is an auxiliary staff, the exact number of which is yet unknown, but in which are included the members of the S.S.

The corps of legal assistants and executives can be divided into Civil Servants on the one hand and auxiliary police, known as 'Hipo', on the other. The majority of these, with the exception of the Director of the Section, Regierungsrat Dr.GESCHKE, are in inferior posts. The centre of this corps is made up of obedient Party followers, members of the Party who, for the most part, have had no technical training at all. Professional police officials are in a minority. It will already have become apparent that in the

The most wicked and worst creatures are BAUER and WEIMANN. They are put on to the most brutal work. If a prisoner keeps silent or is obstinate, he is handed over by the legal assistant in charge who interrogate him for so long, and most at night, that he eventually confesses. Both are typical representatives of the Gestapo regime – narrow, ruthless and brutal to the point of sadism. It is said that they were actively concerned in the execution of the Czech students in November, 1939.

As yet nothing definite has been established about the other divisions of the sub-section I I B. M.

Department III. This deals with defence. The Director is Kriminalkommissar CLEMENS, aged about 28 and with middle-school education. Czech matters, chiefly interrogations of arrested Czech officers, is directed by Inspektor FLEISCHNER, a man of about 50. He is depicted as a bird of prey who tortures his victims with subtlety. The methods of these tortures of the Gestapo are well enough known. As well as these, there are 27 Czech police officials attached to the Gestapo.

Appendix 6

MI14 FILE ON GESTAPO & THE LAW

MI14 (b)

Certain acts, hostile to the government and the people, are considered political crimes in any country; they need no further discussion. But whereas, according to the democratic conception of justice, such offences are clearly defined and graded from misdemeanours to crimes by a precise legal code and a corresponding set of precedents, Gestapo procedure is based on the unlimited interpretation of the above-listed 'political crimes'. Its guiding principles seem to range from opportunist expediency to a rather musty mysticism.

Thus, the Gestapo adds to the more conventional concept of treason and high treason any action, planned or executed, and even any opinion, suspected or expressed, which it considers dangerous or inconvenient to the Nazi party, any of its formations or leading personalities, its uniforms or insignias, and its ritual or traditions. Nor does 'guilt' in the eyes of the Gestapo stop with the committing or planning of such 'crimes'. Passive sympathy with a political 'offence' often suffices to affect intervention by the secret State police.

The next step of repression is made possible by the way in which Nazis have deliberately blurred and mixed together the concepts of Government, State, Nation, People and Party, and infused fictitious interests into the resulting politico-national creation. The safeguarding of such interests may then be construed as including an unlimited range of 'crimes' from communist activities, agitation or sympathies to offences against the privilege of German citizenship and the 'honour of the German Race', and even beyond that, to mere dislike of German folklore, songs, art or any other form of 'Kultur'.

To the crime of transmission, publication and general spreading of anti-Nazi propaganda is added the mere listening to 'illegal' broadcasts, perusal of enemy or opposition leaflets, or reading of banned literature.

Acts which elsewhere would be considered minor economic or financial infractions of the law are in Germany crimes against the Government and the people and as such become the concern of the Gestapo. This category is stretched to cover a list of crimes ranging from offences against foreign exchange and currency regulations and hoarding of goods listed as essential down to any communication or transaction with elements regarded as non-German or anti-Nazi. A peasant who, without a permit, slaughters a pig is prosecuted as vigorously as somebody accused of 'harbouring thoughts unworthy of a German'.

The use of the thin cloak of legality was never more than a convenient pretence and was never guided by considerations of justice. The basic edict of the Prussian Decree of 10 Feb 36 however authorised the Reichsführer SS Chef d. Deutschen Polizei 'to take measures necessary for the preservation of security and order, even <u>exceeding the limits previously defined by law'</u>. Not content with the mock-interpretation of a so-called legal code, the Gestapo could thus proceed to supplement the law by any extra-legal action it considered necessary. Subsequently, a HITLER proclamation of 22 Oct 38 removed even theoretical limitations, such as they were, by pointing to the 'unwritten law' of Germany as expressed in "the will of the Party Leader". The proclamation stated bluntly that 'every means adopted for the purpose of carrying out the will of the Leader is considered legal <u>even though it may conflict with existing statutes and legal precedent'</u>: the Gestapo has received its unlimited 'hunting licence'. Thus, long after the body had been buried, the very ghost of 'Government by law' departed from the German scene.

As may be seen from the foregoing, Gestapo methods have passed through three stages of evolution – undefined interpretation of the law, unchecked supplementing of the legal code, and authorised violation of statute precedent. The Gestapo is now in a position to apply methods of these three successive stages of justice separately or in any convenient combination. Since the Gestapo is in no way subject to veto, review, or advice by the judiciary its powers are absolute and unlimited both in theory and in practice.

SECRET
Postüberwachungsdienst (Postal censorship)
In democratic countries censorship of letters does not exist in peace-time. Even in war-time such intrusion into the private rights of the individual are at best regarded as a necessary evil and limited to safeguarding information that might be of use to the enemy; but in Germany such considerations of civil liberties are no longer permitted to interfere with measures for the maintenance of Nazi power. Postal censorship has therefore become a regular police function.

It is a widely known fact that such censorship based on the 1933 Decree for the protection of people and Government was put into operation immediately after the Advent of power. Details of the early organisations of this control, however, are not available. As previously mentioned (in Para 85) some of the functions of censorship may originally have been carried out by the Verwaltungs-polizei in cooperation with the postal authorities, but the system has, since 1933, expanded so enormously that censorship can no longer be regarded as an administrative function; it has become a powerful instrument for the subjugation of the German people.

Theoretically certain limitations on the power of censorship have been imposed, but they are neutralised by so many clauses open to almost any interpretation that it seems futile to discuss them. In practice censorship by the German security Police is limited only by the machinery and personnel at its disposal. In order to 'legalise' a purely extra legal function of this kind German Police authorities again stress the principle of crime prevention and point to the responsibility of the

Staatsschutzkorps for protecting the German people against all political and criminal attacks.

Three types of censorship of communications must be distinguished: inside Germany and occupied countries, to and from foreign countries and to and from Armed Forces. All three types include the control of every means of communication, postal censorship being, of course, the largest and most important task.

Originally the Police took over only the censorship inside Germany and occupied countries and there are no reasons to believe that this merely took on the form of 'snap checks' against specific persons who were politically or otherwise suspected. On 30 June 1938, it was decreed (MBliV – Miniterialblatt für die innere verwaltung – p.1087/38) that the sole authority for official violation of the privacy of personal communications rests with the Geheire staatspolizeiant and, through it with the Stapo-Leitstellen. This decree was amended on 19 mar 1943 giving the same authority to the Reichskriminal-polizeiant and the Kripo-Leitstellen, but pointing out the technical difficulties which are in the way of postal and other censorship against specific persons. It appears, therefore, that no large-scale machinery was set up inside the country to control all mail and other private communications. Man-power shortage in war-time has probably added to the difficulties and has most likely forced the Kripo and Gestapo to limit themselves to the control of a relatively small amount of letters and to specific instances only.

Mail to and from foreign countries is censored at the Auslands-Briefprüfstellen (Censorship Offices for Foreign Mail) which were as far as can be ascertained set up and controlled, until the summer of 1944, by the former Ahwehr, the Military Intelligence. Thirteen of these offices have been identified, 6 of them located in the old Reich, one in Austria and the others in occupied countries. They control 100 per cent of the letters and telegrams to and from foreign countries. It is not quite clear, yet it is likely, that the Gestapo and the Kripo in the absence of any censorship machinery of their own also made use of the Briefprüfstellen, by indicating specific cases for observation and report.

Concentration Camps

The ruthless methods of the Nazi Police are most apparent in the workings of the Concentration camps, where the Gestapo imitation of the Inquisition rises to its climax. As already explained the Nazi interpretation of the term Schutzhaft (protective custody) means the temporary or permanent detention of persons, a large proportion of whom have never been legally tried or sentenced by a Court of Law. Protective custody has also been extended to include persons who have served their term of imprisonment according to the sentence awarded by a Court, but are further detained by order of the Gestapo (Secret State police), the Kripo (Criminal Police), the SD (Security Service) or the Geheime Feldpolizei (Secret Field Police). It is in the Konzentrationslager (officially abbreviated in Germany by the letters KL, but popularly referred to as KZ – concentration camps) that such persons are detained.

Actual detention orders appear to be issued as follows:

a) The Kripo handles cases involving Borufs or Gewohnheitsverbrecher (Professional or Habitual Criminals).
b) The Gestapo prosecuting all 'political' criminals.
c) The Geheime Feldpolizei (GFP- Secret Field police), as sister organisation of the Gestapo within the armed Forces, may in some instances, through the Gestapo, submit civilians as well as soldiers for detention.

It is not likely that the SD issue direct detention orders. Instead that branch probably submits its finding to the Gestapo with the recommendation for the subjects removal to a Concentration Camp.

To affect the release of an inmate in a Concentration camp, approval must be obtained from the Gestapo and Kripo, and the SD is almost certainly consulted as well.

The number of Concentration Camps in Germany and occupied countries has risen constantly and runs into hundreds at the present time. All available information on them, especially also on their administration and chain of command has been published in B.D.S./G/6: 'German Concentration Camps'. Within the scope of the present book it is only possible to mention briefly the links between the Concentration Camps and the various branches of the German Police.

In paragraph 2, sub-para 4, of the statutory regulation amplifying the decree regarding the secret State Police, issued 10 Feb. 1936, it is stated that the Gestapo-Ant is entrusted with the administration of the governmental Concentration Camps. The bulk of the Concentration Camp guards, however, were not drawn from the Gestapo or any other German Police branch, but were recruited from the Allgemeine-SS and became known as the SS TotenKopf-Verbünde (SS Death's Head Units), notorious for their ruthlessness and brutality. Their Chief, SS OPG Theodor EICKE was made Inspekteur der Konzentrationslager (Inspector of Concentration Camps) and was as such directly responsible to HITLER. It was stated in 1940 that this Inspeckteur and his office were in charge of all direction and administration of the camps. In 1941 EICKE took command of the Waffen-SS Panzer Division 'Totenkopf', and was succeeded as Inspeckteur of the KL's by SS-GF, Genlt. N-SS Richard GLUCKS. (EICKES was killed in 1943 on the Eastern Front).

As the war progressed and the manpower shortage in Germany became more acute, the SS realised the great value of slave labour held in Concentration Camps. All the economic administration of SS and Police was, from 1941 on, concentrated in the Wirtschafts-u. Verwltungshauptaut of the SS (SS-WVHA – SS Economic Administrive Department), which among other offices took over the Haushalt und Bauten (Department of Budget and Buildings) of the Police.

In 1942 the office of Inspekteur der Konzentrationslager was abolished and also incorporated in to the WVHA, and GLUCK became Chief of Antsgruppe D, Führung und Veruultung der Konzentrationslager (Serpervision and Administration of KL's), in the WVHA.

It appears that since then all administrative and economic matters concerning Concentration Camps have been handled by the Antsgruppe D. Further details concerning the WVHA and its link with the Concentration Camps will be found in E.D.S./G/S, The Allgemeine SS.

This change in the administration of the Camps leaves to the Gestapo merely the supervision of KL inmates and political control over the KLs. Exact details are not known and it is likely that even this responsibility for political control is shared with the SD. This control appears to be exercised through the Political Commissar in each camp, who according to reports, is a member of the political section of the Stapo (Lait) stolle, in whose area the Concentration Camp is located.

Appendix 7

MI14 FILE ON AMT IV RE-ORGANIZATION

MI14 (b)
S.I.S/C.X/12799

TOP SECRET
COPY NO: 67

AMT IV: Re-organisation

Since the publication of 'Revision Notes No 2' on Amt IV of the RSHA, new evidence has been received which largely confirms former conclusions and gives a perfectly clear picture of the internal sub-divisions of AMT IV after re-organisation last summer.

It would appear that when the Abwehr was dissolved and the greater part of Abwehr I I I went into Amt IV, this change was combined with a general re-organisation of Amt IV. It was now divided into two sections IV A and IV B. IV A, generally speaking, continued the former activities of Amt IV and was further subdivided into Referate numbered from 1 to 6. It can now scarcely be doubted that all Gestapo (left) stellen in the Reich as well as Abteilungen IV in Einsatzkommandos abroad were re-organised to follow this system of numbering. IV B took over the functions of those parts of Abwehr I I I which were absorbed

by Amt IV, with the exception of III N, which because IV A3, IV
B was also divided into numbered sub-sections ranging from 1 to
4. IV B1 to IV B3 had territorial responsibilities and presumably
were engaged, for the most part, on what had formerly been the
work of Abwehr III F. IV B 4 dealt with passports, identity papers
and visas. This may well mean that it took over the functions of
the former Abwehr III C.

It may be assumed that when IV A or IV B are now referred
to, the new and not the old divisions of Amt IV are meant. This
clears up the apparent anomaly of Abwehr I I I F being absorbed
by Amt IV B 3. In fact, this is purely a territorial sub-division of
the new IV B and has nothing to do with the old IV B. which
dealt with ideological opponents of the Nazi regime.

A table is appended showing in full the new divisions of
Amt IV and their functions. The sub-sections of IV A will be
found to correspond almost entirely with what had already
been deduced from the study of various Abteilungen IV
abroad. There are, however, one or two additional points of
particular interest. Foremost amongst these is, perhaps, the
listing of the 'Free Germany' National Committee as one of the
interests of IV A1 a.

AMT IV
Investigating and combating of opposition
(Gegnererforschung and bekaemfung)

IV A1 a   Communism, Marxism and auxiliary
               organizations ("Free Germany" National
               Committee) in Germany, the occupied territories
               and abroad, war offences so far as they fall into
               the above-mentioned spheres, wireless crimes,
               illegal Communist and Marxist propaganda,
               hostile propaganda (including leaflets), Partisan
               activities (Bandenunwesen) in Germany,
               Lower Styria and Upper Carniola/Carinthia
               (Oberkrain/Kaernten), German and Allied (i.e.
               satellite) prisoners of war in Soviet Russian
               captivity.

IV A1 b	Reaction, opposition, Legitimism, liberalism, pacifism, insidious anti-Nazi activities (Heimtueckeangelegenheiten), disintegration of the war effort and grumbling (Miesmacherei), defeatism, discontented members of the Wehrmacht, including prisoners of war, and their relatives.
IV A2 a	Prevention and combating of sabotage, political assassinations, political forgeries of passports and documents, terrorists, syndicalists.
IV A2 b	Parachute agents, playing back of captured agents (Funkspiele).
IV A3 a	Counter-espionage (Abwehrangelegenheiten), Gesellschaftaespionage, cases of high treason through negligence (fahrlaessiger Landesverrat).
IV A3 b	Economic affairs in Germany, in occupied territories, in relations with foreign countries and vice versa, economic 'Surveillance' in Switzerland, currency offences.
IV A3 c	Frontier matters, local frontier crossings (kleiner Grenzverkehr) and frontier incidents.
IV A3 (IIIN)	Security of communications (Abwehr ueber Nachrichtenverkehr, Verstoesse gegen denselben).
IV A4 a	Catholicism and Protestantism, religious sects, other churches, Freemasons in Germany and the occupied territories, matters of belief (Grundsatzangelegenheiten) in foreign countries as well.
IV A4 b	Jews, emigrants, matters concerning the incomes of enemies of the people and the State (volks-und staatsfeindliche Vermoegensangelegenheiten), cases

of persons being deprived of Reich citizenship in Germany and occupied territories.

IV A5 a   Schutzdienst, special tasks, anti-social conduct towards evacuees, German work-shirkers (deutsche Arbeitsbummelanten), demeanour hostile to the community.

IV A5 b   Party matters and Press.

IV A6 a   Card index and personal files

IV A6 b   Protective custody.

IV 8   (NB The designation looks most unlikely and may be a misprint in the original document).
Foreign workers and foreign prisoners of war, plans to escape and escapes of prisoners of war in Germany and the occupied territories, illicit conveying of letters to and by foreign workers, refusals to work by foreigners.

IV B   deals with all matters which were formerly the concern of the Abwehr III N, except, of course, III N, which is under IV A 3, and the sections of II which deal with military security and remain under the O.K.W.

IV B1 a   France, Belgium.

IV B1 b   Holland, England, North America and Canada.

IV B1 c   Denmark, Norway, Sweden, Finland.

IV B2 a   Eastern territories and the Soviet Union, White Ruthenian and Ukrainian émigrés (Vertrauensstellen).

IV B2 b   The Government General.

IV B2 c   The Protectorate, Slovakia.

IV B3 a   The Balkans (including Hungary and Romania, Bulgaria, Turkey, the Far East)

IV B3 b   Switzerland, Italy, Spain, Portugal, Africa, South America.

IV B4 a   Passports.

IV B4 b   Identity documents, Kennkarten, Auslaenderpolizei.

IV B4 c   Central Visa office.

(N.B. It will be remembered that the work of Abwehr III F in territories not occupied by Germany was taken over by Amt VI Z. The mention of certain such territories under IV B is therefore difficult to explain: the possibility of a certain duplication of work in this field cannot be ruled out).

Appendix 8

MI14 FILE ON THE ORGANISATION OF THE GESTAPO

MI14 (b)
Report No. A.4 5619
The description of the organisation and activity of the German secret police (Geheime Staatspolizei, ab. 'Gestapo') given below was compiled from memory, documents etc. having been destroyed. Thus, the following description is necessarily brief and contains only the most general and basic data on the subject. Several details have been omitted, as it would be difficult to write these without reference to documents.

This description, furthermore, refers to the organisation of the Gestapo preceding the outbreak of the war. The changes which might have taken place in the organisation and activity of the Gestapo during the war, are not known; this is due to the speedy development of the military operations in Poland and the short duration of the campaign. The sparse documentary evidence which came to hand could not be adequately studied and used. But certain data regarding the preparation of the subversive and sabotage action in Poland by the Gestapo and the prominent part which its agents played in it, have been taken into consideration in this description.

The General Organisation of the German Police

The German Police is divided into two main groups:
1. 'Ordnungspolizei' – Public Order Police, which is uniformed.
2. 'Sicherheitspolizei' – Security Police, which is not uniformed.

'Ordnungspolizei" consists of the following branches of Police:

a) 'Schutapolizei' (Schupo) – Safety Police stationed in larger towns.
b) 'Gemeidenpolizei' – Communal Police carrying out its duties in smaller towns and communities.
c) 'Gendarmerie' – Gendarmery acting in small settlements and villages.

Another separate division of the Gendarmery is the motorised Street police (Motorisierte Strassenpolizei), which is responsible for order on the roads and highways.

The 'Sicherheitspolizei' is divided into two branches:

a) 'Kriminalpolizei' – Criminal Police designed for the prosecution of common crimes.
b) 'Politische Polizei' – Political Police whose duty is to prosecute political offences.

The chief of the German Police is the 'Neichsfuehrer de S.S' – Heinrich Himmler, and the following are subordinated to him:

Chief of the Public Order police – Gen.d.Pol. Kurt DALUEGE

Chief of the Security Police – S.S. Gruppenfuehrer Reinhold Heydrich.

The Chief of the German Police directs the whole Police Organisation through the intermediary of two offices, which jointly form the central governing office of the German Police.

'Aust Ordnungspolizei' – for matters dealing with the police responsible for public order.

'Aust Sicherheitapolizei' – for matters dealing with the police responsible for the security of the State.

The duties of the Political Police are carried out by the Secret state Police, the head office of which is the "Gehdmes Staatapolizei Aust".

The duties of the Secret State Police.
The sphere of activity of the Secret State Police is widespread and consists of the detection, prevention and suppression of any action directed against the security of the State or the Party and its representatives.

In particular, the following matters belong to the exclusive duties of the Gestapo:

- high treason,
- political, military and economic espionage,
- sabotage, subversive action and agitation,
- political attempts,
- any activity contrary to the leading policy of the State and of the governing party.

Further they are entrusted with:

- the supervision of the concentration camps,
- the control of the press (censorship) and of public meetings,
- the control of correspondence, tapping of telephone conversations, telegraph and wireless.

Organisation of the Secret State Police
Organisation of the Central Office
The Head office of the Secret State police is:
'Geheime Staatspolizei-Aust', Berlin, B, Prinz Albertstrasse.

Chief: S.S. – Gruppenfuhrer HEYDRICH,

Deputy Chief: S.S. – Oberfuhrer Dr. BEST

I Department (Abteilung I)

Activities: Matters concerning the organisation and administration of German Secret State Police at the Head Office and local branches; protection of the security of Government Offices, Central Archives of the Gestapo, administration of concentration camps.

II Department (Abteilung II)

Activities: Directing political matters connected with the security of the State and Party, and especially those referring to the Communist and Social Democratic Party, the legal Labour Front and the illegal workmen's associations, minorities, public societies, various political, social and intellectual associations and clubs. Matters pertaining to the Church, religious sects, reactionary parties and free-masonry. Supervision of the activity of the NSDAP and her branches.

III Counter-Espionage department (Abteilung III – Spionage-Abwehr.)

Chief: Dr. Best, Deputy Chief: DANZOG.

This department is the main organ of the C.E. Service for the whole of Germany. Its activities consist of enquiring into and liquidating foreign espionage, sabotage and subversive action through its local executive organs and it collaborates in this sphere with the offices of the military counter-espionage service.

The department is divided into a number of sub-departments each of which is concerned with espionage matters originating from a certain territory comprising a group of countries.

The following sub-departments are known.

Sub-Department 'East' (Ost) - Chief: KUBICKI.

This sub-department was concerned with espionage activities of the following countries: Russia, Poland, Czechoslovakia, Hungary, the Balkan States and the Far East. It was further divided into two sections, of which one with Dr. RIEDEL as Chief dealt with Poland, Czechoslovakia, Hungry, the Balkans, while the second with PENNER as Chief dealt with Russia and the Far East.

Sub-Department 'West' – Chief: Dr. CROSS, Deputy Chief Dr. FISCHE

This sub-department was also divided into two sections, and comprised France, while the other dealt with England, Belgium, Holland and Luxemburg.

Sub-Department 'South' (Sud) comprised Italy, Spain and North Africa.

Sub-Department 'Overseas' (Ubersee) comprised North and South America.

Sub-Department 'Coast' (Kueste) comprised the Scandinavian and Baltic Countries.

Sub-Department of Economic Espionage (Wirtschafts-Spionage Abwehr).

Chief: Dr. SCHMIDT

This sub-department is concerned with the suppression of economic espionage and the protection of the security of heavy industry, war industry in particular, and also the protection of the secrecy of their production. Within the competency of this sub-department lay also to prepare the organisation of sabotage and subversive actions abroad.

In carrying out its activities, this department maintained close contact, with the Security Service of the S.S. (Sicher heitsdicnst der Heichafuehrung der SS, abb SD-RFSS).

One of the constituting parts of the Gestapo Head Office is the Commissariat for special purposes, (Sonderkoumissarist gur besonderen Verwendung), which disposes of special cadres of the S.S. for the security of higher officials of the State or the party, for suppressing riots and revolts, carrying out raids, searches and arrests and, if necessary, death sentences. Telegraph, telephone and wireless tapping, as well as the censorship of correspondence, belong to the duties of this Commissariat.

When describing the activities of the Gestapo one should not omit the activity of:

<u>the Security Service of the S.S. (German abb. SD-RFSS)</u>

since both these organisations, while totally different from one another – the Gestapo being a State Organisation and the SD-RFSS a Party organisation – are interlocked and collaborate closely together.

The aims and the sphere of activity of both these institutions are similar and their duty lies in the protection of the Security of the State and of the Party, the only difference between them refers to their field of activity and method of work. While the Gestapo is active when the State affairs in general are concerned, the SD-RFSS acts chiefly on the terrain of the NSDAP and her branches, such as SA, HJ etc. A fact which deserves a mention is the collaboration between the SD-RFSS and the Gestapo in the protection of heavy industry, and especially of the war industry, and in the suppression of economic espionage. Although there is similarity of aims and a constant concurrence of the activities of both these organisations, their work is accurately co-ordinated and no doubling occurs.

The efficiency and the co-ordination of this activity is ascertained by the fact that the Chief of the German Police Himmler is at the same time the Head Commander of the S.S. (Reichsführer der S.S.), and the chief of the Gestapo.

HEYDRICH is the head of the Security Service of the S.S. (SD-RFSS) furthermore nearly all employees and workers of the Gestapo are members of the S.S. and many of them, as for instance the chiefs of the Staatpolizeistellen are at the same time members of the SS-RFSS which is even a better inspired organisation than the Gestapo.

<u>Territorial Organisation of the Gestapo</u>
The Central Office of the German State Secret Police (Geheimes Staatspolizei –Aut) fulfils the part of the General Staff and the

directing centre for the whole net of the local executive posts on the terrain of the German State.

The posts are in hierarchical subordination to the Central office and bear the following names:

- Staatspolizeileitstelle (abbreviation Stapolste)
- Staatspolizeistelle (abbreviation Staposte)
- Aussenstelle
- Grenzdienststelle and Grenzkommissariat.

The Staatspolizeileitstellen (the leading posts of the Gestapo) existed only in some countries and provinces of Germany, excepting Prussia. A number of Staatapolizeistellen were subjected to each of these leading posts which were directly subordinated to the Central Office of the Gestapo in Berlin. However, in Prussia where there were no Staatspolizeileitstellen, the mentioned Staatspolizeileitstellen were subjected to the Chief Berlin Office.

The Staatspolizeileitstellen are in all larger towns of the provincial administrative centres (the Regierungsbezirk). In each district town there are Aussenstellen which are subordinate posts to the above mentioned Staatspolizeileitstellen.

In border areas beside the Aussenstellen, the Grenzdienststellen and Grenzkommissariate are acting, whose duty lies in the protection and security of the frontier areas and the frontier itself. In these areas a special 'frontier Police' (Grenzpolizei) is acting, and it is under direct command of the Gestapo.

The Competency and Activity of the Gestapo

In order that the numerous and far reaching duties of the Gestapo in the political, social and economical life of Germany may be efficiently carried out, this institution enjoys widespread privileges and has the advantage of the close collaboration of all Government and Party Offices.

The Geheimes Staatspolizei-Amt and its local offices apart from employing an official staff disposes of a wide net of secret agents and confidants recruited from all classes of society, penetrating all the vital centres of public life not only in Germany, but abroad.

In relation to all the other branches of Police and local administrative offices the Gestapo is placed in a privileged position and it may require any necessary explanations from them, request them to investigate matters or reserve some of them to be dealt with exclusively by the Gestapo.

The employees of the Gestapo enjoy some rights belonging to the Prosecuting Officers and are authorised to carry out revisions, searches and detentions.

The Gestapo is the central directing office of counter-espionage all over Germany. This refers to political, economic and military espionage.

In order to suppress foreign espionage in the German Forces, the Gestapo collaborates with the military counter-espionage service.

At the headquarters the following departments collaborate:

On the part of the Gestapo: – The III department (espionage-Abwehr) of the Geheimen

Staatspolizei – Amt.

On the part of the Military Authorities: – The III department of the Intelligence and Counter Espionage service (Abzchrabteilung) which forms part of the Supreme Command of the German Armed Forces (Oberkommando der Wehrmaht) in the Ministry of War (Kriegeministerium).

In regard to the territorial executive organs, the collaboration between the Gestapo and the military authorities is ascertained by the local offices of the Gestapo: the Staatepolizeistellen and the military intelligence and counter-espionage service posts: the Abwehrstellen, which are in every military district (Wehrkreiskommando) and are subordinated to the Central Office: the Abwehrteisung.

At the frontier areas, the military intelligence sub-post the 'Eweigstellen' or 'Hebenstellen' collaborated with the local frontier Gestapo offices of the 'Aussenstellen' and 'Grenzdienststellen'.

The Gestapo, which is the central organ of counter-espionage and in its activity comprises the whole of the foreign espionage system, apart from the suppression of its activity on German soil, directs counter-espionage abroad, in order to enquire into the organisations, staff, method and technique of work of the foreign intelligence services.

In addition to the counter-espionage service, the Gestapo directs the political and economic intelligence service abroad and carries on intelligence service work on the frontiers of neighbouring countries.

The political and economic intelligence service is carried out by secret agents and confidants acting under some cover in consular and diplomatic offices, also in social, religious and cultural organisations, as well as in different economic, industrial and banking enterprises.

On the border areas the Gestapo is aided by the local police and employees and guards of the customs offices (Houptcollcoste and Zoilaanto).

Furthermore, one of the main duties of the Gestapo is the organisation and preparation of the subversive and sabotage action in foreign countries, all in close co-operation with the appropriate organs of the military intelligence service.

On the whole, according to the experience gained in Poland, one of the characteristics of the German counter-espionage and intelligence service is its widespread popularisation and penetration. Its action is not only undertaken by a limited group of special government functionaries and secret agents, but by representatives of all classes of society drawn into this activity.

For it is expected from every German going abroad to carry out certain observations there within the limits of his employment, capacity and possibilities, and to inform the German authorities accordingly. Moreover, special missions of intelligence service character are allotted to some of them.

According to our experience and practice, the German espionage system in Poland was based not so much on paid agents as on a wide spread net of confidants recruited from the German minority and prompted to join this action by patriotism and Party ideology.

The German minority living in the frontier areas, who were in close contact with their relatives on the other side and frequently crossed the frontier for family, trade and other purposes – formed for the German Intelligence Service an inexhaustible source of accurate and current information.

Also, representatives of the German population who held sometimes responsible leading posts in commerce, trade, banks and other centres of public life in Poland were of an incomparable informative importance as an intelligence service net for the German authorities.

The numerous trades, commercial and banking enterprises in Poland under complete or partial control, or depending upon German capital, were points of support for German secret agents disguised in various capacities.

The German organisations in Poland, whether of political or non-political character, whether social, cultural, religious and economic associations or just simple singing or physical training circles, they all had a side-line aim. Through the intermediary their members were more or less drawn into the net of the German Intelligence Service. They were thus centres where the preparatory work for sabotage and subversive action was carried out in anticipation of war.

A matter worthy of attention is the fact that this tendency of infiltrating almost every sphere of public life was actually accentuated after the last Great war and originally was the only solution, necessitated by the conditions in which the official German Intelligence Service found themselves at the time.

It should be remembered that the German Army which according to the Clauses of the Treaty of Versailles was reduced to the number of 100,000 men and limited only to defensive purposes, was not authorised to have General Staff and consequently an intelligence service, and was legally allowed to organise only a counter-espionage service.

It is known however, that in spite of these formal obstacles the German Army was constantly and secretly increased and her hidden cadres existed and grew in strength under the cover of police and military training organisations.

Parallel to the development of the Army, the Intelligence Service was secretly organised in the form of counter-espionage organs, or concealed posts in different Government, Party, social and even private institutions, which, so far, had never had any contact with this sort of activity.

Although the later military decrees of 16.3.35 and 21.3.35 which broke away from the restrictive clauses of the Versailles Treaty assigned to the German Armed Forces and consequently to the German Intelligence Service unrestricted conditions of development – yet the German Intelligence Service had not deprived itself of these subsidiary espionage organs. On the contrary, their utility was adequately reorganised, enlarged centralised and subordinated to the proper organ of the Official Intelligence Service.

The widespread military propaganda (Werporpaganda) carried out by the Nazi Government, and lectures on the military knowledge (Wehrwissunschaft) in German Colleges and Universities contributed towards the popularisation and better understanding of the importance of the espionage work among all classes of the German nation, both in Germany and abroad.

All this, together with the numerous and well organised German minorities in some countries, enabled the German minorities to form an extensive espionage system based on a widespread net of confidants. Those prompted to join this action by patriotism, are generally more trustworthy and reliable than the paid agents, and often have better possibilities than the latter of penetrating into the State secrets of foreign countries.

Appendix 9

MI14 ESTABLISHMENT

15.5.40	W.E.C. Meeting No.993 approved the formation of a new section, known as M.I.14, to function under D.D.M.I.(I).

The ever-increasing Intelligence with regard to Germany has made it necessary to separate M.I.3(b), hitherto responsible for this type of Intelligence, from M.I.3, and form it into a separate Section with a C.S.C.1 as head.

The entire function of M.I.3(b), with most of personnel has been transferred to M.I.14.

In effect M.I.3(b), has been developed into a full Country Section. M.I.P. has also been transferred from M.I.3 to M.I.14.

M.I.14 is organised into 5 sub-sections with the following sub-division of duties:

Function	M.I.14(a) -	Strategy
		Operations
		Publications
		Invasion Intelligence

M.I.14(b) -	Order of Battle
	Organisation
	Morale
	Casualties
M.I.14(c) -	Communications
	Topography
	Air Photographs
M.I.14(d) -	Information from Special Sources
M.I.14(e) -	A. A. Intelligence
M.I.P. -	(Press Reading)

Establishment:	G.S.C. I	-	1
	G.S.C. II	-	2
	G.S.C. III	-	6
	St Lieuts.	-	5
	I.Os. (Capts)	-	4
	I.O (Lieut)	-	1
	Clerks	-	14

15.5.40.   Lt.Col. E.W.D. Strong, R.S.Fus. appointed M.I.14 Colonel

10.12.40   W.E.S.C. No.316 approved the following amendment to the establishment to meet further expansion in the work of M.I.14.

Increase:	G.S.C. II	-	1
	I.C. (Capt)	-	1
	Clerks	-	2

10.12.40   W.E.S.C. No.325 approved increase by 1 Clerk

7.2.41   W.E.S.C. No.348 approved the increase by 1 Draughtsman

21.2.41   W.E.S.C. No.355 approved an increase by I.C. (Capt.)

25.3.41   W.E.S.C. No.373 approved an increase by 2 J.C.As.

9.4.41	Lt. Col. C.S. Clarke, Cameron Highlanders, appointed M.I.14. Colonel vice Lt. Col. K.W.D. Strong, R.S.Fus
29.5.41	W.E.S.C. No.397 approved an increase by 1 L.C. (Lieut)
9.6.41	W.E.S.C. No.592 approved an increase by 1 G.S.C.3
5.7.41	W.E.S.C. No.415 approved an increase by 1 Clerk
31.7.41	W.E.S.C. No.431 approved the following changes in the establishment:

Increase	-	G.S.C. II	-	1
Decrease	-	G.S.C.III	-	1

1.8.41	Lt.Col. W.P. Barclay, Black Watch, appointed M.I.14 Colonel, vice Lt. Col. C.S. Clarke, Cameron Highlanders.
18.8.41	W.E.S.C. No. 622 approved the upgrading of 1 I.O. (Capt) to G.S.C.3.
18.8.41	M.I.14 is still organised into 5 sub-sections with functions substantively the same as "15.5.30", but the establishment has been considerably increased following consistent expansion in the work of the Section.

The establishment is now as follows:

G.S.C. I	-	1
G.S.Os.II	-	3
G.S.Os.III	-	7
Lieuts.	-	5
I.Os. (Capts)	-	4
I.Os. (Lieuts)	-	3
J.C.As.	-	2

Clerks   -   18
Draughtsman -   1

17.10.41   W.E.C. Meeting No. 648 and at its meeting No. 655 held on 3.11.41. approved a reorganization of M.I.14 entailing the following amendments to establishment:

W.E.C. 648 –

Increase: G.S.C.I.   -   1

W.E.C. 655 –

Increase: G.S.O.II   -   1
G.S.Os.III   -   2
I.O. (Capt)   -   1
I.Os. (Lieunt) -   2
J.C.As.   -   6

To help to cover the above increase in M.I.14, the following decreases were made in other M.I. Sections:

M.I.2	G.S.C.II	-	1
M.I.10	I.O. (Capt)	-	1
	I.O. (Lieut)	-	1
M.I.12	I.O. (Lieut)	-	1
M.I.3	G.S.O.3	-	1
M.I.P	I.O. (Lieut)	-	1

The course of the war has laid such a heavy additional burden on M.I.14 following incursions of the German Army into the Balkans, Libya and Russia since May 1940, that it has been decided to carry out a certain amount of reorganization within the branch and in particular to add another G.S.O.I to supervise the additional 4 sub-sections, making 9 sub-sections as against 5 prior to reorganization.

M.I.14 is now organized into 9 sub-sections, the present G.S.O.I. will be the M.I.14 Colonel and will retain control of 5 sub-sections dealing with the most important subjects, and the second G.S.O.I will control the remaining 4 and act as Second in Command.

The lay-out and function of sub section is now as follows:

M.I.14 Colonel –

M.L.P.	-	(Reading of Foreign Press)
M.L.14(a)	-	Strategy, Intentions, Operations, "I" Summaries Liaison M.O., J.L.S. etc. J.L.C. papers
M.I.14(b)	-	Order of Battle (including Army and G.A.F. personalities) Liaison with A.I. 3(b) and M.I.3(3).
M.I.14(e)	-	German Anti-Aircraft Italian A.A. defences in Italy and areas occupied by Italian forces.
M.I.14(f)	-	Invasion Intelligence W.O. representative on C.I.C.
M.I.14(g)	-	Organisation of German Army Liaison with M.I.10, A.P.V. and M.E.W.

G.S.O (2nd in Command) –

M.I.14(c)	-	Communications Maintenance problem Liaison with J.L.S. and R.S.S.
M.I.14(d)	-	Special Intelligence (inc liaison with other M.I. Sections as required)
M.I.14(h)	-	Air Photographs Bombing results Defences Liaison with C.I.U.

M.I.14(j) - Research (including morale, tactical, manpower)
M.I.14 Library
M.I.14 Publications
Liaison with I.T.C.

Establishment:

G.S.Os.I	-	2
G.S.OsII	-	5
G.S.OsIII	-	9
St.Lieuts	-	5
I.Os. (Capts)	-	5
I.Os. (Lieuts)	-	5
J.C.As.	-	8
Clerks	-	18
Draughtman	-	1

1.11.41 Lt.Col. G.O. Spence, Ox & Bucks L.I., appointed M.I.14
Colonel vice Lt. Col F.B. Barclay, Black Watch

28.5.42 Lt.Col. C.E.R. Hirsch, Welch R., appointed M.I.14 Colonel vice Lt. Col. G.O. Spence, Ox & Bucks L.I.

2.10.42 W.E.I.C.(A) No. 4 approved the following amendments to establishment:

Increase: G.S.OsII - 2
Decrease: G.S.OsIII - 2
(In effect the G.S.OsIII i/c of sub-sections M.I.14(d) and (g) were upgraded to G.S.O.II).

24.4.43 A third G.S.O.I appointed to M.I.14 to take over sub-sections now controlled by the Senior G.S.C.I., leaving the latter free to act as head of M.I.14

24.4.43 W.E.I.C.(A) 36 and W.E.I.C. "A" 37 of 29 April 1944 approved the following amendments to the establishment to provide the British Army element for the Combined Order of Battle Group.

C.O.B.G. has been formed to reconcile divergencies of opinions between the British and American estimates in German man-power and casualties. C.O.B.G. will be comprised of 2 Echelons:

Forward
Echelon: War Office (M.1.14(C.O.B.G.)

Rear Echelon: War Department, Washington, who will also provide a complement of Officers.

Increase:	G.S.C.	- 1
	I.O. (Capt)	- 1
	I.Os. (Capts)	- 5 (will be Polish Officers)

27.5.43   W.E.C.I. "A" No.41 approved the following amendment to establishment:

Increase:	G.S.O.II	- 1
	I.O (Lieut)	- 1
	J.C.As.	- 2
Decrease:	I.O. (Capt)	- 1

16.7.43   W.E.C.I. "A" 49 approved the following amendment to the establishment of M.I.14(b):

Increase:	G.S.Os.III	- 1
	I.Os. (Capts or Lieuts)	- 3 (may be A.T.S.)
	J.C.As.	- 2
	Draughtsman	- 1

16.7.43   W.E.I.C. "A" approved the setting up of a new Section to be known as M.I.15 (see Appendix) with a G.S.O.I. head to take over the duties of M.I.14(e) dealing with A.A. Intelligence. This type of Intelligence had developed in importance and extent beyond the scope of a sub-section to deal with.

This reorganisation entails transferring the following personnel from M.I.14(e) to M.I.15:

G.S.Os.II	-	1
G.S.Os.III	-	1
I.O. (Capt)	-	1
I.O. (Lieut	-	1
J.C.As.	-	1
Clerks	-	3
Draughtman	-	1

8.7.43   W.E.I.C. "A" 47 approved the following amendments to the establishment of C.O.B.G. (now known as Military Intelligence Research Section (M.I.R.S.):

Decrease: From M.I.14(b) - St.Lieut. - 1
Increase: M.I.14 (C.O.B.G.) - Jnr.Comdr.(ATS) - 1

28.7.43   Lt.Col. J.D. Wyatt, Northants, became M.I.14 Colonel, vice Lt. Col. C.E.R. Hirsch, Welch R.

19.8.43   W.E.I.C. "A" 54 approved the following amendment to establishment:

Clerks - 4

30.9.43   W.E.I.C. "A" 62 approved the following amendment to M.I.P. establishment:

Decrease: I.O. (Lieut) - 1

7.10.43   W.E.I.C. "A" 63 approved a proposal to alter the title of M.I.14 (C.O.B.G.) to Military Intelligence Research Section M.I.14(M.I.R.S.)

26.10.43 W.E.I.C. "A" 67 approved the regrading of all I.O. (Captain) or I.O. (Lieut) appointments in M.I. Directorate as "I.O. (Captain or Lieut)".

11.11.43 C.8 approved the following amendment to establishment:

Increase: J.C.A - 1

16.11.43 C.8 approved an increase in the establishment by 3 Clerks.

1.1.44 The lay-out and duties of M.i.14 by sub-sections is as follow:

M.I.14 Colonel (G.S.O.1) Head of Section
G.S.O.1(A)   -
M.I.14(a)   -   Strategy Intentions Operations in Russia and S. Mediterranean
M.I.14(b)   -   Order of Battle and Locations Army personalities

M.I.14 (M.I.R.S.) -   Captured documents
M.I.14(c)   -   Operations in W. Mediterranean Communications, troop movements and maintenance in all German occupied countries
M.I.14(d)   -   Nazi Party Nazi Personalities S.S. Policy and other para-military formations Pigeon Intelligence Study of Special Intelligence

G.S.O.1(B)   -

M.I.14(f & j)	-	Tactics, morals, manpower Publications Liaison with Schools of "I" and with M.T. Invasion of and Raids on U.K.
M.I.14(g)	-	Organisation and equipment
M.I.14(h)	-	Defences and Installations Air Photographic I (including coordination of M.I. Directorate requirements).
M.I.P.	-	Press Reading Establishment:
G.S.os.I	-	3 (one M.I.14 Colonel)
G.S.Os.II	-	8
G.S.Os.III	-	9
St.Lieuts.	-	4
I.Os. (Capt or Lt)	-	21 (6 Polish I.Os. in MIRS)
J.C.As.	-	22
Clerks	-	37
Draughtsmen	-	2

8.3.44 W.E.I.C. "A" 86 approved a proposal to delete M.I.14 (M.I.R.S.) from M.I. Directorate and become a separate Outstation establishment with a C.S.O.I head (See appendix)

The above entails the following amendment to M.I.14 establishment w.e.f. 7.2.44:

Decrease:	G.S.O.II	- 1
	G.S.O.III	- 1
	I.O. (J/Cdr ATS)	- 1
	I.Os. (Capts or Lts)	- 6 (Polish Officers)
	J.C.A.	- 1
	Clerks	- 12 (7 translators

8.3.44   W.E.I.C. "A" 86 approved the regrading of the 4 staff Lieuts. In M.I.14 to I.Os. (Capts or Lieuts) following the regrading of all Staff Lieuts in M.I. Directorate.

3.5.44   W.E.I.C. "A" 96 approved the following changes to establishment:

Decrease:	I.O. (Capt or Lt) transferred to M.I.R.S.	
Increase	G.S.O.II	- 1
	G.S.O.III	- 1
	I.O. (Capt or Lt)	- 1
	J.C.A.	- 1
	Clerk	- 1
	Draughtman	- 1

The above increase was necessitated by greatly increased work following development of operations in Western Europe.

A new sub-section has been formed (M.I.14(k) by splitting M.I.14(c). In future M.I.14(c) will deal with the German side in France and M.I.14 (k) with the German side of operations in Italy.

11.5.44   Lt. Col. A.F.H. Fausett-Farquhar, Gordon Highlanders, appointed M.I.14 Colonel, vice Lt. Col. J.D. Wyatt, Northants Regt.

4.7.44   W.E.I.C. "A" 103 approved the following change in establishment:

Increase:	I.Os. (Capts or Lts)	- 2
	J.C.A.	- 1

25.7.44   W.E.I.C. "A" 106 approved the regrading of 1 G.S.O.2 as G.S.O.2 (may be A.T.S.)

15.9.44   W.E.I.C. "A" 112 approved the following change in establishment:

Regrade: 16 I.Os (Capts or Lts)   as
          16 I.Os (Capts or Lts) – may be A.T.S.

15.9.44   At a meeting of the Directors Committee (1/ Estab1147). It was agreed, with Treasury approval, to approve adding a deputy directorate (D.D.M.I. (Germany)) Colonel, who became the head of M.I.14 and M.I.15.

The case for adding another Deputy Director to the Directorate is that M.I.14 has become so large in staff and important in function with the development of the war in Germany that the head of M.I.14 must have direct contact with D.M.I.

M.I.14 is therefore transferred from D.D.M.I. (I) to D.D.M.I. (G)

The following change is affected to M.I. 14 establishment:

M.I.14 Colonel becomes D.D.M.I.(G)

Decrease: 1 C.S.O.I

27.9.44   Lt.Col. W.B.P.P. Aspinall, I.C. became M.I.14 Colonel vice Lt.Col. A.M.F. Fausset-Farquhar, Gordons, appointed D.D.M.I.(G) (Colonel)

25.10.44   The following decrease in establishment agreed between M.I.14 and c.8.

Decrease: 1 J.C.A.

13.10.44   The following change in establishment agreed upon between M.I.14 and c.8.

Decrease: 1 J.C.A.

1.1.45   The lay-out and functions of M.I.14 are now as follows:

M.I.P. – (Reading of Foreign Press)
G.S.O.I(A) –

M.I.14(a)	-	G.S.O. II head – Strategy, Intentions, Coordination of work of section
M.I.14(b)	-	G.S.O.2 head – Order of Battle and Location Army Personalities
M.I.14(c)	-	G.S.O.2 head – Operations in Western Europe Communications and troop movements
M.I.14(d)	-	G.S.O.2 head – Nazi Party (including preparations for post-war activities) Nazi Personalities S.S. Police and other para-military formations. Pigeon Intelligence Study of Special Intelligence Post-Hostilities Planning.

G.S.O.I(B) –
M.I.14(f)

and (j)	-	G.S.O.2 head – Tactics, Morale, Manpower, Casualties Liaison with Schools of "I" and with M.T. Invasion of and Raids on U.K.
M.I.14(g)	-	G.S.O.2 head – Organisation and Equipment Liaison with M.I.10 and M.E.W.

M.I.14(h)	-	G.S.O.2 head – Defences and Installations Air Photographic Intelligence (incl. Coordination of M.I. Directorate requirements).
M.I.14(k)	-	G.S.O.2 head – Operations in Mediterranean and Eastern Europe Maintenance in all German Occupied Countries Establishment:
G.S.Os.1	-	2
G.S.Os.2	-	8 (1 may be A.T.S.)
G.S.Os.3	-	9
I.Os (Capts or Lts)	-	20 (may be A.T.S.)
J.C.As.	-	21
Clerks	-	21
Draughtsman	-	3

3.1.45   W.E.I.C. "A" No. 130 approved the following changes in establishment:
Decrease: I.O. (Capt or Lt may be ATS) - 1

This I.O (ATS) has been attached to Air Ministry from M.I.14 for work on "CROSS BOW". The appointments of other personnel working on this subject are included in establishment of Miscellaneous Appointments (Homs). It was therefore considered that this appointment of I.O. (ATS) should be deleted from M.I.14 and added to Miscellaneous Appointments (Homs).

(Note: "CROSS BOW" was the code-name for the Committee set up to study German long-range weapons, i.e. V.1 and V.2)

28.2.45   W.E.I.C. "A" No. 138 approved the following permanent increase in establishment. They had previously been approved by W.E.I.C. "A" No. 96 (3.5.44), subject to review.

Increase:	CSO II	-	1
	CSO III	-	1
	I.O. (Capt or Lt)	-	1
	J.C.A.	-	1
	S/Sgt	-	1
	Draughtsman	-	1

These appointments were necessary to deal with operational intelligence in Western Europe. They will be needed as long as operations continue.

18.5.45   C.8 approved the following change in establishment:

Decrease: Civilian Draughtswoman - 1

30.5.45   W.E.I.C. "A" No 151 approved the following change in establishment:

Decrease: Sgts. - 2

These appointments were surrendered to meet an increase in personnel for M.I.3 to cope with heavy demands for Russian Intelligence.

12.6.45   W.E.I.C. "A" No. 153 approved the following change in establishment:

Decrease: I.Os. (Capts or Lts) - 2

28.7.45   C.8 approved the decrease of one RC III

28.8.45   Consequent upon certain reallocation of duties between M.I.2, 3 and 14, W.E.I.C. "A" No.164 approved the following changes in establishment:

Increase:	CSO II	-	1
	CSO III	-	3

J.C.A.	-	1
E.S.C."A"	-	1
Sgt	-	1
Spl.	-	1
TC III	-	1
Typist	-	1

The above appointments, together with the responsibility for dealing with Intelligence relating to Western European countries were transferred from M.I.3 to M.I.14, sub-section M.I.14(k).

The responsibility for Czechoslavakia was transferred from M.I.14 to M.I.3(b). No personnel were transferred.

M.I.14 to be known in future as M.I.4/14, with a view to eventually dropping the "14".

M.I.4/14

15.9.45   C.8 approved the decrease of one J.C.A.

1.10.45   C.8 approved the deletion of one J.C.A.

1.10.45   Consequent on O.M. 2413, involving reductions in the M.I. Directorate, W.E.I.C. "A" No. 173 approved the following:

Decrease:	CSO II	-	1
	I.O (Capt or Lt)	-	9
	J.C.A.	-	10
	W.O. II	-	1
	S/Sgt	-	1
	Sgt	-	1
	R. & F.	-	2
	Draughtswoman (ATS)	-	1
	TC II	-	2

7.11.45   W.E.I.C. "A" No.177 approved the following decreases in establishment:

Decreases: GSO II - 2 (w.e.f. 26.10.45 – 3.11.45)

I.Os (Capts or Lts) - 2 (w.e.f. 3.11.45 – 7.11.45)

I.O. (ATS) - 1 (w.e.f. 12.10.45)

20.11.45   Lt.Col. F.M. de Butts, Somerset I.I. approved GSO I, M.I.4/14 vice Lt. Col. W.B.P.P. Aspinall, I.C.

27.11.45   W.E.I.C. "A" No. 177 approved the following addition to establishment:

Increase: Sgt (unpaid)   -   1

An English-speaking Belgian N.C.O. capable of reading and drafting letters in Flemish, French and Dutch, is required to assist in investigating records of acts of courage and enterprise by civilians in Belgium, Holland and France in connection with Carrier Pigeon activities with a view to official recognition. This N.C.O. is being provided and paid by the Belgian Ministry of National Defence in London.

1.1.46   w.e.f. 1 Jan 46 M.I.4/14 became known as M.I.4

ABBREVIATIONS

AFHQ	Allied Forces Headquarters
AI	Air Intelligence
AI10	Cover name for SOE
ACSS	Assistant Chief of the Secret Service
AKA	Also Known As
AM	Air Ministry
AMA	Assistant Military Attaché
AMID	Air Ministry Intelligence Branch
BEF	British Expeditionary Force
BL	British Library
BNL	British Newspaper Library
BPP	Bayerrische Politische Polizei (Bavarian Political Police)
BT	Board of Trade
BUF	British Union of Fascists
BVP	Bavarian People's Party
C	Head of SIS
CAB	Cabinet (UK)
CE	Counter Espionage
CCS	Combined Chiefs of Staff
GCHQ	Government Communications Headquarters
COHQ	Combined Operations Headquarters
CIA	Central Intelligence Agency (formerly OSS)

CID	Committee of Imperial Defence
CIS	Combined Intelligence Section
CIGS	Chief of the Imperial General Staff
COI	Coordinator of Information
COS	Chief of Staff
CSC	Controller Special Communications
CSS	Chief of the Secret Service
CPGB	Communist Party of Great Britain
DAF	German Labour Front
DCI	Director of Central Intelligence (USA)
DDCI	Deputy Director of Central Intelligence (USA)
DGI	Director General of Intelligence (MOD)
DGPID	Director General Political Intelligence Department
DGSS	Director-General of the Security Service (MI5)
DDGSS	Deputy Director-General of the Security Service (MI5)
DI	Defence Intelligence
DIS	Defence Intelligence Staff (now DI)
DJIB	Director Joint Intelligence Bureau
DNI	Director of Naval Intelligence
DNVP	German People's Party
DMI	Director of Military Intelligence
DDMI	Deputy Director of Military Intelligence
DMO	Director of Military Operations
DMOI	Director of Military Operations & Intelligence
DORA	Defence of the Realm Act
DULAG	Durchgangslager – Transit POW camp (airmen)
ETO	European Theatre of Operations
FANY	First Aid Nursery Yeomanry
FBI	Federal Bureau of Investigation (USA)
FLA	First Lord of the Admiralty
FO	Foreign Office
GCCS	Government Code & Cipher School (now GCHQ)
GL	Nazi Party Regional Headquarters
HMG	His Majesty's Government
HO	Home Office
GESTAPO	Geheime Staatpolizei
IB	Intelligence Branch (War Office)
ISIC	Inter-Service Intelligence Committee
ISLD	Inter Services Liaison Department

ISRB	Inter Services Research Bureau (aka SOE)
JIB	Joint Intelligence Bureau
JIC	Joint Intelligence Committee
JIO	Joint Intelligence Organisation
JIS	Joint Intelligence Staff
JPS	Joint Planning Staff
KPD	German Communist Party
KRIPO	Detective Branch of Criminal Police (Germany)
KZ	Concentration Camp
MA	Military Attaché
MCD	Minister for Co-ordination of Defence
MCO	Military Control Officer
MDA	Ministry of Defence Act 1946
MEPO	Metropolitan Police
MEW	Ministry Economic Warfare
MI1	Military Intelligence 1
MI2	Military Intelligence 2
MI3	Military Intelligence 3
MI4	Military Intelligence 4
MI5	Military Intelligence 5 (aka Security Service)
MI6	Military Intelligence 6 (aka SIS)
MI7	Military Intelligence 7
MI8	Military Intelligence 8
MI9	Military Intelligence 9
MI10	Military intelligence 10
MI11	Military Intelligence 11
MI12	Military Intelligence 12
MI14	Military Intelligence 14
MI15	Military Intelligence 15
MI16	Military Intelligence 16
MI17	Military Intelligence 17
MI19	Military Intelligence 19
MOD	Ministry of Defence
MOS	Ministry of Supply
MIRS	Military Intelligence Research Section
MOI	Ministry of Information
MP	Military Police
MP	Member of Parliament

NCO	Non-Commissioned Officer
NKVD	Narodny Kommissariat Vnutrennich Del (Russian Secret Police)
NSDAP	National Socialist German Workers Party (Nazi)
NVS	Nazi Welfare Association)
OFLAG	Offizierslager – officers' POW camp
OIC	Operational Intelligence Centre (Admiralty)
ORPO	Uniformed ordinary German police force
OSS	Office of Strategic Services (later renamed CIA)
PCO	Passport Control Office
PDU	Photographic Development Unit
PIU	Photographic Interpretation Unit
PMS	Intelligence Section; Ministry of Munitions
POW	Prisoner of War
PRO	Public Record Office (now TNA)
PRU	Photographic Reconnaissance Unit
PWE	Political Warfare Executive
RAF	Royal Air Force
RAFIS	Royal Air Force Intelligence School
RAFP	Royal Air Force Police
RN	Royal Navy
RSHA	Reich Security Main Office
SA	Sturmabteilung (Stormtroopers)
SAS	Special Air Service
SBS	Special Boat Squadron
SD	Sicherheitsdienst (SS Intelligence Department)
SDP	Social Democratic Party (Germany)
SHAEF	Supreme Headquarters Allied Expeditionary Force
SIB	Special investigation Branch (RAF Police)
SIPO	Joint Department controlling Gestapo & Kripo 1936/39
SIS	Secret Intelligence Service (formerly MI1(c), aka MI6)
SOE	Special Operations Executive
SS	Schutzstaffel
STALAG	Stammlager – ordinary ranks POW Camp
STC	Supply & Transport Committee
STO	Supply & Transport Organisation
TNA	The National Archives

TSD	Topographical & Statistical Department (War Office)
WAAF	Women's Royal Auxiliary Air Force
WO	War Office
ZO	Z Organisation – SIS network headed by Col. C Dansey

SOURCE NOTES

1 - Benefit of Hindsight
The Papers of Major-General Kenneth Strong, KBE, CB, Imperial
    War Museum
Foreign Office Political Files, Germany, TNA FO 371/17756

2 - Heads in the Sand
The Papers of Major-General Kenneth Strong, KBE, CB, Imperial
    War Museum
Remilitarization of the Rhineland, TNA FO 371/19892
Military Intelligence Organization, TNA WO 106/6083
Files on Germany (Political), TNA FO 371/17756

3 - Sleepwalking to War
Manchester Guardian, Frank Jellinek, 28 April 1937
The Times (London), George Steer, 29 April 1937
Vivian, Security Documents in HM Embassy, Rome, 20 February
    1937, TNA FO/850-2 Y777
Vivian, Security Measures at HM Embassy, Berlin, 22 July 1937,
    TNA FO 850/2 Y832
United States Holocaust Memorial Museum, Hannover Gestapo
    to Berlin Gestapo, RG-11.001M.02 Reel 6, Folder 449
The Papers of Major-General Kenneth Strong, KBE, CB, Imperial
    War Museum
Foreign Office Political Files, Central Department, Jewish Affairs,
    TNA FO 371/21636-21639

4 - The Watchers
Portuguese Secret Service (PVDE) Archives, Ministry of the
Interior, Lisbon, Portugal
Foreign Office Political Files, Germany, TNA FO 371/17706
The History & Organization of the Gestapo, Volume 1, MI14,
November 1941
MI14 File on Hermann Göring, TNA WO 208/4463
MI14 File on Dr R Dials, TNA WO 309/768
File on Dr R Diels, TNA, FO 371/17706
MI14 File on Heinrich Himmler, TNA WO 208/4474
The Rohm Plot, TNA FO 371/17706-17708

5 - Plot and Counter-plot
The Venlo Incident, TNA FO 1093/201
Payne Best Papers, Imperial War Museum, London
Payne Best Papers, Intelligence Corps Museum, Chicksands,
Shefford
Evidence of Walter Schellenberg to enquiry of Dutch States,
General, Volume 1b, exhibit No 43, Imperial War Museum
Cadogan MS diary, 4-5 November 1939, CCAD, ACAD 1/8

6 - Down in the Basement
History of the Development of the Directorate of Military
Intelligence, TNA WO 106/6083
The Papers of Noel Gilroy Annan, GBR/0272/NGA, King's
College Archive Centre, Cambridge
Brian Melland obituary by Wheeler-Bennett, The Times (London),
29 July 1971
Should Strategists veto The Tunnel? by W S Churchill, Weekly
Dispatch, 27 July 1924
Why Not a Channel Tunnel by W S Churchill, Daily Mail,
12 February 1936

7 - Gestapo GB
David Eccles to Gladwyn Jebb, 4 July 1940, TNA FO 1093/23
'C' to Sir Alexander Cadogan, 7 July 1940, TNA FO 1093/23
'C' to Sir Alexander Cadogan, 19 July 1940, TNA FO 1093/23
German Invasion Plans for the British Isles 1940, Bodleian
Library, Oxford

Report by R H Denning, DO War Office, TNA WO 193/141
Memorandum to Home Secretary 17 May 1940, TNA CAB 67/6/31
Notes on Invasion; GHQ Home Forces, 6 June 1940, TNA WO 199/1705
Report on Preparations for Defence, GHQ Home Forces, 4 June 1940, TNA WO 199/1712
Report of the Combined Intelligence Committee, 22 June 1940, TNA AIR 40/1137
Report of the Combined Intelligence Committee, 27 June 1940, TNA AIR 40/1637
If the Invader Comes, 19 June 1940, TNA CAB 21/1473
Handwritten Note by Winston Churchill, TNA PREM 7/2
Memorandum from Winston Churchill, 9 July 1940, TNA ADM 223/484
Churchill to Colonel Jacob, 16 September 1940, TNA CAB 120/438
Minutes of the Chiefs of Staff Committee, 17 September 1940, TNA CAB 79/6
Barge Concentrations, Report to the Admiralty, 21 September 1940, TNA MT 6/2755
File on Arnold Littman, TNA KV 2/2837

8 - The Last Ditch
Papers of Noel Gilroy Annan, Ref GBR/0272/NGA, King's College Archive Centre, Cambridge
The History and Organisation of the Gestapo, Volume I, MI14, November 1941
Papers of Major-General Kenneth Strong, KBE, CB, Imperial War Museum
Die Sonderfahndungsliste GB, 1940, ID: DA585 A1 G37 (V), Record No: 649516, Hoover Institution, Stanford, California

9 - House in the Country
Lt Colonel C S Clarke, TNA WO 208/2004
Lt Colonel C S Clarke, London Gazette, 28 April 1939
'Spy-Pigeons' by Captain Brian Melland, CIC Report, 2 July 1941, TNA WO 208/3556-85
Spy-Pigeons, Messages 23-855, July 1941, TNA ADM 199/2475

Amt IV of the RHSA, Volumes 6 & 7, TNA KV
Activities of Dept IV of the RHSA, TNA CAB 146/448

10 - **The Torturer**
Gestapo Interrogation Methods, TNA, HS 8/852 (SOE file)
File on Walter Habecker, TNS KV 2/2752
Golden Fleece: Kriminalkommissar W Habecker, Report No BSC
  684, CIA Archive, Washington DC

11- **The Man with Nine Lives**
The Papers of Airey Neave MP, Parliamentary Archive, Ref AN
File on Harold Cole, TNA KV 2/415-417
File on Helmuth Knochen, TNA KV 2/2745

12- **The Butcher of Prague**
File on Operation Anthropoid, TNA HS 4/39 (SOE file)
Czech Intelligence Papers, TNA HS 4/79 (SOE file)
File on Reinhardt Heydrich, TNA WO 208/4472
Operation Archery Casualties, TNA DEFE 2/83
The Cooler; S.O.E file 22666/A, TNA HS 9/549/6

13 - **Tom, Dick and Harry**
The Papers of Airey Neave MP, Parliamentary Archive, ref AN
Historical Record of MI9, TNA WO 208/3242
RAF POWs in Germany, TNA WO 208/3245
History of IS9 (WEA), TNA WO 208/3246
History of IS9 (CMF), TNA WO 208/3250
POW Camps in Germany, TNA WO 208/3269-95
MI9 Headquarters War Diary, TNA WO 165/39
Official History of the North Compound, Stalag-Luft III, TNA
  AIR 40/2645
Hamburg Trial of Gestapo Agents & Testimonies, TNA WO
  235/425-429
File on Ogruf Gottlieb Berger, TNA KV 2/172

14 - **Turning the Tables**
The Sagan Case, TNA WO 208/4301
The Hamburg Trial of Gestapo Agents, TNA WO/235/425-429
Statement of Walther Grosch, TNA AIR 40/2266

15 - An Unsatisfactory Conclusion
MI14 appreciations from 1 January to 11 June 1944, TNA
WO/208/4312
The Interrogation of Adolf Eichmann, RG 79.11/A/3062/1, Israel
State Archives
File on Heinrich Mueller, Records of the CIA, RG 263

Epilogue
General A M Patch to General D D Eisenhower, 25 May 1945,
Shapell Manuscript Collection
The Diaries of Sir Guy Liddell, Head of Counter-Espionage MI5;
TNA KV 4/466-468
File on Ernst Kaltenbrunner, TNA KV 2/269-273
Interrogation of Heinrich Himmler, TNA WO 32/19603
Papers of the International Military Tribunal & Nuremberg
Military Tribunals, University of Southampton Special
Collections, 1945-1949, GB 738 MS 200
The Indictment against the Gestapo, presented by Col. Robert
Storey, 20 December 1945 & 2 January 1946, AP-IMT
Testimony of Dr Werner Best, 31 July 1946, AP-IMT
Defence Closing Speech; Counsel for the Gestapo, Dr Rudolf
Merkel, 23 August 1946, AP-IMT
The Nuremberg Judgement, 30 September 1946, AP-IMT

BIBLIOGRAPHY

Allen, William, *The Nazi Seizure of Power; The Experience of a Single German Town*, New York, 1984

Andrew, Christopher, *Secret Service*, London, William Heinemann, 1985

Andrew, Christopher, The *Defence of the Realm: The Authorized History of MI5*, London, Allen Lane, 2009

Annan, Noel, *Changing Enemies*, London, Harper Collins, 1995

Aronson, Shlomo, *Beginnings of the Gestapo System*, Jerusalem, Israel Universities Press, 1969

Beevor, Antony, *The Second World War*, London, Weidenfeld & Nicolson, 2012

Birkenhead, The Earl of, *Halifax: The Life of Lord Halifax*, London, Hamish Hamilton, 1965

Bishop, Chris, *Hitler's Foreign Divisions: The Waffen SS 1940-45*, London, Amber Books, 2005

Black, Peter, *Ernst Kaltenbrunner*, Princeton, Princeton University Press, 1984

Bishop, Patrick, *The Cooler King*, London, Atlantic Books, 2015

Booth, Nicholas, *Zigzag*, London, Portrait, 2007

Bower, Tom, *Klaus Barbie: Butcher of Lyon*, London, Michael Joseph, 1984

Bradford, Barbara, *The Reluctant King*, New York, St Martin's Press, 1989

Breuer, William, *The Spy Who Spent the War in Bed,* Hoboken, John Wiley & Sons, 2003

Bullock, Alan, *Hitler: A Study in Tyranny,* London, Pelican Books, 1962

Bunting, Madeleine, *The Model Occupation,* London, Harper Collins, 1995

Butler, Rupert, *The Gestapo,* London, Amber Books, 2004

Calic, Edouard, *Reinhard Heydrich,* London, Military Heritage Press, 1982

Curtis, Michael, *Verdict on Vichy,* London, Weidenfeld & Nicolson, 2002

Dawidowicz, Lucy, *The War against the Jews: 1933-1945,* London, Bantam Books, 1975

Delarue, Jacques, *The History of the Gestapo,* London, Macdonald, 1964

Deschner, Gunther, *Heydrich: The Pursuit of Total Power,* London, Orbis, 1978

Deutscher, Isaac, *Stalin,* London, Penguin, 1966

Dorril, Stephen, MI6: *Fifty Years of Special Operations,* London, Fourth Estate, 2000

Foot, M R D & Langley J M, *MI9: Escape & Evasion 1939-45,* Boston, Little Brown, 1979

Foot, M R D, *The Special Operations Executive 1940-46,* London, Pimlico, 1999

Fraser-Smith, Charles, *The Secret War,* London, Michael Joseph, 1981

Fry, Helen, *The London Cage,* Yale, Yale University Press, 2017

Gellately, Robert, *The Gestapo & German Society,* Oxford, Clarendon Press, 1990

Gill, Anton, *The Great Escape,* London, Headline, 2001

Halifax, Earl of, *Fulness of Days,* London, Collins, 1957

Holmes, Richard, *The World at War,* London, Ebury Press, 2007

Jeffrey, Keith, *The Secret History of MI6,* London, Penguin, 2010

Lampe, David, *Last Ditch,* New York, G P Putnam & Son, 1968

Longerich, Peter, *The Unwritten Order,* Stroud, Tempus, 2001

Longmate, Norman, *If Britain Had Fallen,* London, Greenhill Books, 2004

McDonough, Frank, *The Gestapo: Myths & Reality,* London, Hodder & Stoughton, 2015

McKinstry, Leo, *Operation Sealion,* London, John Murray, 2014

Macintyre, Ben, *Agent Zigzag,* London, Bloomsbury Publishing, 2007

Montefiore, Simon S, *Stalin: The Court of the Red Tsar,* London, Weidenfeld & Nicolson, 2003

Morton, Andrew, *17 Carnations,* London, Michael O'Mara, Books, 2015

Murphy, Brendan, *Turncoat: The Strange Caseof Traitor Sergeant Harold Cole,* London, Macdonald & Co, 1987

Neave, Airey, *Saturday at MI9,* London, Hodder & Stoughton, 1969

O'Connor, Bernard, *Bletchley Park & the Pigeon Spies,* USA, 2018

Reid, Patrick, *Colditz; The Full Story,* London, Macmillan, 1984

Roberts, Andrew, *Holy Fox: The Life of Lord Halifax,* London, Weidenfeld & Nicolson, 1991

Roberts, Andrew, *Hitler & Churchill,* Weidenfeld & Nicolson, 2003

Roberts, Andrew, *Churchill: Walking with Destiny,* London, 2018

Roberts, Andrew, *Leadership in War,* London, Allen Lane, 2019

Service, Robert, *Stalin: A Biography,* London, Macmillan, 2004

Smith, Michael, *Six: A History of Britain's Secret Intelligence Service,* London, Dialogue, 2010

Smith, Michael, *Foley; The Spy who saved the Jews,* London, Biteback Publishing, 2016

Pawle, Gerald, Pawle, *The Secret War,* London, George G Harrup & Co, 1956

Seba, Anna, *That Woman: The Life of Wallis Simpson,* London, Weidenfeld & Nicolson, 2011

Strong, Kenneth, *Intelligence at the Top,* Boston, Doubleday, 1968

Urbach, Barbara, *Go Betweens for Hitler,* Oxford, OUP, 2015

West, Nigel, *At Her Majesty's Secret Service,* London, Greenhill Books, 2006

Wiesenthal, Simon, *Justice Not Vengeance, London, Weidenfeld & Nicolson, 1989*

Williams, Susan, *The People's King,* London, Allen Lane, 2003

Wood, Anthony, *Great Britain 1900-1965,* London, Longman, 1978

Zeigler, Philip, *King Edward VIII,* New York, Alfred A Knopf, 1990

INDEX

Hutton, Christopher (Clutty) 170–1

Informationsheft GB (Gestapo Guide to Britain) 91
Inverlair Lodge 158–63
Italy 14, 26, 28–9, 95–6, 166, 193

Japan 26, 28, 95–6
Jeffreys, John 108
Jellinek, Frank 31
Jong, Edgar 50
Jordan, Jessie 92

Kahane, Joseph 134
Kahr, Gustav 17–18
Kaltenbrunner, Ernst
Kell, Sir Vernon 57
Kendrick, Tommy 33
Keyes, Admiral of the Fleet Sir Roger 72–3
Klop, Lieutenant 62–8
Koch, Julius 46
KRIPO Detective Branch of Criminal Police (Germany) 54, 58, 113, 175, 176, 185, 187
Kristallnacht (Crystal Night) 39, 41, 69
Kubiš, Jan 153–7

Langley, Captain Jimmy 136, 166–8
League of Nations 11, 22–4
Ley, Dr Robert 34, 58
Liddell, Guy 181, 201
Lidice 156–7
Lisbon 43–5, 85–6

Liss, Ulrich 38
Littmann, Arnold 93
Lloyd George, David 73, 82
Lorenz SZ42 on-line teleprinter cipher machine 110–11
Ludecke, Winfried 46–7
Ludendorff, General Erich 17
Ludovici, Arnold 94
Luftwaffe 13, 31, 35, 45, 61, 85, 87, 95, 99, 101, 110, 120, 174, 179
Luteyn, Anthony 165–6

MacLaren-Clarke, John 'M.C' 41–2, 44, 81, 112–13
Mason-MacFarlane 38
Masterman, John 43
Mein Kampf 18
Melland, Brian 81, 112, 139
Mercer, Cecil 55
Merkel, Dr Rudolf 203–6, 208
Military Intelligence (MI) 24–7, 76, 101–2, 109, 111, 167, 181, 183–4, 203
MI1 25
MI2 25–6
MI3 26–7, 34–5, 45, 74, 77, 190
MI4 26
MI5 27, 56, 90–4, 112, 139, 143–5, 181–2, 184, 195, 201, 203, 208
MI6 25, 60, 62, 65, 85–6, 90, 92, 94, 106, 111, 116, 118–19, 139, 181, 184, 195
MI9 114, 136, 138–9, 145, 166–72, 176, 179, 184
MI14 61, 74–83, 96–9, 106, 111–22, 123, 125, 139, 168,

Also available from Amberley Publishing

BACKING BLETCHLEY

The Codebreaking Outstations, from Eastcote to GCHQ

Ronald Koorm

Also available from Amberley Publishing

BRITISH MILITARY INTELLIGENCE

OBJECTS FROM THE MILITARY INTELLIGENCE MUSEUM

NICK VAN DER BIJL

Available from all good bookshops or to order direct
Please call **01453–847–800**
www.amberley-books.com

Also available from Amberley Publishing

'FASCINATING' *DAILY MAIL*

D-DAY
THROUGH
GERMAN
EYES

HOW THE WEHRMACHT
LOST FRANCE

JONATHAN TRIGG